Based on a true story of abuse and betrayal

HUNTER MARSHALL

ACKNOWLEDGMENTS

To my awesome son, for being the smart, loving, and kind person he is —
To a very special woman I call Mom, who has never given up
on me, even when I've felt like giving up on myself —
To my friends and family (you know who you are) who have
believed in this project even when I didn't —
An extreme thank you to my editor Caprice Whitmire for, once again,
saving my bacon
And, it goes without saying, but I would be remiss if I didn't mention the
greatest cover designer and one of my best friends, Jessica Tahbonemah
with The Magic Quill Graphics for making the photo and cover stand out
so well.

PROLOGUE

December 9, 2006

I should be sleeping, but I can't. My emotions are All. Over. The. Place. I want to cry, scream, and disappear all at once. One minute I'm in tears, and the next I'm so angry that all I want to do is hit someone. In the last twenty-four hours, my life, along with that of my son, Tyler, has been completely upended. My husband, Grey, admitted he's been cheating on me, and the bastard had the audacity to tell me it's my fault. Can you believe that?! Yeah, like I held a gun to his head and made him put his penis where it has no business being! Exactly how does that work? He even claimed he was going to "get rid of me" as soon as I get my degree.

I'm utterly heartbroken. He says we're through. I hope he changes his mind. I know, I know...what am I thinking, right? How do you just completely stop loving somebody though? I can't downshift that fast.

See? Told you my emotions are all over the place. I went from pissed off to a blubbering idiot in less than ten seconds.

I want him back.

I want our family to be just that—a family. I want Grey to care about the vows he made to me, get rid of the girlfriend, and come knocking on the door to beg me for another chance. Somehow, though, after our awesome conversation, I doubt that will happen.

I am such a failure! Why can't the men in my life love me? I'm just not loveable, I guess.

I don't like any of this. I don't know what I'm going to do. How am I going to finish school? Mom told me we're just going to get me through finals, have Christmas and New Year's, and go from there. Somehow, I think she was trying to make the pain go away—or at least make it more bearable.

And this was after my parents had the horrible job of dropping another bombshell in my lap. Oh, I forgot to mention another tidbit, right? Well, not only is Grey cheating on me, but the girlfriend is PREGNANT! Grey told me on more than one occasion that he didn't want any more kids…maybe that's just with me.

What makes the situation even more heartbreaking is Tyler asked whether he should call his daddy "Daddy" or if he can call him Grey. I don't really care what he calls him. It's not like Grey has ever had much to do with him anyway.

Annnnd there I go…pissed off again! You'd be proud of me, though. After my spectacular conversation with Grey, I was so pissed that I took our wedding picture from my mom's china cabinet and, with mom's approval—she handed me the butcher knife and cutting board!—I castrated Grey right there. I went so crazy I cracked the cutting board and bent the poor butcher knife! Oh, but it felt *good*. At least, for the moment.

For now, Tyler and I are staying with my parents. That could have something to do with Tyler acting as if nothing has changed when, in all reality, his life took a drastic turn. He doesn't seem bothered at all, at least not yet.

I asked my dad to give me a blessing. Afterward, I prayed, and cried, and prayed some more that I'll have the strength to handle all that I'm going to have to do over the next who knows how long.

Tomorrow, I have the wonderful task of finding an attorney. Oh, yeah—Grey wants the divorce, but he doesn't want to pay for it. He seems to think I have more money at my disposal than he does. Right—I've been Mrs. Rockefeller all along, Honey. Before I set up an appointment, though, Grey *will* know that the only thing I want from him is sole custody of Tyler. He might fight me on that, but then again, he might not, because if *I* have sole custody then *he* gets to pick and choose when and if he wants anything to do with his son. Won't be any different than the last five years of the kid's life, anyway.

I'm going to talk to Tyler's teacher as well. I need to fill her in on what's happening and have her look out for any behavioral issues she may see crop up. And I want to reinforce that Tyler is only allowed to leave school with me or my parents. Grey doesn't have a driver's license and there is *no way* I'll allow my son to be picked up by anyone I don't know—even if Grey is with them.

I'm so tired, but it's almost time for Tyler to get up, so it looks like yet another sleepless night for me. I'm afraid I'm going to have to get used to these because I feel as if I'm never going to sleep again.
Talk to ya later,
Hunter

CHAPTER ONE

In February 1998, RJ and I had been together for three years. One night, a couple weeks after Valentine's Day and a year after our engagement (we were engaged my senior year in high school), he told me he needed to date other girls in order to make sure I was the *right one* for him. Somehow, I knew it wasn't my disability—my Cerebral Palsy—that caused this reaction. RJ had always told me I didn't give myself enough credit when it came to my strengths. He knew I didn't like people knowing about my disability and that I spent tons of time trying to hide it, but he said it was one of the reasons he loved me. He just needed time.

I thoroughly *hated* being the heartbroken college sophomore living less than ten minutes away from the man I had promised to spend the rest of forever with. Why had God done this to me? Why had he introduced me to such a good person, only to take him away with no warning? I wanted an eternal family, and I struggled with the idea that RJ was not sure that was what he wanted. Why couldn't he see that being sealed as husband and wife was the closest to Heaven a human could get in this life? I'd dreamed about being sealed for time and all eternity since I was a little girl, and now my love wasn't sure. Couldn't God let up a little and give me some mercy, some grace? Frustrated and angry, I needed a breather from RJ, God, and the whole plan I had for myself, so I decided to take matters into my own hands.

~~~~~~

For the next several weeks, I did not go anywhere or do anything, except school and homework. Those held no appeal for me either, though. My best friend, Lindley, had taken about as much moodiness from me as she could stand. One night she called me and said we were going out and there wasn't anything I could do to get out of it. We started off small, going to the bowling alley to play a few frames.

Pretty soon, I found myself frequenting The Alley on a weekly basis. Rather than bowl, though, Lindley and I both found the pool hall more inviting and, in no time at all, were brilliant with a pool stick. Playing pool eased some of the pain and rejection I felt from RJ. We played many weekends with a guy we knew from high school named Hank. He taught me how to hold the pool stick, as we had to get creative due to the Cerebral Palsy that encompassed my right side and affected my ability to hold anything in my right hand the way everyone else did. I found a way that worked, but it wasn't the norm. It was my new-found love of pool and my friendship with Hank that put me in the direct path of a blonde-haired, blue-eyed, handsome cowboy named Grey Andrews.

~~~~~~

One night in April, when we were, as usual, at the bowling alley and pool hall, I heard, "Hey, sexy girl. What're you doin'?" I turned and saw Grey Andrews staring at me so hard I was afraid his eyes might pop out of his head. He reeked of cigarette smoke and smelled like a brewery mixed with Stetson cologne. I hated the smell of cigarette smoke, and combined with the cologne and alcohol, it made me want to gag. I was completely and utterly repulsed by him; I couldn't believe he had the audacity to say something like that, especially since, last I heard, he was dating someone I knew from high school.

"What does it look like we're doing?"

Ignoring my question, he asked, "Mind if I play with you?"

I'd heard through the grapevine that Grey wasn't a nice guy. He had just returned from a stint in active duty Army and had decided not to reenlist. He used his charm on any female who would give him the time of day, but that night, he seemed okay to me. It didn't hurt that he was cute, either.

Trying not to let the smell get to me, I agreed to let him play. He was pretty good with the pool stick, and taught me a few tricks. Grey didn't seem to notice the way I held the pool stick, or anything else different about me. That was a plus.

Trying to keep up the conversation, I asked, "So, where's Kendyl?"

"How do you know her?"

"She went to highschool with Lindley and me." Grey looked at Lindley like he didn't know she had been there until that moment.

"Well, we broke up."

"Oh? Why?" Curiosity got the best of me.

"She cheated on me."

"Oh. That sucks. I'm sorry."

"Oh, well." Grey didn't seem hurt too badly over it. "That's life."

We continued to play regular Eight Ball and then switched to Cutthroat so we could include Lindley. She looked none too thrilled to have Grey hanging out with us, but I was enjoying his attention.

As the night wore on, however, Grey started getting on my nerves as he got cockier with every win. Every time he sank a shot, he did a little victory dance like football players do when they make a touchdown. *Embarrassing much?* Not to mention, he kept looking at me as if he wanted to eat me for breakfast. He had an air about him that said, "I'm God's gift to women." Although he lavished tons of attention on me, I wasn't sure if I liked this side of him.

"We need to leave," Lindley suddenly blurted. I knew she was right, but I wasn't sure how to make an escape without being rude. Finally, though, I couldn't stand Grey's stares or victory dances any longer. Trying to be nice, I said, "Grey, it's getting late and we really need to go."

"What? You have a curfew or somethin'?"

"Yeah."

"Oh. So, you're one of the good little Mormon girls, huh?"

In an instant, Grey had gone from being nice to degrading my very beliefs. I was angered by his comments and actions. "What? You think you're God's gift to women, don't you? You're not! You are an asshole!" Saying nothing else, I stormed out with Lindley laughing hysterically behind me.

~~~~~~

When July rolled around, it not only brought the heat of summer, but also Reghan's wedding day. Why did Reghan always get the boys and all the firsts even though I was older? Comparing myself to her was something I'd done since we were little. Not only did she get to do everything first, but she was taller, skinnier, and prettier to boot. As my mom and I helped her get ready in the bride's room, feelings of inadequacy, jealousy, and the stark reality that I was and possibly always would be at the bottom of the Marshall Family totem pole overtook me. I willed my tears to stay at bay, at least until the reception was over.

"Are you nervous?" I did my best to be the big sister, supporting Reghan and keeping my feelings to myself.

"Yeah, kind of." Reghan could tell I was having a difficult time but didn't bring it up.

"I love you, you know." That was my last comment as my dad came to get her for her walk down the aisle.

~~~~~~

It was late by the time we wished the couple well, sent them off to their honeymoon, and cleaned everything up from the wedding reception. I had fought back tears throughout the ceremony, pictures, and reception. I didn't want anyone knowing that I was suffering, nor did I want them asking questions. All I could think was, *it should've been RJ and me getting married, or, at the very least, planning our own wedding.* I wasn't a drinker, but at that point, I would do whatever I could to numb the feelings that consumed every fiber of my being.

I knew RJ's older brother, Brax, had a friend that was old enough to buy alcohol. Trying not to second guess myself, I called Brax. "Hey. It's been a while." I tried sounding happy.

"Hey, Hunter. What's up?" I could tell Brax wasn't alone.

"Yeah. I'm not so swift. My sister's wedding was today, and I am so…" I couldn't finish my sentence. I did not want him to hear me cry.

"Hey. Are you okay?" Concern laced his voice. Although RJ and I were no longer together, Brax had been a good friend to me anyway.

"I wish I could just numb all these feelings that won't go away! Why am I not good enough for anyone?"

"You know that's not true. My brother is a total jackass!" Brax tried to make me feel better, but the more he talked, the more I wanted to get plowed, and having never taken so much as a sip of anything with alcohol in it, I had no idea what to expect; just that I didn't want to feel anymore.

Out of the blue, I asked, "Can your friend get some wine coolers for me?"

"Are you serious?"

"Yes. I want to get completely drunk so I don't feel crappy anymore! When you get it, meet me at The Alley, okay?"

13

I was almost giddy about getting drunk. *This must be what rebellion feels like*, I thought as I drove.

~~~~~~

The next morning, as I cracked open one eye to the blinding Sunday morning sunlight, I recalled what I had done the night before. It only took three wine coolers to give me a feeling of euphoria or buzz. I didn't throw up like I'd heard most people did. I didn't have a massive headache either. I remembered Grey being at The Alley; I remembered flirting, flirting with him and loving his attention. I remembered those blue eyes and the heavenly smell of Stetson that permeated him. As I thought back over the previous night, I recalled that he didn't smell like a nicotine factory as he usually did.

Getting drunk didn't make me feel better; feeling like a nobody was never going to dissipate. I felt like I would never find my one and only. At least I was able to forget for a little while, and having a hot cowboy hanging on my every word didn't hurt, either.

As Sunday wore on, I began feeling guilty about my binge drinking. It went against everything I believed. How could I forget, even for a moment, what I wanted my life to be like? I prayed that I could withstand the need to numb my negative feelings.

~~~~~~

Deciding I didn't want to be alone for the rest of my life, and believing RJ was never coming back, I started dating again. By October, I was seeing a guy named Scott, who I liked a lot. He was a friend of Brax's and had begun hanging around the pool hall, but he smoked and drank and didn't have the same ideals regarding marriage and family that I did.

I hadn't touched a drop of alcohol since that fateful night in July, which was difficult because Scott loved drinking. Somehow, I influenced him enough that he didn't drink a whole lot when we were together. Since we went to The Alley almost every weekend, we ran into Grey a lot. Grey and Scott didn't seem to like each other much, and Grey did nothing to hide the fact he wanted me all to himself. Making Scott jealous became a favorite pastime for Grey, and I didn't exactly hate that. Grey's bad boy air still had the power to intrigue me.

~~~~~~

One day, out of the blue, Scott stopped taking my phone calls, and he had the nerve to hang up on me the couple times he did pick up! I wasn't sure what caused him to ignore me, but if being dumped by RJ had taught me anything, it was that I couldn't stop living just because I didn't know what was going on.

I started a new job as a bridal consultant in February, taking orders for wedding invitations, napkins, cake toppers, and such. It was much more exciting than flipping burgers like I'd done the previous three years. I loved this new job, but with it and school, I had little time for anything else. What little time I did have was spent at The Alley with Lindley and, of course, Grey and Hank. I didn't know then that the boys knew each other so well in high school, nor did I know they were best friends. I wasn't sure if he and Hank came because Grey knew I would be there or because he was hoping I would be. Either way, he made it easy to forget about Scott *and* RJ.

On the last weekend in February, however, Grey threw me for a loop. He showed up at the bowling alley with a girl I had never seen before. When he saw me, his face lit up. "Hey, you!"

"Hey, yourself. Hey, Hank." Hank was talking to the girl, but I could tell by the way she possessed Grey's hand that she was with *him*, not Hank.

15

After a few minutes of chitchat and realizing Grey wasn't going to introduce us, I piped up, "Hi. My name's Hunter." The girl was nothing like other girls I had seen with Grey. She wasn't skinny, nor was she the drop-dead gorgeous type either.

"Lynese," she replied while batting her eyelashes. Then she said, "I'm Grey's girlfriend." She drew out girlfriend, probably to make certain I *knew* she was Grey's. I was completely surprised! He had a girlfriend and he hadn't told me?

"Well, it's nice to meet you." I hid the jealousy in my voice the best I could. Where had that come from? I didn't want to analyze my feelings, at least not at that moment. Instead, I asked Grey, "So, where did the two of you meet?" Lynese was talking with Hank and looked like she could care less what Grey was doing.

"At Renegade." It was a local dance club a lot of college students and younger crowds frequented.

"How long have you been dating?"

"A few weeks. Why? You sound jealous." Grey looked like he was about to laugh.

"Not jealous, just curious."

"Do you like her?" Why he cared what I thought was anyone's guess.

"I guess. What are you smiling at? Don't you think you should be spending time with her and not over here talking to me?"

"Oh. She doesn't care. It's not that kind of relationship anyway. I just think it's cute that you're jealous…and you claim not to like me!"

My issue with him, at that moment, was that he acted as if he wasn't attached to her. What hadhe meant by "not that kind of relationship?" I would find that out soon enough.

~~~~~~

Two weeks later, Lindley and I were playing pool when Grey walked over to me, lifted me off the ground in a huge bear hug, and promptly kissed me on the cheek. He'd never done that before and it made me wonder what he was thinking.

"Where's Lynese?" I asked, struggling to regain my composure. I didn't want him to see how the kiss had rattled me.

"We broke up." He didn't act all that heartbroken over it, either.

I decided right then and there that I needed to clear things up with Scott. I called and left a message: "Scott, this is Hunter. I don't know what's wrong, but I *deserve* to know what's going on with us. Unless I hear from you by Friday night, I will assume we are done. I won't do this anymore."

By Friday night I still hadn't heard from Scott. As I walked in the door after work, the phone rang. Hoping it was Scott, I answered, "Hello?"

"Hey, sexy." It was Grey.

"How did you get my number?"

"Hank gave it to me. I've had it for a long time, but something told me that I needed to call you tonight. What are you doing?"

"I am going to kill that little..." I stopped before I said something I might later regret. I'd given it to Hank a while ago so we could plan our weekends, but I didn't expect he would give it to Grey. I wasn't sure how I felt about Grey yet, but I was certain that him having my phone number wasn't a good thing.

"Whoa, slow down there. I begged and begged until he finally gave in. Don't be too hard on him. He was only helping out a desperate friend." Thinking I hadn't heard his question, he asked again, "What are you doin' tonight?"

"Nothing."

"Aawww!" I could almost see the devilish grin on his face. "Why don't you come to the bowling alley with Hank and me?"

"I just want to stay home tonight. Alone." I put emphasis on *alone*. I huffed and rolled my eyes again as Grey continued talking. I knew I wasn't getting out of this one.

"I don't think so. I'm coming to get you." He hung up before I could object.

Deciding he would probably make good on his word, especially when it was something he wanted, I changed my clothes and waited for Grey. I was completely shocked when he came to the door for me. I wasn't surprised, however, that Hank was with him. Hank was always with Grey.

"Do you think Scott will show up?" Grey asked as we walked to his truck. I didn't answer. I really didn't want to talk with Grey about Scott, nor did I really want to think about the pain I was feeling. I really was just looking for a low-key night, so I wasn't at all prepared for what happened later.

Grey, Hank, and I were shooting pool when a guy approached us. I had never seen him before, but apparently he knew who I was.

"Are you Hunter?" His breath smelled as if something died in his mouth. I could also tell he smoked by the nicotine stains on his teeth.

"Yes." My stomach roiled. "Do I know you?"

"I'm a friend of Scott's. Carter. He has a message for you."

"Okay." I drew the word out.

"He says it's over."

With fire in my eyes, I asked Carter where Scott was. Pushing past him, I headed outside. When Scott saw me, he gunned his engine and sprayed gravel in all directions as he sped away. *Son of a bitch*! I stormed back inside.

Grey noticed my cherry red face and my ragged breathing. "Are you okay?" I pushed his six-foot-five frame out of the way as if he was no heavier than a feather.

As I sat sulking on one of the empty pool tables, I was unaware that this night would change my entire future. Grey knew he couldn't just come out and tell me he had feelings for me. I wasn't the type of girl he usually dated. I was a good girl. He played cute and begged me to play pool, but I shut down. I never blew him off if I had a chance to beat him at his game, but I wasn't in the mood.

I moved to a nearby table and watched the guys play a couple of games. I guess Grey thought he had let me stew long enough, so when he finished the last game he walked over and asked, "Hey there, sexy. Are you okay?"

I looked around as if he were asking someone else, rolled my eyes, and said, "Fine. Why?"

"You don't look okay."

"Oh yeah? Why do you care?"

"We're friends, aren't we?"

"We are?" He looked at me, hurt.

"Yeah, I guess."

"If you want to talk, let's get out of here and go for a drive."

"You don't really want to talk, and you know it. I can see right through your friend-like façade. All you really want is to—let me see, how did you put it—get in my pants?"

"I'm not like that anymore." He sounded like he was trying to convince himself more than me. I had noticed, however, that he didn't have the same foul mouth as when we first met, at least not all the time. Nor did he smoke, drink, or smell like a brewery when I was around.

"I don't know. I don't feel much like being nice, and I have no intention of pretending that I'm okay."

"Who says you have to be nice, or pretend?"

It *was* late; I decided a drive wasn't in the cards for me. I asked Grey to take me home, but not before promising to spend the next day with him. And, of course, Hank too.

Later, as I was getting ready to call it a night, my brother, Derek, knocked on my bedroom door. For the first time in twenty years, I had my own room—my own space. I wasn't sure I liked being alone.

"What you doin'?" Derek asked.

"Nothing. Why?"

"What's the matter? You look like someone just killed your best friend."

"Remember that guy I was dating just before you came home?"

"Yeah. Scott, right?

"He dumped me tonight."

"Are you kidding me?! That is so wrong!"

"You're telling me. He didn't even have the decency to tell me himself. He sent his friend, Carter, to break the news."

"Whaaa?" Derek was so stunned he couldn't even finish his sentence.

"Yup."

"Well, what about that guy who came to get you earlier? Who's that?" He winked as he smiled.

"Oh. You mean Grey? He's just a friend. We play pool sometimes at the bowling alley."

"Huh. The way he looked at you did not say, *Hey, let's be friends*. It was more like, *You are HOT. I want to eat you for a snack!*"

"I don't think so, Derek. You've been out of the dating scene far too long." I couldn't help but giggle.

"No, really, Hunter. He couldn't keep his eyes off you. You two are going to get married," he sang at me.

"What? No! Are you crazy?"

"Some people think I am, Sis, but the way he was watching you… I can see you two being more than just casual."

"You have lost it, Bro! All that hot air in Spain must have taken what was left of your smart brain cells."

I was beginning to wonder if maybe Derek was right. Grey *had* done a total 180 and didn't seem like the same person I met when he was dating Lynese. He said he had been going to church and reading *The Book of Mormon.*

That night, I fell asleep with a smile tugging at the corners of my mouth while dreaming of a tall, blonde-haired, blue-eyed cowboy.

~~~~~~

As promised, I spent the next day with Grey. Having only seen the outside of Grey's house, I was totally unprepared for the clutter and dust that covered almost every inch of the interior. Because I hadn't met Grey's family and wanted to make a good impression, I didn't so much as flinch. "Hey, Ma!" Grey hollered as we walked into the house. "Hey, Sis!" There was a woman sitting on the floor watching *Xena: Warrior Princess.*

"This is Hunter. Hunter, this is my sister and my mom." I turned as an elderly woman walked into the room while Grey was introducing me.

I replied with a friendly hello, but they were engrossed in the show on the television, and neither acknowledged my presence.

Upstairs, Grey's room looked more like an apartment than a bedroom. He had everything!—from a television and DVD player to a mini fridge with snacks. Grey and Hank decided to watch *Terminator,* but because I was emotionally exhausted from the night before, I quickly fell asleep next to Grey. Sometime later, I woke up to hear them talking. Grey said, "Isn't she the most beautiful thing you've ever seen?" Hearing him say those words made my heart happy. He thought I was beautiful? I smiled, not letting on that I was awake. As I lay there, my feelings toward Grey began to change. I no longer wanted to be just friends. I wanted to see if there was more to it than that.

"If you hurt her," Hank threatened, "I will kill you. She's been through a lot and doesn't need to deal with *your* reputation."

"Dude, I won't hurt her. It's because of her that I've started going back to church and reading the scriptures. She makes me want to be a better person."

"I hope, for your sake, you aren't jerking her around."

That was the end of their conversation, but I was on cloud nine. Could Derek be right?

~~~~~~

There wasn't a huge announcement when Grey and I officially started dating in April of 1999. We began spending all our free time together getting to know each other—talking about family, friends, the military, and even what we wanted in our futures. The military was something I was against.

"The idea of being the girlfriend of a soldier scares me. What happens if you get called to active duty or decide you want to be active duty?"

"I wouldn't make the decision to be full-time active duty without talking to you first, but I don't see the harm in being in a reserve unit."

"I know you want to. It just scares me. Promise me that if we are going to be together, you will talk to me before making a decision like that."

I didn't know it then, but he had already turned in his application for the Army National Guard. It should have raised a red flag when he didn't respond, but it didn't. Grey also knew I'd been engaged before, so he broached anything about the future carefully. I was shocked, however, when, out of the blue he told me we were going engagement ring shopping. There we were, only a month into our courtship, and he wanted to go ring shopping? I was scared, to say the least. Thrilled, but scared.

I talked with my mom about this at length, especially after Reghan announced she was expecting her first baby. Of course, more of my "not enoughness" surfaced.

"You know, I think you and Grey are moving too fast, but if being together is what you both want, there is nothing wrong with being married civilly and making a temple marriage something you aspire to, as long as you and Grey want the same thing."

"It scares me, Mom. What if this fails too? I don't think I can take that."

My mom then repeated something she had been telling me my entire life. "You need to pray about it."

I had been praying about it the entire time Grey and I had been dating, but after my mom and I talked, I prayed even harder. I felt this was something I was supposed to do. I didn't know why yet, but I *knew* marrying Grey was the right path at that time. I was falling in love with him, and fast. I just continued to hope he would be the knight in shining armor who would take me to the temple and be sealed, not only for time, but also for eternity.

~~~~~~

On ring shopping day, Grey surprised me by driving to Temple Square in Salt Lake City, only thirty-minutes from where we lived in Springville. I couldn't help but wonder if we were moving too fast. I wasn't sure I was ready to hope that another engagement wouldn't fail.

"What's the matter?" Grey asked when he saw the worried expression on my face.

"Oh, just thinking."

"If that's all you're doing you wouldn't have that *I want to barf* look on your face. Now spill."

"I'm scared."

"Of me?"

"Yes. No. I don't know. I think I'm scared this engagement will fail like with RJ. Or maybe I'm afraid it won't."

"That doesn't make any sense. I am not RJ, nor will I *ever* do what he did."

However, the matter of being sealed in the temple brought all my fears and doubts to the surface again. We talked about that, too, and Grey reassured me that, although he had issues he needed to resolve, he wanted the same thing.

I did my best to put my insecurities out of my mind as we looked for a wedding set at Diamonds Are Forever in Salt Lake. I wondered why he needed me there to find the perfect ring.

Grey didn't spend much time looking at rings before he picked one. It was the smallest and cheapest of the rings we looked at, but I didn't care. Since we were already there, I decided to peruse the men's rings and get an idea of which I wanted to buy for him. Of course, I was going to get it when he wasn't with me. There was more of a surprise that way.

Because Grey had bad credit and no job, we ended up using my credit to set up a payment plan and I paid the down-payment on my own engagement ring. This bothered me a little, but not enough to draw attention to it.

~~~~~~

Over the next several weeks, I found myself wondering why Grey hadn't given me the ring. When I asked him, he answered with things like, "When I'm ready," or, "Not today." At the end of April, we, along with Hank and Lynese—yes, the same girl Grey introduced as his girlfriend—decided to attend Cabaret at Brigham Young University. This annual dance was the equivalent of a high school prom, with dinner served to the attendees—a big deal for the college, and even bigger for those who were asked.

Going dress shopping with my mom was a lot of fun. We found a dress at JC Penney in the mall that Mom and I deemed

"Grandma's curtains." At first glance, I was repulsed by all the colorful flowers scattered across the lacy overlay.

"No way! That looks like something Grandma would hang in her windows!"

"Just try it on," mom urged.

I was pleasantly surprised at what I saw when I looked in the mirror. Definitely *not* "Grandma's curtains."

~~~~~~

The day of the dance, I was jittery as all get out as I sat in a chair while my mom put my hair up and applied my makeup with an expert hand. I wondered what Grey would think while I watched the transformation take place. Hopefully, he wouldn't see "Grandma's curtains" as I had. His reaction, though, was nothing like I expected.

"Wow! You look beautiful!" He couldn't take his eyes off me.

"Thanks." The butterflies that had taken up permanent residence in my stomach wouldn't subside. Nerves? Where had those come from? It was only Grey, for Pete's sake. He had never made me nervous before. The nerves were good nerves, though, as I realized I was falling hopelessly, head-over-heels in love with him. After RJ, I didn't think it was possible, but there I was, doing exactly that!

We didn't want to wait in line for pictures at the dance, so my mom, a professional photographer, took our pictures right in the house. Following the pictures, Lynese and I decided we would rather take fast food up to a beautiful spot in Provo Canyon than go to a fancy restaurant for dinner with the guys. We also chose to get fast food because we were trying to save money, and it was so much cheaper than eating at an elegant restaurant. The four of us had so much fun talking, laughing, and joking that we lost track of time and had to hurry to the dance.

As Grey and I danced to the song "Here I Go Again" by Whitesnake, I looked up into the face of the blue-eyed cowboy I swore I would never fall for. *How had this happened?* I thought as we swayed back and forth. The night wore on in pure bliss. We danced, laughed, walked around, and talked about everything and nothing. I was in heaven!

CHAPTER TWO

A week later I was at work when I suddenly felt sick. Knowing what the cause was, I asked to leave early. I'd started having ovarian cysts that wouldn't burst the year before, and every now and again the nasty beasts would plague me badly enough to cause me to curl up in a ball of tears. After arriving home, I took some medication and, with a heating pad on my stomach, fell asleep on the couch.

A little while later, as I was on the edge of sleep, I heard my mom say, "I won't wake her up, Grey."

"But I need to see her." He was whining, but why?

At that point, I was awake. "Hey," I said rubbing the sleep from my eyes.

"Are you okay? I called your desk and they said you'd gone home sick."

"I'm fine. I just don't feel well." I lay back down while Grey sat next to me with my feet on his lap.

While watching *Meet Joe Black*, a movie Grey wanted to see, he picked up my left hand and slipped the engagement ring onto my finger. "Here," was the only word he uttered.

I couldn't believe he had *finally* given me the ring, but at the same time, I was disappointed by the way he did it. As far back as I could remember, I dreamed of my knight in shining armor getting down on one knee and professing his love to me. What girl hadn't?

Forget getting down on one knee! Grey hadn't even bothered to *ask* me.

"Why now?" I asked, trying not to show my disappointment.

I wasn't prepared for the words that came out of Grey's mouth. "So you'll quit bitching at me. And so I don't have to hear that I shouldn't be doing this from my mom and sister!"

"Your mom and sister? What do they have to do with it?" His first comment rang in my ears. *Did he really feel like I was only after him for marriage?*

"The day we got the ring, I accidentally left it in my coat pocket and my sister found it. She flipped! The bitch started ragging on me about how I am too young and too irresponsible to be getting married. Where the hell will we live? How would I take care of you? That sort of shit." His filthy mouth was back.

"Is that why it took you so long to give it to me?"

"Yeah, and I don't want to deal with it. They'll give me shit, so when we're at my house, don't wear it."

I was confused. I purposely *didn't* bring the ring up after he got it because I didn't want him thinking I was a nag. And now there he was calling me one? It didn't dawn on me at that moment that I should have been worried. I wanted so badly to belong to someone that I overlooked this, as I would a lot of things Grey said and did.

A few minutes later my mom appeared. I hoped she hadn't heard our conversation, but all she said was, "You should have seen how nervous this guy was when he came over here the other night to ask for your dad's blessing. I thought he was going to wear a hole in the carpet, pacing so much. I finally told him he needed to ask your dad to go for a drive with him. They were both happy when they came back, so—" If she'd heard any of it, she didn't let on.

"Who's that talking about me?" My dad came in the front door and saw Grey and I sitting on the couch. He turned to me, "Hunter, this young man lied to me about you."

I looked from my dad to Grey, horrified. "What lie?"

"Well, he told me that he loves and wants to marry my daughter."

I wasn't as excited as I should have been. Grey's bitch comment kept creeping into my mind.

~~~~~~

By the middle of June, Grey and I had set our wedding date for August 12, 1999. I didn't want to burden my parents with the cost of another wedding, so I was determined to pay for as much of my wedding as I could. I started working at Arby's, along with my other job, to pay for our part of the wedding.

On June eighteenth, I went to Grey's house to surprise him for his twenty-third birthday. I tried to blindfold him, which he didn't like. "What the hell are you doing?" he demanded, not at all happy.

"It's a surprise. No questions." I laughed as he grudgingly let me put a blindfold on him. We drove out to a park and campground called Bear River, just outside of town, where a few of our friends waited. With Lindley's help, I blew up and taped twenty-three balloons to the table and surrounding trees. As I removed the blind-fold, everyone yelled, "Surprise!"

Grey looked dumbfounded. "Happy Birthday!" I stood on my tiptoes and gave him a kiss on the cheek. But the look he gave me stopped me dead in my tracks.

"What the f*** is this?!" He was angry, but why? I hated the F-bomb, but this was just the beginning of hearing that word, as it would burn in my ears for many years to come.

Feeling as if I'd been slapped, I squeaked, "I wanted to do something nice for your birthday."

Grey looked at me, almost apologetic, and answered, "Thank you. I'm just not used to this kind of thing. No one, not Mom, or my brother, or my sisters, remembered that today was my birthday."

A weenie roast, cake, and presents followed. As the night wore on, Grey kept being lovey dovey, but I couldn't shake the feeling that something wasn't right. I guess he was trying to make up for being mean.

~~~~~~

When I returned home that night, my parents were waiting up for me. "Honey," My dad looked almost sad, "we need to talk to you."

"Okay..." I wondered what about.

"Why don't you sit down," Mom responded. I was worried. The only time my parents talked with me like this was when something was serious. "We need to talk to you about Grey."

I immediately froze. "We've heard the way he talks to you, and he's not always nice. And the way he does things like smack you on the behind when he thinks no one is watching. There are also things that I'm not sure you know about." Mom's face was drawn.

"Like?" I was getting defensive.

"Well, I've heard he has assaulted girls in the past and he has cheated on more than one of them."

"Where did you hear that?" I asked almost angrily.

My mom replied, "That isn't important. What is important is that you are aware of what has been going on. He's been spotted with other girls, too."

"Have you seen any of this?" I countered.

"Well, no, but the way he acts around you and talks to you, it's not a far stretch," my dad chimed in. "Has he told you any of his military stories?"

Grey had told me those stories, but I chalked it up to him being Grey. Oh, the stories! He told anyone who would listen that he had been hired by the government to spy on terrorists while he was still in basic training, and when he was eighteen, he jumped out of a 747 at 20,000 feet, but his parachute didn't open until 9,000 feet. He claimed it was the only time he could kiss his own ass good-bye. He said he had to have both his knees replaced with titanium because he shattered his in the fall. "Yes. I know they are exaggerated. So what? He likes telling stories."

"Honey, we're concerned that, if he tells stories like that to get attention, what other things does he lie about? You say he stopped smoking, but he smells like cigarettes whenever he's here." This came from my mom.

"We've noticed, too, you don't hang out with Lindley much anymore. It's as if you have chosen him over anyone else."

If I was honest with myself, especially after what happened earlier, they had a point, but I was *so* tired of being alone, and my feelings for Grey were anything but platonic.

I responded through clenched teeth, "You said we could get married!" I glared at one parent and then the other.

"Calm down!" my dad commanded in his father-like tone "And you will not speak to your mother and me that way!"

"I'm sorry, but I love him. What do you want me to do? Call off the wedding?" I was feeling remorseful.

My mom was thinking that exact thing, but she didn't say it. Instead she said, "Maybe give it a little more time. Don't get married in August. Wait six months and see if you still feel the same. You guys dated very little before your engagement, and we think waiting might be the best thing."

"I don't want to wait. Reghan *always* gets to do things before me! She got engaged before me, got married before me, and is having a baby before me. Why can't I do something I want to do for a change, without everyone knocking it?" I knew I was being immature, but I didn't care.

Alone in my room, I reached a decision. I *wanted* to rebel! Marrying Grey would be the only really rebellious thing I had ever done!

Growing up in my family hadn't always been a picnic. I was the child my parents thought would do and say whatever they wanted, if only for their approval. I wondered if they thought I wouldn't because of my disability.

~~~~~~

I was born on August 28, 1978, three months before my actual due date. Weighing in at a hefty two pounds, the doctors didn't know whether I would live or not, nor did they give much hope for it. I spent the first 75 days of my life at Primary Children's Hospital in Utah; when I was two and a half months old, the doctor told my parents that they were sending me home because I did much better when Mom was around. However, they told my mom and dad that if they brought me back, I would more than likely die.

A few days after arriving at home—being the stubborn stink I was—I decided I wasn't going to eat. As a young mother with three other children at home, my mom was scared to death. Not knowing what else to do, she called the doctor at Primary's. "

"Burn a hole in the nipple of the bottle," he said. "I don't want to see her back here."

Throwing all caution to the wind, my mom did as he instructed, then looked at me and said, "It's drink or drown, baby."

When I reached six months old, I wasn't sitting, or even attempting to, like most babies my age were. My parents knew there was something wrong with their daughter, but it wasn't until I was three that they found I had Cerebral Palsy affecting my right side. However, with mom and dad's encouragement and my mom's tireless efforts, I learned to do everything with my left hand because, due to the golf ball size hole in the left side of my brain, I had to rewire things to the right.

Learning to walk wasn't easy, but I first learned on my knees. Mom always said I had the dirtiest little knees of any child she had ever seen. I then transferred to a walker to help support me. At age four, I had a heel cord lengthening procedure done on my right foot to help me walk straight and without a walker. The doctors didn't know how disadvantaged I would be, so, although my brother Derek and I were less than nine months apart, I started kindergarten a year after he did. Surprising all the doctors, physical therapists, and occupational therapists who worked with me, I hit every developmental milestone and more.

~~~~~~

As far back as I could remember, my dad teased me about getting married. He jokingly told me that when my fiancé proposed, I would have to make sure he was okay living with my parents, because I was too scared to stay away from home.

Even if I had to pay for the entire wedding and put everything together myself, I was going to marry Grey and prove to my parents that I **would** get married and there was **no way** we would live with them. I would also prove Grey wasn't who they thought he was. However, being raised to pray about important decisions, I once again found myself on my knees asking Heavenly Father whether I should marry Grey. I didn't get a "yes you can" or "no you can't" answer. I still felt it was something I needed to do.

~~~~~~

The first part of July brought huge changes to my immediate family, which, in turn, put a damper on the wedding plans Grey and I were making. The owner of the land we lived on demanded we vacate the property within two months, including the trailer we lived in. After talking it over with Grey (my parents weren't interested in the planning phase anymore), we made the decision to change our wedding date to September 20, 1999.

"You know, when I was about twelve or thirteen, I had a dream that September 20th was going to be my wedding day. It's kind of funny that *now* it will be!" I was trying to stay positive in spite of the changes, but could tell by the scowl on Grey's face he wasn't having any of it.

"Why can't we just elope?" he complained.

"Elope? Why would you want to do that?"

"It seems like a bunch of shit to me, this the whole wedding planning thing." His brow creased in anger. Grey swore a lot. Every other word out of his mouth was either vulgar, colorful, or both. There seemed to be something more to his grumpiness, however.

Not knowing how to broach the subject, I bluntly asked, "Is there something bothering you? It's not the wedding, is it?"

"No, why?"

"You seem kind of testy. Every time I try to talk to you about anything, you get all weird."

With that, Grey handed me an envelope from the United States Army. My hand began to shake, and my mouth went dry. "What's this?" I asked, although I knew what it was.

"Well," Grey drew the word out, "I've been dreading telling you about this since the day you agreed to marry me, because I didn't want you bitching at me about it."

"What! When did you do this?!" I was pissed! How could he make such a crucial decision without talking to me first?

"I've been thinking about it for a while, but I applied for it a couple of days before we got engaged. I had every intention of telling you, but I couldn't find the right time."

"So? You know my feelings about being a military wife! Why would you do this knowing you were about to ask me to marry you? Why, damn it?!" I took deep breaths, thinking I could stop the panic attack that threatened to erupt.

"I knew you'd act like this. That's why I didn't want to tell you. Why the hell can't I do this? It's not like I'm going active."

It took me a few minutes to get my emotions under control. "Okay, this means you go one weekend a month and two weeks a year, right?"

"There's more." Grey couldn't look me in the face.

"More? Like what?"

"I have to go to Boise for a month. I leave the first part of October for some schooling they want me to do."

"A month?! Right after our wedding? Can I go with you?" At this point, the panic was in full swing!

"No. We're staying in the barracks, and only Army personnel are allowed in them." Grey didn't seem so agitated after getting the news off his chest, but my head was swimming. *Another roadblock? This is not fair! I should be able to go with him! After all, we will barely be married two weeks by his departure date!*

"Hunter, are you okay?" Grey asked tentatively.

"Am I okay? Seriously?! We still don't have a place to live, my parents don't want us to get married, and you do *this* without talking to me?" I was trying hard to control my temper.

"I'm sorry," he whined. Could he be any more childish? "But I knew what you would say."

Not wanting to let him have it, especially in front of other people, I asked, "Is this why you want to elope?"

"Kind of. This…and your parents hate me."

"They don't *hate* you. They just can't figure out why you must exaggerate things to get people to like you, among other things."

"Oh, so now you believe them? You believe the rumors?" He sounded hurt.

"I didn't say that."

We let the matter drop. The doubts that had started to form hit me full force again. If he could join the military without consulting me first, what else was he doing that he didn't tell me? I did my best to squelch any doubts and kept plugging away, but they crept up constantly.

~~~~~~

As the day grew closer for my family to move, I grew increasingly nervous. There was still no decision regarding where *I* was going. Grey didn't appear to care one way or another where I ended up, as long as he didn't have to make any decisions.

After looking through countless rentals, I called the place that sold us our first home. Because we were in a crunch for time, Grey and I bought it sight unseen, with the understanding that the seller would replace the carpet and linoleum, but it was up to us to tear it out.

Our small, three bedroom, single-wide trailer had bluish-gray paint on the outside, a patio and a front porch, and a shed off to the side. The inside, however, left a lot to be desired. Not only did the place smell like pee, the walls were dark brown wood paneling, making it seem darker inside than it really was. The lighting was awful too. The grates over the heating vents were missing, and so was the enclosure over the water heater in the hallway. There weren't any doors on the kitchen cabinets, and the counters were chipped white paint with mold forming in every corner. It was just plain old. With a little paint and some tender loving care, we hoped we could give it a homey feel and make it ours.

Over the next two weeks, Grey spent most of his time at the trailer pulling up carpet, while I was at work. Hank's dad was a residential painter, so we received a great deal on the white paint we used to brighten the place up.

Grey, Hank, Lynese, and I worked feverishly to get the painting done and the carpet in so I could move in at the beginning of August. Meghan, my friend from high school—and the only one of my friends Grey seemed to like—moved in with me until Grey and I got married, as to not tempt fate. We made a rule that after dark, Grey and I weren't allowed to be in the trailer alone.

~~~~~~

On July 31st, just after nine in the evening, Grey, Hank, Lynese, Meghan, and I sat back and admired our handywork. The dark, drab walls were now a bright white, just the homey feeling we had been working to achieve. The carpet in all the rooms was teal colored shag, and the linoleum in the kitchen was white with gray flecks that looked like tiny flowers.

"I cannot believe we got this done," I sighed.

"I know," Meghan responded. "I was beginning to wonder if we would have it done in time. They sure took their own sweet time getting the carpet and linoleum in though!"

"No kidding," Hank chimed in as he placed his hand on Lynese's leg. There was something different between those two. I glanced at Grey to see if he noticed. He did.

"Okay, you two," Grey asked, "what are you hiding?"

"Ummm..." They were both stuttering like they had gotten caught with their hand in the cookie jar. Lynese replied, "We're getting married!"

"What?! When did this happen?" I countered. Lynese pulled her wedding ring from her pocket.

"Oh, we have been toying with the idea of dating since Cabaret, and things fell into place from there," she stated. It wasn't a huge surprise to me, considering the day I met Lynese she'd spent most of her time with Hank.

"When's your wedding?" Meghan inquired, wanting to be a part of the conversation.

"October twenty-fifth," Hank returned.

"What the f***? I won't be there!" Grey was angry. "Who's going to be your best man?"

"I don't know yet. I wanted you to, but you won't be back from military training yet."

"Well, that's shitty," Grey barked, "You can't wait until I get home?!" He was angry enough that no one knew what to say or how to answer. Instead, we gave the happy couple our congratulations, ignoring Grey's attitude.

Hank and Lynese left a few hours later. Sensing that I needed to talk to Grey, Meghan headed to her bedroom. When we were finally alone I asked, "Grey, are you okay?"

"I'm fan-f***in-tastic. Why?" He still acted like he wanted to bite somebody's head off.

"You're not yourself. You haven't been for several weeks." Concern was evident in my voice.

"Well, how the hell would you feel if your own best friend decided to get married even though they *knew* you wouldn't be there? I thought for sure that, because he's going to be my best man… It's always been implied that I would be his. Damn it all to hell!"

"I understand why you're hurt but getting angry at Hank isn't going to change things." I did what I could to console him, but he wouldn't let me hold his hand or give him anything resembling affection.

"Oh, you don't have a clue! You're just the damn good little Mormon girl, who has no idea about anything."

If Grey was trying to make me feel as bad as he did, he had succeeded. He didn't bother apologizing, and went home without even so much as a peck on the cheek, swearing a blue streak the whole way to his truck.

~~~~~~

The next several weeks went by in a blur for me, and before I knew it, it was September. Between work, spending time with Grey, and wedding plans, I was thoroughly exhausted. Grey and I didn't talk about his decision to join the Army Reserve anymore. He knew how I felt, but there was nothing I could do about it if we were going to be married. It wasn't like he would go back on his word to the military.

Because our wedding was on a shoe-string budget, I used the same color scheme as Reghan had for her wedding - hunter green and burgundy. That way I could use the same bouquet, table settings, cake topper, etc. I also borrowed her wedding dress. My bridesmaids wore burgundy dresses and the groomsmen wore hunter green cummerbunds and ties. The only thing that was different was the DJ. Meghan's brother-in-law offered to do it if I provided all the CD's. Even the venue was the same.

Not wanting to ask my mom to take our engagement pictures, we had Meghan take some snapshots, hoping at least one would turn out for our invitations. We chose a photo invite with the words imprinted on it, because it was faster and cheaper. I still worried they wouldn't be done in time, because the wedding was only a month away.

~~~~~~

September 4. 1999 was my birthday and although the twenty-first birthday was supposed to be great, mine brought nothing but dread. I didn't know if Grey had remembered or whether my family cared. There was a lot of tension in my family with the continued planning of my wedding, so I didn't see or talk to them much.

After getting ready for the day, I stopped to purchase my daily sixty- four ounce mug of Pepsi, and then picked Grey up so he could drop me off at work. With it being my birthday, Grey said he wanted to borrow my car, and I wasn't allowed to ask any questions. I was simply to be ready to go when he picked me up from work. I couldn't wait for the day to be over.

When Grey came to pick me up, he had a mischievous look on his face. "What?" I asked, smiling.

"Nothing," he said, but the wicked grin was still there.

"So, where are we going?"

"Home."

"Yours or mine?"

"Ours." I had a difficult time with *ours.*

We rode in silence the few miles to the trailer. "Okay. Close your eyes, and NO PEEKING," Grey commanded.

We walked toward the trailer, with Grey guiding me and instructing me. As he opened the front door, I caught a whiff of something cooking, but nothing surprised me more than when I opened my eyes. On the table was a huge box and a chocolate cake. My favorite!

"When did you do this?" I asked, almost in tears.

"Why do you think I borrowed your car today? I needed some excuse to come here."

"Thank you." I gave him a hug and a lingering kiss.

"Wow! If this is all I need to do to be kissed like that, I'll have to do it more often," he replied, cheerfully.

"You'd better!"

Just as Grey put the finishing touches on the meal, there was a knock at the door. In walked Derek, Reghan, Mom, and Dad.

"Happy Birthday!" they chorused. A round of hugs followed.

Grey, seeing it was my family, left the room. I was, of course, wondering why he would do that if he wanted to change how my parents felt about him, but I didn't say or do anything; instead I turned to my guests.

"Thanks, you guys!" I opened their packages: a pair of silver and gold toned cowboy boot earrings and a brown leather jacket I'd wanted for a long time. "These are awesome!" Even though everyone put on a happy front, a definite tension filled the room. In fake politeness mode, we were more like strangers than family.

"Well," Dad chimed in, "Looks like you guys are eating, so we'd better go."

"You guys are more than welcome to stay," I replied, hopefully.

"No, we need to get Reghan home anyway," my mom declared. Reghan was looking quite pregnant.

"Oh, okay." It was difficult to mask the disappointment in my voice.

Just then, my mom pulled me aside. "Sweetheart, are you sure this is what you want? Are you sure you are ready? It's not even that your dad and I don't think you're ready, but you know our concerns regarding Grey." Yes, I knew *very well* what they thought of the man in my life. "We are concerned that you chose Grey as a rebound from RJ." Mom's eyebrows furrowed as she spoke.

"I AM NOT on the rebound!" I had to bite my tongue as not to say something I might regret. "I love Grey and I am going to marry him in two and a half weeks, and that's it!"

"I didn't think we would be able to change your mind, but we want you to know that we love you and want to see you happy." And with that, Mom motioned to the others, but not before saying, "Even though I don't like what you are doing, I DID promise to take your wedding pictures and pay for half the venue, so that's what I'm going to do."

For some reason, not having the support I so desperately needed and wanted from my family was taking its toll. But then again, they might have a point. Grey *was* out of work. I didn't think he'd quit smoking or drinking, either. Maybe he wouldn't change. I was questioning EVERYTHING! Grey and I, Mom and Dad, truth and lies... EVERYTHING!

~~~~~~

"You told me you haven't been smoking!" I nearly screamed at Grey.

"I haven't."

"What the hell?"

"I haven't! Why don't you believe me? Man, you can be a colossal bitch sometimes!"

"Then why do you smell like cigarette smoke?"

"We are at the bowling alley! Even you smell like cigarette smoke after coming here."

"Are you kidding me?! You expect me to buy that?! The difference is, my breath doesn't smell like nicotine. Yours does. I told you if you start smoking again, I won't marry you! Is this your way of telling me you want out?" I was pissed enough that, although I wanted to cry, I couldn't.

"NO! I want to marry you!" A whole slew of explicit words left his mouth, then he said, "This is my last one, I swear! I don't even have any more."

The next few days went by without much contact between us. Once again, I struggled with the decision whether or not to call off the wedding, and it was coming up fast. I loved Grey, but at the same time had doubts. It didn't make for a great way to start our life together.

~~~~~~

One night, over a chick flick and popcorn, I confided in Meghan. "What should I do? I still want to marry him, but he lied!"

"I think you should still marry him. If he says he's done smoking, then he is."

"How do I know that?"

"You don't, but you have to start trusting him sometime. Besides, your wedding is a week away and you already sent out the invitations. What are you going to do? Send out un-invites?"

I didn't even want to go there. After a prayerful night, not a whole lot of sleep, and no answers, I decided to continue with the wedding.

The next day, I went over to Grey's house after work. "Hey." I couldn't dismiss the way butterflies appeared in my stomach just by looking at him.

"Hey." He gave me a hug, not knowing whether I'd let him kiss me or not. I didn't. "How's it going?"

After what he had just put me through? Was he serious? "I'm fine." However, I didn't feel fine. I was fighting a war within myself. A war against what I wanted and what I believed.

"So," Grey said, "about the wedding—are we, or aren't we?"

Was *that* all he could say? I sat down on the top step of the dilapidated porch. I hoped I never had to live in that house. I loved my soon-to-be-mother-in-law but felt she deserved to live in something a lot nicer than an old, filthy house with paint peeling off the wood on the outside and dust and filth on the inside.

I looked at Grey and asked, "Is that all you can say? You know how I feel about your smoking, and here you are still doing it! Did you ever quit?"

"Yes, but I was getting nervous."

"How long?"

"A couple of weeks."

I could tell by the way Grey looked at me that he was lying. I feared he had never quit. I loved him, though, and if he told me he wouldn't smoke again, I'd let it go.

"Do you still want to marry me?" I was almost afraid to hear his answer.

"Yes! I've never wanted anything more in my life!"

"Promise me, here and now, that you will never pick up another cigarette, and I won't call off the wedding."

"I promise."

"And promise to *never* call me a bitch again."

"I promise." He even gave me the scouts honor salute.

"By the way, you have Meghan to thank for still getting the best thing that will ever happen to you." Without another word, I gave him a kiss and left.

~~~~~~

I woke up the morning of the eighteenth—two days before my wedding with a sore throat, feeling achy and feverish. *Oh please, please,* I prayed, *let this stay low key, at least until after our vows.* (I didn't realize until later what sort of sense of humor Heavenly Father had). Something told me I needed to try on my wedding dress. And it was urgent! The reason I had that thought was made clear to me a few minutes later.

"Hey Meg, are you up?" I knocked on Meghan's door. I heard a muffled response from the other side.

"I have a feeling I need to try on my dress."

I hadn't tried on the dress I had borrowed from Reghan in four months, and, with all the stress, I was afraid of what I'd find. "Meghan, did you hear me?" I hollered a little louder.

"I'm up. I'm up!" A not-so-chipper, sleepy-eyed Meghan answered the door. "What is it?" she asked, not the least bit enthused about getting up early.

To her, I looked the same as I had when I tried the dress on the first time, four months before. However, putting on the dress wasn't the problem; zipping it up was.

"Suck it in!" Meghan gritted her teeth.

"I AM!" I sucked my gut in so much it hurt. After three tries, we decided it was a lost cause. "Damn, WHAT AM I GOING TO DO?!" I was almost in tears. There was no way I was going to get another dress in two days! Why hadn't I thought to try it on a couple weeks before?

"Stupid, stupid, stupid," I berated myself, under my breath.

"Hey," Meghan tried comforting me, "It's going to be okay."

"Yeah? How do you know? It's as if I'm butting my head against a wall at every turn. Every time things look like they are coming together, something or someone botches it." Then I expressed the one thing that had been eating at me. "What if this isn't supposed to happen?"

"Don't talk like that! You are letting the opposition get in the way." Meghan's voice rose a notch.

"Well, then, what do you expect me to do?" I had almost given up.

"Hey! Isn't the owner of Weddings Are Forever in your ward?"

"Yeah, why?"

"Maybe you could check with her. I know they sometimes have dresses that don't sell and have to either donate them to Goodwill or The Salvation Army or give them away."

Within thirty minutes, Meghan and I were standing in Weddings Are Forever. "Hunter," the owner said after hearing my sob story. "I think I might have something that will work, but you'll need to try it on."

"How much?" I asked, with a crestfallen expression.

"Let's see if we can make it work first." In the fitting room, my hopes fell as I put on the gorgeous white dress with long, lacy sleeves and a full skirt with delicate beading all around the edges. "I can't get it zipped all the way." I couldn't hide the tears glistening in my eyes, but not yet spilling over.

"You know, if we let all the seams out, it should work. Your wedding is in two days, right?"

"Yes. Do you think you can get it done?" I was desperate.

"Let me get a hold of my tailor and see what she can do. She should be able to have it done by tomorrow, because all she's doing is pulling out all the stops."

"How much do I owe you for all your help?"

"Nothing. Let's just say this is our wedding gift to you."

After hearing that, I couldn't stop the tears that had been threatening all morning. I'd always wanted my own wedding dress, and it looked like I was going to get it! Weddings are Forever called later that day and told me I could come in the next morning at nine o'clock, allowing time for changes, if necessary.

As luck would have it, the dress fit—barely. Even with all the seams let out, I could barely breathe, but I was not going to look a gift horse in the mouth. The next thing on my last-minute wedding errand list was to finish paying the reception hall bill. There I was, the day before my wedding, going into the very place I would give myself to the man I wanted to be with forever.

I stepped into the hall and I couldn't help but look around—everything was beautiful! There were white, twinkling lights everywhere, along with a wooden bench and a trellis with burgundy and white flowers entwined up and down it. The owners had already started setting up chairs for the twenty-five people who were invited to the ceremony.

As far as Grey was concerned, all of the details of the wedding were my responsibility. The only thing he was adamant about was being able to shove cake in my face. Fortunately, when I asked the owner about the policy, she was firm in her explanation; she felt it took away from the sanctity of marriage. Therefore, anyone using her facility was prohibited from doing anything of the kind.

Grey, of course, was mad about that because, as he put it, "That was the only thing I was really looking forward to." At that moment, I was too star-struck to understand the full meaning of that statement.

~~~~~~

Meghan and Kieran (my best friend since eighth grade) decided they needed to throw a bachelorette party for me. Seriously, you only get married once, right? They, of course, didn't tell me, but they told Grey he couldn't see me after six o'clock that evening because it was Party Time. Grey wasn't too happy about it, but he conceded. Besides, I believed it was bad karma for the groom to see the bride at least twelve hours before the wedding, and we were shooting for twenty-four.

46

I was surprised to see Kieran when I got home from getting some last minute errands done. I'd invited Kieran to be one of my bridesmaids, but she wasn't sure whether she would be able to make it. Reghan was my matron of honor, and I didn't want anyone else to be my bridesmaid. Meghan was going assist the caterers with the reception refreshments and assist Reghan with anything she needed.

"Hey! What are you doing here?" I squealed.

"Surprise!" Kieran answered. "You can't get married without a bachelorette party. And there was no way I was missing your wedding!"

"What party?" I looked at them both suspiciously. "What did you guys do?"

"Well, we are going to order pizza and have an *almost* all-nighter, then tomorrow we are taking you to lunch at Central Park just before you go to the reception hall to get ready," Meghan replied.

"Why not pull an all-nighter?" I asked. I was getting nervous, almost scared—the day was getting close and I couldn't help but feel apprehensive. What if my mom was right? Was Grey a cheater? Was he snowballing me to only make it *look* like he was changing?

"Woo-ooh! Anyone in there?" Kieran snapped her fingers at me.

"Oh. Sorry, I was just thinking." I didn't want to ruin the party for my friends, so I kept my fears to myself. "Hey! Let's get this party started!" I did my best to have a good time and not let on that anything was amiss.

"What makes the two of you think I'm going to be able to sleep at all? I am so nervous." As we watched an all-time favorite movies *Eight Seconds* one of my all time favorite movies that for sure would make me cry, my thoughts turned to Lindley. Lindley should've been there. The problem was I didn't know where to find her; I'd heard that she'd moved with her parents to Pleasant Grove, only a few minutes away, when their house sold. She still worked at Deseret Industries, but I didn't know her schedule.

I was so distracted I didn't hear Kieran say, "Kyle is back from his mission." He was Kieran's boyfriend, and she'd been waiting two long years for his return. "Hunter, did you even hear what I just said?" Kieran scowled.

"No, sorry. I have a lot on my mind."

"Yeah, like your wedding night!" Meghan spoke up, then started to giggle. Before too long all three of us were busting it up.

"You know you can't wait…" Kieran teased.

In truth though, I was terrified. What if I wasn't any good? He was the experienced one. What if I did it wrong or did something he didn't like?

Seeing the worried look on my face, Kieran said, "Hey, we're only kidding. The only reason we are teasing you is because we love you and you're the only one of us that's even close to that."

CHAPTER THREE

I awoke on September 20, 1999, my wedding day, and the first day of the rest of my life, feeling like I was about to make a huge mistake. I rolled out of bed onto my knees and asked Heavenly Father to give me comfort in knowing I was doing what I needed to at that point in my life.

"Wake up, wake up, wake up!" Meghan and Kieran burst into my room but were shocked to see me on my knees.

"Now, *that's* the best way to start your day" Meghan smiled. Especially the first day of the rest of eternity! But it's time to get up!"

"We let you sleep in because you tossed and turned most of what was left of the early hour.." Kieran piped up.

"So, what's first?" Although Reghan was the matron of honor, it was up to my friends to make sure everything went off without a hitch since my sister was expecting. "Well, after I shower and get dressed anyway."

"First, we are getting our nails done. Meghan made the appointment several days ago. Then we are going to lunch, and after that, the reception hall," Kieran replied.

"You do realize that I will go see Grey before the wedding, don't you?" I gave them a look that said, *I WILL get my way, especially today."* I didn't want them to know about the fear that he might not go through with the wedding that kept rattling inside my brain.

"Well. We *did* tell him twelve hours, and by the time we get done with all the girly stuff, it'll be at least fourteen." Kieran said.

"I didn't think he'd go even two hours with no contact so this is kinda shocking." Meghan laughed.

~~~~~~

A couple hours later found me sitting on the edge of Grey's mom's couch. "Hey, sleepyhead, wake up," I whispered into Grey's ear.

Grey groaned, "What?" Once his eyes opened enough to see who it was, he perked up. "Hey babe! What are you doing here? Isn't it bad for the groom to see the bride before the wedding?"

"I know, I know. I just wanted to see you one more time before…you know."

"Before you are stuck with me forever." With that statement, he put my mind at ease without even realizing it.

"Yup. Hey, the girls are waiting for me. I'll be the nervous blonde in white." I kissed him passionately before I left.

~~~~~~

I was completely nervous by the time my sidekicks and I got to the reception hall; I started to panic. "You are okay," I chided myself. "You have prayed about this, and this is what you are supposed to do."

"Did you say something?" Kieran inquired.

"Nah. I'm just giving myself a little pep-talk."

"Nervous?"

"Extremely. Am I doing the right thing? It seems like everyone, most of all my parents are totally against this."

"Okay. You've prayed about it and have gotten a good feeling, right?"

"Yeah, but what if it's just because I want it so badly and not because it's what Heavenly Father wants?"

"You're second guessing yourself. Today is not the day to do that. You are getting married. Focus on that, not what might or might not happen."

"You are so right. I should be excited and happy!" I gave Kieran a hug and opened the door to the bride's room. I gasped as I stepped inside. *This would be the last place I'd be a single woman*, I thought as I looked around the brightly lit room.

Getting ready for my wedding without my mom was difficult for me. She'd been there on Reghan's wedding day, from start to finish. I didn't even know for sure whether my parents were coming or not. I hadn't talked to them a lot over the last few months. Even though my mom had promised to take my wedding pictures, I knew that, because of the way they felt about me marrying Grey, they might not come at all. The only thing I could do was wait, hope, and try not to think about it.

Reghan arrived about thirty minutes before the ceremony. She was wearing a long-sleeved, burgundy maternity dress that, for a maternity dress, was cute. "Hey, sis!" she said as she gave me a careful squeeze, not wanting to ruin my hair and makeup. My dress was the last thing to put on because I wanted the ability to breathe as long as possible. "Nervous?" Reghan asked.

"I was, but not anymore. Giddy is more like it. Do you know where Mom and Dad are?"

"They're on their way. They had to stop and get Mom some pantyhose."

"They better hurry." We were putting on my wedding dress when my mom arrived. "Hi, Mom." I hugged her, not caring whether I messed anything up or not. "I'm glad you're here. Where's Dad?"

"He'll be here shortly. How are you?"

"I'm really nervous…excited, but nervous."

"Well, sweetie, I may not agree with what you are doing, but you are my daughter. And yes, nerves are normal."

"I just wish you had been here to help me get ready." No matter how hard I tried, I couldn't hide how hurt I was.

"I couldn't. You have to understand, I feel like this is your funeral, not your wedding." Dead silence followed.

Thankfully, my dad chose that moment to enter. "Hi, Daddy." I hoped he couldn't see how hurt I felt.

"Are you ready?" he asked.

"As ready as I'll ever be." Meghan came in at that moment to let us know it was time. When given the cue, I put my arm through my dad's, took as deep a breath as my dress would allow, and began my walk down the aisle to "From This Moment" by Shania Twain and Brian White. This was the only walk down the aisle I would ever take. I was still battling with myself—until I saw him, and all my doubts fled. The apprehension was immediately replaced with an overwhelming sense of love for the man I was about to commit eternity to.

"Dearly beloved, we are gathered here today to witness the union of these two young people..." the bishop began. I didn't hear much after that but held onto Grey as if my very existence depended on it.

"Anyone here who doesn't want this to take place speak now or hold your peace." I didn't realize I was holding my breath until a sigh of relief escaped my lips when no one objected. To keep myself from thinking too much, I locked eyes on Grey's handsome face. Knowing that he wanted to be with me made all the doubts and fears almost frivolous.

I found myself dreading the *till death do you part* phrase, but it never came. *For your time on this earth* took its place (I understood what that meant, and it scared me. We were not sealed—there was no assurance that we would be together for all eternity even if we were sealed). When we exchanged rings, Grey slid mine on without a hitch, but because I didn't want my Cerebral Palsy to show, I spent more time worrying about whether it did or not and fumbled with his ring. Embarrassment washed over me, but I ignored it and hoped no one else noticed.

When the bishop said, "You may kiss the bride," it wasn't the breathtaking kiss I had come to expect. It was more like Grey might kiss his mother rather than his wife; however, the last part the bishop said made me smile.

"May I introduce to you Mr. and Mrs. Grey Andrews!" Whoops, hollers, and catcalls followed.

Heavenly Father must have a sense of humor because, just as we were taking the pictures, my throat began to burn; I felt a fever coming on and my voice vanished. I had prayed that whatever illness I'd been fighting would wait until *after* the I do's and that was exactly what happened. Boy, I didn't feel good!

While planning the wedding, I gave us two hours between the ceremony and the reception, thinking the pictures would take a while, but they only took about thirty minutes. Dang! I wished I'd known this because not only did I feel like warmed-over doggy doo, but I couldn't breathe either. I hoped the next several hours would fly by.

During the down time, Grey's sister asked if he wanted anything to eat; she was going into town to get something for herself and my mother-in-law. I didn't hear his response, but apparently, my mom did. Since she couldn't stand being around him any longer than she had to, and worrying that I wasn't eating, she asked if I was hungry (I wasn't). She told me she, Dad, and Reghan were going to get something to eat because Reghan needed to eat. They brought food back for me anyway. The way my stomach revolted when I took the first bite, I *knew* I was really sick. It wasn't just nerves.

~~~~~~

Just before the reception, my mom and I got into a heated argument—not the first or the last regarding Grey. I felt horrible enough that all I wanted to do was get through the next several hours, so I could crash. Not wanting to cause a scene, I quietly but bitterly explained to my mom that I was tired of only hearing negative things from her; she would accept both or neither of us.

My mom knew it wouldn't happen because, "Hunter would *always* come home." I was not one to stray too far from my parents, and my mom knew that.

The reception came and went with all the usual reception events: from standing in line and greeting well–wishers, cutting and feeding the cake to each other, and throwing the bouquet. I was so glad when I was able to remove my dress. Being able to breathe was magnificent! I knew we were far from being able to leave, however; we still had everything to clean up after the reception.

I wanted to cry when I saw my car. "Damn it! Why did they have to do this?" I wailed. Not only was it up on cinder blocks, but there were condoms filled with shaving cream inside the car and Vaseline and shaving cream smeared all over the outside; not to mention, Vaseline under the door handles. We took it down off the blocks and quickly removed the 'balloons.' Phew! Thankfully, none of them broke in the process. We cleaned off as much of the Vaseline and shaving cream as we could with the cleaning supplies we had available to us, but there wasn't much we could do.

It was after eleven o'clock by the time we could leave. Grey and I stopped at an all-night car wash to clean the rest of the goo off my car. There was so much of the slimy stuff all over the hood, the trunk, on the doors and under the door handles that, even after three super-duty washes, the filmy mess could still be felt, especially when opening the door.

~~~~~~

I was terribly sick and so tired by the time we arrived at the Comfort Inn, so much so that I didn't have the energy for the wedding night jitters brides were supposed to have. Although I seriously felt like crap, I didn't want to ruin it for Grey. Having never done this before, I took my cues from him. I'd waited my entire life for this moment. The moment the man of my dreams and I would come together as husband and wife. As we were changing, Grey informed me that he didn't like any of that *girly* stuff. He said he preferred his women in a huge t-shirt and boxer shorts or sweats. That made me think though, because I wasn't fat but nor was I skinny either. Why would he want that, especially on his wedding night? When packing, I put in a very tasteful black negligee with a lace wrap. I decided to wear it anyway.

When I came out of the bathroom, his reaction was so much worse than what I expected, even knowing he'd rather have me in boxers and a t-shirt. I thought he might change his mind, especially on our special night. "Why the hell are you wearing that? Did you not hear a damn word I said?" he demanded. Under his breath, I heard, "Stupid bitch." Totally hurt by his reaction, I kept quiet. "Come here," he growled, but not seductively like I had always imagined. After getting under the covers, Grey said, "I like my women to go down on me." He knew I'd never been with anyone before, but he didn't care.

"You mean you want me to...?" I swallowed, trying to dislodge the lump forming in my throat.

"Oh, for hell sakes! Come here and I'll show you what to do."

Not wanting to disappoint my new husband I did as he instructed. When I didn't move fast or deep enough, he lost his patience and shoved my head down until I gagged.

"You better not puke," he snarled. He'd never used that tone before and it scared me. Before I could recover, Grey exploded into my mouth. It took every ounce of willpower I possessed not to throw up right there.

When I finally got his taste out of my mouth, Grey sneered, "Now comes the part you'll like, but it might hurt." There was no foreplay or kissing, and the deed was done. Less than a minute later, Grey turned on the television and proceeded to ignore me. He didn't bother to ask whether I was okay after all that. I tried to cuddle with him, but he barely acknowledged my presence; he just continued watching whatever show he'd found.

I knew it wasn't supposed to happen the way I experienced it. *What was wrong with me? Did I disgust Grey?* My insignificance threatened to engulf me as I lay crying, making my already aching head worse. I wanted to die! With depressive thoughts running through my head, I fell into a fitful slumber.

~~~~~~

The next morning, I woke up before Grey. I did my best to put our first time out of my mind—maybe the next time he would show me how making love *should* be. As he began to stir, I turned toward him and croaked out a, "Good morning, husband." I hoped he'd ask how I was feeling, but he grunted at me instead.

Then, out of the blue, he said, "You'd better not get me sick!"

Never mind that I felt worse than I had the night before; he was more concerned about whether I would make him sick. Where was my sweetheart? Who was this stranger that had taken his place?

When we arrived home, Grey immediately stomped into our bedroom and slammed the door, rattling the trailer; I presumed he was going to finish unpacking.

Meghan could tell something was off because she asked, "What's up with him?"

"I don't know. He's been acting kind of weird since last night after...you know... Maybe it's because I feel like garbage and he sees that. Maybe I wasn't good enough. Maybe it's because he knows he leaves in two weeks and doesn't want the needy drama he's so sure he's going to get from me."

Meghan shrugged, "So...how was *it?*"

I knew what she meant, but because I didn't want to go into the gory details I said, "I am not talking about that with you."

An hour later, I found Grey still in the bedroom. "Hey, you. What're ya doin'?"

"Just gettin' this shit put away. Why?" He growled, sounding nothing like a man who'd just gotten married.

"Do you want to open our gifts before we leave?"

"I don't give a shit." He leaned down and kissed me on the cheek; it felt more of an obligatory peck than something he *wanted* to do. "Maybe we shouldn't go to South Jordan. You look like hell."

"Gee, thanks." I tried to sound like I was teasing, but I felt like dirt. He hadn't shown any real concern except that I might make him sick. So why did he care whether we went to South Jordan or not?

A few minutes later, we opened our wedding gifts. Most were cards, some with money, and some without. Other than that, we received a set of mixing bowls, sheets, and, my favorite gift, burgundy and hunter green Double Wedding Ring quilt made by Grandma Kacie, my mom, and a bunch of women that lived in the same building as Grandma.

Suddenly Grey burst out, "What the f***! That's it? All those people I stood and shook hands with, and we get a measly hundred bucks?"

"Grey!" I looked at him in utter astonishment. "What's the matter? You've been acting really strange since last night."

"Nothing. I just think I deserve more for all the hand shaking and ass kissing I did."

I was so dumbfounded that I wasn't sure how to respond. I didn't know what he was thinking, and couldn't get him to open up to me. I was sick enough, and Grey was so despondent that we cancelled our weekend to South Jordan.

I got more ill as the weekend wore on, but not sick enough that Grey didn't get his needs met. Most of the time it was a wham, bam, thank you, ma'am with a little hickey action on the side, but what Grey deemed a little hickey was a HUGE bruise on the side of my neck. I was instructed, however, NEVER to leave even a tiny one on him where anyone might see.

~~~~~~

Grey's departure date crept up faster than I expected. I was not looking forward to the next month without my sweetheart, but I would make it, I hoped. As I helped Grey pack, I couldn't stop the tears that I'd tried so hard to hide the last two weeks.

Grey didn't seem too unhappy that he was leaving. In fact, he was excited. After he finished packing, we spent the rest of the night cuddling on the couch, watching movies — much to my surprise! Grey hadn't been lovey-dovey since before our wedding. It was all about sex. Nothing more.

~~~~~~

When Grey's departure date arrived, I asked Meghan to go with me to take Grey to the airport. If left up to Grey, we wouldn't even park, but dump him off at the curb. I was having none of that, however. I was a newlywed and, instead of getting to know my husband as a married person, I was sending him off and entrusting him to people I didn't know.

I insisted we go inside and wait with him until he boarded the plane. He wasn't happy about it but didn't say anything.

When Grey's boarding number was called, my panic rose. What was I going to do without him? With the distance he'd been enforcing the last two weeks, what if he decided he didn't want me? What if he decided he didn't want the sanctity of marriage? Unless it was an emergency, I was to neither write nor call while Grey was away. His strict instructions. He said he'd call when he could, but would he? He gave me a quick peck on the cheek, gave me a cocky grin and headed down the boarding ramp.

"All right, Mopey." Meghan turned to me. "We can either go get your favorite chocolate cake or go shopping. What do you say?"

Not wanting to dampen Meghan's good mood, I asked, "Why not both?" Even though I *hated* shopping and I wanted nothing more than to go home and hide under my blankets and pillows sprayed with Grey's Stetson cologne for the next month, I knew I couldn't. A month wasn't that long, right?

The entire month of October crawled for me. Grey called me about ten days after he left, and acted as if talking to me was a pain, but I wasn't ready to let him go just yet. "So...how are you?" I asked.

"We are so busy. I barely have time to breathe, much less take any time for myself," Grey replied. "How are things there?"

"I'm okay. I really miss you though."

"Yeah. Me too." He didn't sound like he meant it.

"Do you get to do anything else? Down time? Anything?" I couldn't imagine that even the military wouldn't allow them time for themselves.

"Well, yeah. I've been to the bar a couple of times."

He must've heard the apprehension in my voice because the next sentence out of his mouth was, "Don't worry. I don't drink. In fact, they have nominated me the designated driver."

The news gave me some relief. "What have you been doing besides pining for me?" Grey inquired, thinking he was being funny. For some reason that question upset me.

"I don't sit at home every night, if that's what you're getting at. I spend time with both Grandma Marshall and Grandma Kacie. I've been to see your mom a couple times, too. She misses you almost as much as I do."

"Well, I better get off here. Give my mom a hug for me." With a quick "bye," he hung up.

It bothered me immensely that he didn't say, "I love you," or anything else endearing, but I couldn't let myself dwell on it.

~~~~~~

On October twenty-fifth, I found myself getting dressed up to go to Hank and Lynese's wedding and reception. Alone.

I'd thought about not going, because they were more Grey's friends than mine, but since we were married, and he couldn't be there, I felt it was my duty as his wife to represent us. Afterward, I went home, changed into pajama bottoms and one of Grey's t-shirts sprayed with his cologne, and sat down to watch *Dirty Dancing*.

Just as I was settling in, there was a knock at the door. It was a little late on that Thursday night, but I wasn't prepared for the person on the other side of the door. After telling her that I was Grey's wife and he was away at training, she grudgingly handed me the item she held in her fist. I definitely wasn't prepared for what I saw. The paperwork handed to me was a court document naming Grey as the father of a child and asking for child support—a little girl who, if the papers were correct, was almost a year old.

My stomach clenched, and the room began to spin as I made my way to the couch. Whoever the person was wanted Grey to pay back child support to February. That meant Grey either knew about the baby when we got together, or he had no idea there was a baby.

I did the only thing I could think of now. When Meghan answered, I blurted, "You will not believe what I am holding in my hand!"

"I don't know. What?"

"It is a court document claiming Grey is a father. The baby girl is almost a year old, and the mother wants child support!"

"Are you serious?" Meghan couldn't believe it. "Do you need me to come home? I'm just hanging out at my sister's house anyway."

"No, but would you deem this an emergency? Grey said not to call unless it's an emergency." I was hysterical. I could not believe my husband would keep something that important from me.

"How long does he have to respond to the letter?"

"Twenty days."

"He'll be home next weekend, right?"

"That's what he said when I talked to him, but he also said he wasn't sure what would happen. That's how the military runs things, he said. Who knows when I'll see him? It's not like he's gone out of his way to make sure I'm still here anyway."

"If I were you, I would call. This is HUGE! He never told you he got a girl pregnant. That stinks! Maybe that's the real reason why he started smoking again, or why he was a real peach for the two weeks before he left.."

"Or never quit and there's more secrets.." Anger rose to the surface. I decided to leave it alone but wait to see if Grey would call.

Two days before he was due to return, he finally called, only the second time since he left. When I noticed it was Grey on the caller I.D., I put my anger in check. "Hey, honey, how are you?"

"Fine. You?"

"I'm doin' okay, I guess. I miss you like crazy and can't wait to see you. You're still coming home the day after tomorrow, right?"

"Yes, and I'm bringing some friends with me."

"Who?" I *really* didn't want other people in my house. We were newlyweds and Grey had been gone for what felt like forever. I wanted time alone with my husband. Was that too much to ask?

"Just some friends I met here. They are bringing me home, so don't be a bitch!"

Why would he say that?. "Be nice? You sound like I'm going to bite their heads off and spit down their throats as soon as I meet them."

"Hunter," he warned, "they aren't members of the church, aren't married, but live together, and I don't want you trying to convert them or change them or anything like that. In fact, take down the pictures of Christ and the temple so they aren't offended."

"WHAT?" So much for keeping my anger in check. "I WILL NOT take those pictures down. Besides that, they are just dropping you off, right?"

"Uuuuhhh. No. I thought they could stay the night, so we can go out that night."

"Fine. But I'm not taking down any pictures." I was adamant about it. "They know you are a member of the church, right?"

"Yes."

"Then they shouldn't have a problem. If they do, they can stay somewhere else."

"You don't have to be that way about it."

Because I didn't want to belabor the subject to death, I abruptly changed it. "You got court papers served to you the other day."

"Court papers? For what?" He had the audacity to sound baffled.

"Child support." I waited to see what his response might be. Of course, he was mystified. So I asked, "You don't *know* you fathered a baby? How could you do that and never tell me?"

He knew he'd been caught. "I...um...I..." Grey cleared his throat. "I was going to tell you, but just haven't found the right time."

"The right time? That little girl is nine months old! We've only been married six weeks! That means you knew when we started dating or at the very least, when we got engaged."

"Yeah, but I didn't think she would do anything. When I signed the birth certificate, under duress I might add, she said she wanted nothing from me. She's a bitch who's just after my money."

"Your money? You don't even have a job yet!" The heat rose in my cheeks. "And you believed that she wouldn't do anything? Do you know if the kid is even yours? Did you take a paternity test? Grey, what the hell?"

"Don't pull that 'you don't have a job' shit on me. I didn't need to take a paternity test. She wouldn't have cheated on me."

"How in the hell did this happen? What? You only use protection now because you don't want to make the same mistake again?"

"It broke."

I found myself wondering whether he was being truthful.

"Can we talk about this when I get home? I've got to go to formation."

He hung up, no goodbye, no I love you...nothing. Again!

Over the next two days, I did my best to forget about Grey's indiscretion and focused on the good part. My honey was coming home! I spent the time between work and the very little sleep I did get cleaning the trailer from top to bottom, making sure the spare bedroom was ready for his friends.

~~~~~~

The day of Grey's arrival, I waited patiently as the hours crept along. I passed the time writing in my journal. Writing had become my outlet, helping to alleviate the loneliness that having my sweetheart gone had caused.

Finally, around five o'clock that afternoon Grey called...FROM HIS MOM'S HOUSE! Was he serious? For reasons I didn't understand he wanted me to stay home and wait until he decided to show up.

Without telling him, I drove the two miles to his mom's house, hoping he would be surprised and pleased to see me. I couldn't stop the thudding of my heart or the butterflies in my stomach as he strode down the stairs just as I was opening the front door. He looked hot, wearing his ARMY physical training shirt, Wranglers, and a tan cowboy hat. *Where had he gotten the money for that?* I wondered.

His reaction left me heartbroken. "I thought I told you to stay home and we would be there in a while," he thundered at me, not bothering to introduce me to the six-foot-tall blonde guy or the short, brown-haired woman standing behind him on the stairs.

"I wanted to surprise you! I couldn't wait to see you." Grey wasn't happy. Not knowing whether he'd welcome a hug or kiss, I kept my distance.

"Well, since my wife is already here, we should probably go home." Grey turned to the two people behind him.

Finally, the guy said, "Hey, Grey, you gonna introduce us to your wife, or do we have to do it ourselves?"

"Oh. Sorry, man," Grey replied, calming down. "Hunter, this is Darren and Cristine, the ones I told you about. Guys, this is Hunter."

We left shortly thereafter. I asked Grey to ride with me, but he was determined to ride with Darren and Cristine. Not wanting to be put in my place again, I quietly left in my car and tried hard not to cry. *Why does he act as if he isn't happy to see me?*

Later that night we went to the bar to play pool and dance. Grey acted more like he had when we were dating, but he was still distant with me. I hoped he'd talk to me when we got home, but instead I was diverted by Darren, who did his best to convince me that being a member of the Church of Jesus Christ of Latter-day Saints was bad, and following his way—Paganism—was better. I spent the next two hours listening to him put down anything and everything I believed in, while my husband completely ignored me to entertain Cristine.

~~~~~~

"So, what do you think of Darren and Cristine?"

Was he for real? This definitely wasn't what I'd planned for his first night home, but not wanting to anger him, I answered, "They're okay."

"Just okay?"

"Do you really care what I think about them?"

If he were honest, he would say no, but he didn't so... "I don't like the way Darren puts down everything we believe in, while you allowed it to continue! You left me alone with him, which I hated. Then, you expected me to be okay with you and Cristine being alone, while Darren gave me his speech? They are not your friends. After they leave, you will never hear from them again."

"You don't know anything about them! You only met them today. How do you know what they will or won't do?" He was furious. I could see that, but he'd asked me what I thought.

Just then Grey blurted out, "I don't want to be here! I want the hell out!"

Hoping I heard wrong, I asked, "What?"

"You heard me. I don't want to be here."

"Where do you want to be then?"

"I don't know. I'm just not used to being married or having to answer to someone else."

"Is that why you brought them here? So you'll have a way out if you decide I'm not what you want?"

"I guess."

I couldn't believe he had admitted that. "Well, let me tell you something, you son of a bitch," I snapped, my anger rising fast, "I have been here, alone, working my ass off, hoping you wouldn't get used to being single again. And at the same time, I was struggling to figure out how to get used to not being alone. If you want to leave, don't let the door hit your ass on your way out!"

With that, I turned my back to him, knowing sleep wouldn't come anytime soon for me. This was NOT how I had wanted his homecoming to be.

CHAPTER FOUR

One day, during the first part of December, Grey and Hank stopped to see me at work. Grey was more excited than I'd seen him in a long time. "Hey, what are you doing here?"

"We got jobs!" Grey acted like a kid in a candy store.

"Both of you? Where?"

"The glass shop here in town. They need people to cut and carry the glass for windshields and stuff."

I wasn't sure I wanted the two of them working together because they messed around more than they worked. But, hey, I wasn't going to rain on their parade. At least there would be more money coming in, I hoped.

The next Sunday, which was only a few days later, Grey and I were asked to meet with the bishop after church. I was concerned about what he wanted. What if he gave us a calling? I wasn't sure I could handle a calling.

"How are you, Brother and Sister Andrews?" he asked as we sat across from him.

Grey didn't say anything, and because I didn't want him to know how we really were, I answered, "We're okay."

"Well, let's get right down to business, then. We'd like the two of you to team-teach the four-year-old primary class."

My gut fell to my feet, but being raised never to turn a calling down, I answered, "Okay."

Grey acted as if they'd given him a death sentence, but he agreed to it as well. On the way home, though, he let me know what he thought of the whole situation.

"Why the hell did you tell them we would do it?" he ground out.

"I was responding for myself. You could've said no," I retorted.

"And look like a jackass? No way. You're gonna have to teach. I don't know anything about it, and besides, that's the boring part anyway."

"That's fine." I didn't want to start a humongous fight, so I agreed. I continued having doubts as the next Sunday drew nearer and nearer.

Our first Sunday teaching was fun for me because I got to see how Grey handled little kids. They were so enamored of him that he got them to sit still for the entire class period.

~~~~~~

Days turned into weeks, and Grey and I entered a routine as a married couple. During the week, Hank picked up and dropped Grey off, usually at his mom's house. Grey started spending most of his time at his mom's, unless he was at Hank's dad's house after work. His sister got a new computer, and Grey spent a lot of time chatting with friends on the Internet—friends he said he met in Boise. One day though, Grey's sister called me. "Hey, Hunter. Who's Sheryl?"

"Sheryl? I have no idea. It has to be one of Grey's friends from Boise."

"Yeah, maybe. I'll ask him," she said before she hung up.

When Grey came home, I asked him about Sheryl. He explained that she was a friend from Boise that he had a lot in common with, and he enjoyed talking with her. I tried not to let the fact that he'd rather talk to another woman bother me. *At least he wasn't cheating,* I thought, but he seemed to be addicted to the internet.

Little did I know, it wasn't the internet but Sheryl he was addicted to. I didn't dare say anything more about it because I didn't want to set him off, so I let the matter drop. I wanted Grey and me to be married, but since his return from Boise, he treated me more like his harlot and servant than his wife—only good for working, cooking, cleaning and sex. But whenever I brought up how I felt, he would tell me I was completely out of my mind.

~~~~~~

I had always loved the time between Thanksgiving and Christmas growing up. When my siblings and I were younger, our family would make a whole bunch of Christmas candy: peanut butter cups, peanut brittle, caramel, divinity, fudge, and anything else we could come up with. We'd sing Christmas carols at nursing homes and hospitals; wherever we could find someone alone or in need.

Although most of us were married and had our own lives, we got together for a couple of nights to wrap candy and go caroling before Christmas. We bundled up as warmly as we could and set out to make someone else's holiday special. Seeing others smile was worth the frozen hands and faces.

One night we chose to go caroling, but Grey opted to stay at my parents' house. "It's too cold," he grumbled. Instead of causing an argument, I went without him. By the time we returned, I could barely feel my toes, much less my fingers.

Grey acted all put out because we were gone too long and didn't hesitate to let me know how pissed he was. "Geez, took you long enough!" There was that condescending tone he used whenever he didn't get his way.

"It was fun," I replied. Trying to be playful I put my ice-cold hands-on Grey's warm cheeks. "Ahhh! Warmth," I teased.

"Damn! Your hands are cold! Get those off me." He pushed my hands away. "Can we go now?"

I wanted to stay and have hot chocolate, but I didn't want Grey to feel anymore put out than he already did. I was totally looking forward to joking and laughing with my family, but once again, Grey came first.

~~~~~~

For as long as I could remember, I dreamed of going up to the mountains with my sweetheart and cutting down a Christmas tree, or him having the kind of relationship with my family that I could send him along with the rest of the men in my family, while the ladies stayed at my mom's and made Christmas candy with Grandma Kacie. Unfortunately, I wasn't naive enough to believe that would happen. And it didn't.

Grey wasn't much for celebrating any part of Christmas, so he waited to get a tree until a few days before. He purchased the cheapest, tiniest one he could find. I was crushed when I saw what he'd brought home. It was the sparsest tree I'd ever seen. I hoped with a little decoration and love, I could make it into some semblance of a Christmas tree.

~~~~~~

Christmas morning at our house was more somber than exciting. It was after ten o'clock before I could get Grey out of bed. He wasn't at all excited about opening presents with me. When we finally got around to it, I let him open his gifts first because I wanted to see his reaction. I gave him a new pair of Wranglers, along with a new button-down shirt he'd been hinting at. He showed no enthusiasm, not even when I opened mine from him.

It was a gorgeous, silver-plated, round necklace with matching earrings. I started to cry, which angered Grey. "What are you crying for? What? Isn't it good enough for you?!" He would never understand that, to me, the gift meant he still loved me.

I wore my gift proudly while we visited Grey's family. After exchanging gifts with them, we went to my mom and dad's house. Both of my grandmothers were there. On every holiday, someone in the family went to Park City, where Grandma Marshall lived, to pick her up, because she was in her nineties and didn't drive anymore. Grandma Kacie lived in town in an apartment complex specifically for the elderly.

"Hey everybody!" I beamed as Grey and I walked through the door.

My family didn't need to know what had transpired between Grey and me that morning, and there was no way I was going to say anything. Even before Grey and I got married I'd made a promise to myself that it didn't matter how bad or good things were between Grey and me, I wasn't ever going to bring our problems to my parents. I hadn't done it yet; I wasn't going to start.

As the day wore on, my mom, both grandmas, and I worked feverishly in the kitchen while the men and boys watched a football game, coming into the kitchen to sneak food whenever they thought no one was looking.

I stared longingly as I watched my dad kiss my mom lovingly every now and again, usually while swiping food. Not to mention all the other displays of affection going on around me. Grey hardly said a word to me. Maybe he felt my family's dislike for him, although the only member of the family that gave him the cold shoulder was my younger brother, Damien. For reasons that weren't at all clear, Damien seriously hated Grey, and he had no qualms about showing it whenever they were in the same room.

After dinner, everyone gathered in the living room to exchange gifts. Two gifts my parents gave us were a pressure cooker (something I'd wanted for a long time) and two movies, *Overboard* (my favorite) and *Liar, Liar*.

~~~~~~

Grey and I spent New Year's Eve with Hank and Lynese. Lynese worked as a front desk clerk at the Sleep Inn just off the highway and, because of her discount, we got a great deal on a room. We decide to split the cost. There wasn't going to be much sleeping, if any. The motel had the typical amenities: a television in an entertainment center, ice bucket, internet, and access to the swimming pool and hot tub until eleven o'clock at night.

After checking in, we chose to go to the pool and check out the hot tub. The way Grey bantered with and teased me made the last few months seem like a distant memory. We spent a couple hours in the pool and hot tub, then headed back to the room so we could watch a movie or two before midnight, ringing in the year 2000.

I thought spending New Year's Eve with his friends might loosen him up, and it had, at least for a few minutes.

"Grey," I took a stab at getting his attention.

"Huh?" He was miles away.

"Are you having fun?" When he didn't answer, I pulled sexy out of my bag of tricks and kissed the back of his neck, ever so lightly.

He, of course, wasn't paying attention and yelled out, "HEY! What the hell are you doin'?!"

The tears burned, but Grey hated it when I cried, so I wiped at them angrily. I didn't want him to see the new low he'd knocked me to.

"What the f*** do you want?" Grey demanded, irritated.

"Didn't you hear me ask you if you're having fun?"

72

"No. And, yeah, I'm having a great time." He didn't sound like it.

We must've met our quota of communication for the day because Grey and Hank began discussing what movies they wanted to watch. I made up a lame excuse about going to get ice, but no one, least of all my sweetheart, cared. I didn't have any idea what was causing him to snap and lose his temper so much, especially with me, but it was getting tiresome. Real fast. Twenty minutes later, I let myself back into the room.

"Geez woman, what took you so long?" Grey thought he was teasing, but I was in no mood for it. Not anymore. His mood changed from night to day so quickly, especially around me, that I never knew when it was safe to banter back. Ignoring Grey's comment, I questioned, "So, what are we watching?"

"The boys picked *Blair Witch Project* and *Amityville Horror*," Lynese replied, doing her best to act disgusted, but by the way she and Hank were all over each other, I didn't think she minded. I didn't respond; instead, I grabbed my t-shirt and boxers on the pretense of changing. All I really wanted was to be alone. I was in no mood to pretend I was okay.

As the hours passed slowly, I kept to myself while the others picked apart the movies with lewd comments. "Hey, did you see that chick's ass?" Grey laughed. "Check out her tits, man!"

"I know! Right?" Hank responded. Lynese didn't seem at all bothered by the crude comments the boys were using to describe the actresses.

"She'd be a great screw. Huh?" Grey asked Hank. This went on through both movies. No one noticed I wasn't joining in or that I was depressed; they didn't seem to care. It was disconcerting, knowing my husband didn't notice that I was not okay. I wanted to go home, but we all came in the same car, so that wasn't going to happen. Finally, midnight came and we watched the ball drop in Time Square on the television. Hank and Lynese kissed like any brand-new newlyweds who still had stars in their eyes.

Grey, on the other hand, kissed me on the cheek. *What the hell? He didn't just kiss me the way he might kiss his best friend's sister, did he?* I didn't want to deal with his temper tantrums, so I plastered on my best smile and whispered, "Happy New Year, Sweetie."

The way Grey looked the next morning, I was pretty sure he had stayed up most of the night, if not all of it. When we returned home around ten o'clock, Grey complained he was tired and went to bed without saying anything else to me.

He seriously thought he was the only one who didn't sleep the night before? How did he think I knew he stayed up all night? We were supposed to be at my parents' house at two o'clock that afternoon for New Year's Day dinner. I was tempted to make an excuse, but I knew my mom would see right through it and want to talk about it.

Dinner was much the same as Christmas, except Grey paid attention to me. It wasn't good attention either. He didn't care who saw, but every chance he got he either slapped me on the rear end or called me *Sexy Woman* with a crude sneer.

I could tell by the looks that passed between my parents that they wanted to say something, but they didn't. I knew negative attention wasn't good, but I was so starved for acknowledgement from Grey that I took any kind I could get.

~~~~~~

Two weeks later, Grey came home in a tizzy. "The boss wants me and Hank to come early tomorrow. He said to be prepared for some changes."

Due to Grey's less than stellar employment history, I worried about what *some changes* meant. He'd only been there about six weeks.

Grey dropped that bomb on me, then promptly informed me that he needed to go talk to his sister. He spent too much time at his mom's house on the stupid computer and I knew *talking to his sister* was code for chatting, mostly with his Precious Sheryl.

I was so used to being left behind I didn't even flinch when he let the door slam behind him. It was easier to let him go than to get him to listen to how it made me feel. If I tried stopping him, he would blow up at me, and it never prevented him from leaving anyway. Just more heartache for me.

With Grey gone, I tuned the radio to my favorite country station and curled up on the couch to write while waiting for him to come back. I started writing in a journal about anything and everything when I was eight. Lately, I only wrote when things were bad. Even though we'd only been married five months, I wondered all the time whether Grey loved me.

There were times I thought I should leave, and then Grey could have his Precious Sheryl. I wondered if Grey regretted marrying me. I bet he wished he could marry Sheryl. Even not knowing what she looked like, I seriously didn't blame him. I wasn't skinny or pretty. All I saw when I looked in the mirror was a fat, ugly, deformed piece of shit Grey had taken pity on.

I didn't know if I would be able to have children and hated myself for it. Every time I asked Grey, he swore he and Sheryl were only friends, that she was simply someone he could talk to. Apparently, he couldn't talk to me!

I found myself scribbling furiously every rotten feeling I'd had in my journal, and every rotten feeling I had at that moment. When I finished, I did my best to wait up for him, but ended up falling asleep on the couch.

~~~~~~

Right after I arrived at work the next morning, my phone rang. Just as I'd feared, Grey and Hank were fired. Because I was at work, I couldn't go off half-cocked like I wanted to right then. To make matters worse, Grey was at his mom's when I got off work. I was angry enough that I wasn't letting him do whatever he wanted. He heard me drive up and acted all innocent when I walked in. He wasn't even on the computer. His mom was the only one there besides him. "Hi, honey," he said a little too sweetly. Why was he acting like we were happy newlyweds? I'd been trying to get him to do that very thing for four months!

"Hi," I replied cautiously. "What are you doin'?"

"Mom didn't have to work, so I thought I'd come see her."

"Oh?" I wasn't sure I believed him, but at least he was talking to me. And, nicely at that! "Does she know you got fired?"

"Not yet. Don't say anything. Please?" He *was* being nice. Made me wonder what tricks he had up his sleeve.

"Fine, but you really should tell her."

"I will. How was work?"

He wanted to know that? I had my doubts, but I answered, "It was okay. Slow."

"What are you doing now?"

"I was going home, but you spend a lot of time here. I thought I'd check on you first." He was being nice enough I dared ask, "Come home with me?"

"I need to wait till my sister comes home. I've got some questions for her."

Because we were having a real conversation and I didn't want to mar the vibe we had going, I didn't push the question thing. Instead I replied, "Okay. Don't stay too late." Grey actually let me kiss him. I was so elated that we'd had a conversation without negativity that I didn't let the fact he would most likely chat with Sheryl bother me.

~~~~~~

Sometime during the train wreck I called my marriage, Grey decided that maybe getting a paternity test was a good idea, and acted like it was his idea. *Was he kidding?* Instead of bringing it up, however, I found the number and gave it to Grey to make an appointment, which he was able to schedule in February, 2000. I wasn't sure why he was in such a good mood, but I took advantage of that fact and told him I wanted to be there. He conceded without even a mild temper tantrum. What was going on? I would soon find out.

We arrived at the lab, and I was more nervous than Grey. Why was that? Maybe because I wanted so badly to be the mother of his children and I feared the news would fracture our already fragile relationship? It only took ten minutes to collect Grey's DNA. It would take another forty-eight hours for the results. That meant we might find out Monday, but most likely Tuesday. We were in a better place than we'd been in a long time, so much so that I spent the weekend basking in my love for my husband and hoping that the good feeling would last.

Monday morning was another crazy day at work when Grey called me with the paternity news. "I told you I didn't need a damn paternity test. It's over 99% accurate that she's mine."

"I wanted to be sure." I responded.

"Well, now you know. I wish her parents would've let me sign termination papers instead of that damn birth certificate. They held me there at the hospital until I signed. *She* understood why I didn't want this following me. She was okay with it. This is all coming from her parents."

"Now what?" I asked, trying to keep the good vibe we had going.

"I should be paying child support, and they want to go clear back to her birth. What do they think, that I'm made of damned money?"

"You don't have a job, but I read in the documents that they go off what you can potentially make in a year at full-time and minimum wage." After doing some quick math in my head, I explained, "That's over $11,000 a year. We don't even make that much."

"Good thing they can't come after your paycheck." Grey snickered.

"Why didn't you tell me about her as soon as you found out?" I knew I was pushing my luck asking that, but things were good, so I had to try.

"I told you I was waiting for the right time." I could hear the edge in Grey's voice. "What do you want me to do? I made a f***ing mistake."

I didn't like the way he called the child a mistake, or his choice of words, and told him as much.

"When do you want to tell your mom and my parents?" My next question. That was all it took—talking about my parents caused our good vibe to fly right out the window.

"My mom already knows. And, as far as your dumb ass parents? Why do they have to know any of this?" The *not-so-nice* Grey was back.

His response floored me. "Your mom knows? When did this happen?"

"She knew before the baby was born," he was flippant.

"Wait a minute? Your family has known about the baby all along? And you couldn't find the time to tell me?" I didn't hide the hurt in my voice.

"I *had* to tell them. She's family to them."

"What is she to me then? Chopped liver?" I was doing my best to control the quivering in my voice, but the tears were thick in my throat. I couldn't deal with it at that moment, so I burst out, "I've got to get back to work. I'll see you when I get off." I didn't wait for a response before hanging up the phone and making a beeline for the restroom. I couldn't stem the flood of tears that were coursing down my cheeks. How could he tell his family and not me?

~~~~~~

Grey decided that, because he had to pay child support, he deserved to see his daughter. He tried several times after getting the paternity test results back to call, with no luck. Finally, after several attempts, on February eighth, he left a message on their answering machine. "This is Grey. You probably know that, though, because I've called several f***ing times over the last few weeks. Since tomorrow is my daughter's birthday, I want to see her. I will be there at seven o'clock tomorrow evening, so have her ready. I want to get her a gift as well. Call me back and we can talk about what would be appropriate for a one-year-old."

Thinking that he probably wouldn't get a phone call, we went to Wal-Mart for a gift anyway. Because Grey hadn't spent much time around little kids, he had NO idea what to get. It landed on my shoulders, finding an age appropriate present for a one-year-old little girl I didn't know. Fun times. I decided on a baby doll that made crying and laughing sounds. Grey didn't care what I chose, and he was awfully distant. More so than he had been previously. I spent the rest of the evening giving Grey the distance that he acted like he wanted. One minute, though, he wanted nothing to do with me, and the next, he wanted to cuddle.

The next day, Saturday, which was usually Grey's favorite day of the week, we had the entire day to dwell on what might or might not take place. I kept busy cleaning house while Grey spent a lot of time outside, smoking, I was sure. I didn't want to make the day any harder on him, so I didn't broach the subject at all.

Just before six o'clock, Grey, out of the blue, said, "I think I should go alone."

I was taken aback. "What? Why? I'm part of this, too, you know, and I didn't ask for it."

"Is it so bad that I want to see *my* daughter without having to worry about how it's making you feel?" He lashed out.

"Are you serious? You haven't cared how I've felt about pretty much anything since you came back from Boise." I could feel all the hurt, anger, and fear I'd been dealing with rise to surface.

"I don't want to fight about this. You can be a bitch when you really want to, you know."

I gathered all the strength I possessed to act as if it didn't matter. "Fine. Whatever."

Grey didn't need to look up the address; he knew right where it was. Not two minutes after exiting the pickup, Grey came back. He was angry and, without a word, handed me a slip of paper. It read: *I got your message and after talking to my lawyer, you can't see her without a court order. Go ahead and leave her present.* There wasn't a signature or anything, but there was a picture of the baby. I really didn't want to see what the child who didn't belong to me—but *did* belong to the man I loved—looked like. My curiosity won, however. There was no doubt who fathered her.

"How can she do this to me?" Grey growled through gritted teeth. "It's all her parents...they don't like me, so I bet they made this all up just to keep me the f*** away! Well, that ain't happenin'!" He turned the truck around and peeled out of the driveway, spewing gravel everywhere.

~~~~~~

I worked my butt off while Grey either spent his days at Hank's dad's house, supposedly working in the shop, or at his mom's house chatting with Sheryl. The more time that went by, the more time he spent on the internet.

Finally, after getting totally fed up with the situation, I decided to see what was so *special* about Sheryl. I decided to go on a weekend to ensure Grey wasn't around. Because it was his sister's computer, I had to get her to enter the password.

There were two emails he had written to Sheryl, and both made me extremely angry and incomparably sad. One said Grey loved Sheryl as he'd never loved anyone—the same thing he said to *me* once upon a time. The other read that 'Andrews' would look good as her last name. I didn't allow myself to think about how Grey

80

would react to what I was about to do because, at that moment, I felt so hurt and betrayed I didn't care.

After writing an email of my own to Sheryl, telling her Grey was married and NOTHING would come of their relationship, I showed Grey's sister how to delete his emails, messenger account, and change the password on the computer. I then spent the rest of the weekend trying not to think about Grey's reaction.

~~~~~~

Grey stopped at his mom's first, presumably to check in with his Precious Sheryl. The only way I knew he'd been there was the way he stormed in the front door and ripped into me. "Who the hell do you think you are?" he yelled. "YOU had no f***ing right to go into *my* personal email and delete everything!"

I was scared, but I couldn't let it go. If I did, it would open the door for Grey to treat me like a doormat more than he already did. "Who am I? In case you've forgotten, I'm your *wife*. I have every right to know whether my husband is cheating on me! All I want to know is, why?"

"Because. She cares about me. What I want. What I *need*." His tone was still higher than normal.

"And I don't?" my voice rose another octave.

"No." He threw pictures of who I could only assume were of Sheryl; the glossy images falling at my feet. Where he got them, I didn't know. I bit my lip and stifled the scream that threatened.

"Who is this?" Anger prevailed, as I picked up the picture from the floor.

"Who do you think?" Grey taunted. By the look on my face, Grey knew the next thing he said would hurt me even more than seeing the pictures did. "Ya know, it's pretty sad really. . ."

"What?"

"Having sex with you. I have to look at Sheryl's hot, luscious body and pretend you're her. You are repulsive to look at, and even kissing you is like kissing the ass end of a cow." He didn't act at all apologetic as he watched my face to crumble.

My first instinct was to cry, but there was no way I was letting him see how badly I was affected. Instead, I ripped the pictures up and chucked them across the room, surprised that Grey did not stop me. "If that's where you want to be, don't let me stop you. I'll even buy the damn plane ticket!" There was nothing left for me to say, so I looked Grey full in the eye and walked away. I didn't know whether he would leave or not, but at that moment, I was finding it hard to care. I couldn't turn my brain off as question after question took up residence there. *Why did Grey try so hard to marry me if he didn't want me? Was he ashamed of me? Kissing me made him sick? Did he really have to have a vivid picture of Sheryl in his head when we had sex?* I loved him so much, but maybe that love was and always had been one sided.

I spent the next few days trying to act as if everything was okay. My mom always said I was the type of person to wear my heart on my sleeve. Of course, she saw through it. I couldn't stop crying as I told her the whole miserable tale. I cried until there were no more tears left.

I couldn't believe I'd broken the promise I made to myself. I wasn't planning on saying anything, but she saw right through my brave front. I felt like I was going to explode. I had to talk to someone. Her hands were tied though, because of our conversation at my wedding. I knew there was nothing she would or could do.

~~~~~~

Because I was trying to forget all the hurtful, demeaning words my husband leveled at me, I decided to take Grey out for

Valentine's Day. His favorite place was Texas Roadhouse in Salt Lake. Although I'd worked all day and was tired (not including the emotional exhaustion I'd been dealing with the last two weeks), I wanted to do something nice for him. Why? I didn't know. I wanted to let him know that, regardless of how he felt about me, I still loved him. I hoped he might remember a time when I was the next best thing to buttered bread, if there was such a time. As a gift, I gave him a chain bracelet that had *I Love You, Happy Valentine's Day* engraved on it. "What for?" was Grey's response when I let him in on what we were doing for Valentine's Day.

"I thought we could use a night out. Just the two of us."

"Whatever. Looks like I don't have a choice anyway." He grudgingly went with me, but as our date continued, all he was concerned with was when we could go home. Valentine's Day didn't turn out the way I hoped. He, of course, didn't think it was important enough to get me anything or even tell me "Happy Valentine's Day." Why did I try so hard?

Having a crappy date didn't stop Grey from wanting sex, however. Having been raised that you didn't turn your husband down when he wanted to be intimate, I gave in. As always, it was all about Grey's needs. I had learned over the last several months that it was easier to give Grey whatever he wanted, even if that included letting him release where I hated.

That night, though, he did something different and worse than anything he'd made me do thus far. I was lying on my back, praying for it to be over quickly, when I felt Grey's huge, meaty hands grab me around my throat. I laid there thrashing, gasping for breath, fighting to make him let go as he thrusted inside me. I saw Grey's face contort with pleasure as he finished, then everything went black.

This became a regular ritual as Grey decided he liked living out his fantasies. I'd been married less than a year and already felt like a cheap slut. No wonder he called me a bitch all the time. Why did he treat me so badly? Because I allowed it. I felt I deserved nothing better.

~~~~~~

The next day we met with the bishop because, since Grey didn't have a job anymore and we couldn't live on what I made, the church helped with our financial situation. The bishop asked how we were doing. He knew Grey still smoked, but nothing about the Sheryl ordeal or the fantasies Grey had. Grey took this as his queue to blow up at me right in front of the bishop. He said whatever he could to justify his relationship with Sheryl. He proceeded to add insult to injury, putting me down from how I kept house to my not being *available* whenever he wanted sex. We argued about everything from Sheryl to the temple. Our bishop asked who Sheryl was, and Grey had no qualms about reiterating they were only friends; it wouldn't have mattered what I added, because Grey had the bishop eating from his hand. Grey was so incensed that no one—not me, not the bishop—could get a word in edgewise.

The bishop helped Grey get a small job that would help cover the $200 per month payment on the trailer. Grey helped a neighbor gut out his double-wide because he wanted to sell it. They usually worked Monday through Friday from about six-thirty in the evening until sometimes ten or eleven. During their work hours, he gave Grey tips on how to get a good job and keep it. I was grateful to the bishop for being willing to stick his neck out for Grey. Maybe it had to do with the very desperate fight we started in his office. Or maybe the bishop felt sorry for me, having to carry our whole financial situation.

After meeting with the bishop every week for the next six weeks, he suggested we go to marriage counseling. At the suggestion of counseling, Grey balked and was adamantly against it.

The bishop gave us some advice of his own. He told me I needed to back off regarding the temple. He explained our marriage was too fragile and he worried we might take that step before either one of us was truly ready, especially if we didn't fully understand what we were doing and why we were doing it. His advice to Grey was that he needed to do some serious thinking about whether he wanted to be with me, or even married at all. That if he didn't, I deserved to be loved by someone who *wanted* to love and be with me through the eternities. Grey was told to go nowhere near a computer for a while.

I tried not to worry so much or push the temple issue. Grey went to church every once in a while and helped teach the class—if you called making faces and being disruptive helping—but he still smoked and I was almost certain, drank. At least the internet was a moot point because we didn't have a computer, and I hoped if he tried to go to his mother's house, his sister would turn him down flat!

CHAPTER FIVE

Greg, my oldest brother, decided to come for a visit in March. He hadn't been back in Utah for a few years — since moving to Arizona. I worried a lot about the pending visit because not only did Greg smoke, he was also single.

Grey and I were doing somewhat better, I thought, but we were far from where we should be. He didn't swear at me as much, and I knew he couldn't chat. My biggest fear was that Grey might see Greg's single life and decide that was what he really wanted. What if he wanted to go back to Arizona with Greg?

The visit with Greg wasn't all that bad, mostly because he seemed rather annoyed with Grey and his so-called military stories. When Grey started telling his stories, Greg either pretended he was listening or ignored him altogether.

The only things they had in common were smoking and the military. Grey followed Greg outside every time he needed a cigarette, which happened quite often. I honestly hated it, but what could I do? I'd promised the bishop *and* Grey I wasn't going to push the temple or smoking issues.

A couple days before Greg was scheduled to leave, my parents decided that, because all members of the original Marshall Family were present, we needed family pictures. When Grey and I arrived, the tension was so thick it could be cut with a knife. I wondered if it was because Grey wasn't the favorite of anyone in my family. Except for Grandma Kacie (she always tried to see the best in people and had, from the beginning, given Grey the benefit of the doubt), my family made it clear they did not like him. Was it because Grey had a "To hell with it. I don't wanna be here" attitude? During this time, Derek at least treated him as if he belonged, but everyone else only tolerated him; nothing more, nothing less. The photo shoot took longer than my mom wanted, so by the time we were finished, everyone was on edge.

On Greg's last night home, we met at my parents' house to play games. Playing games was something my family did a lot when we kids were growing up, but as everyone married and moved away, there wasn't time for it. The tension of the day before dissipated as we laughed, talked, and bantered with each other. Even Grey was having a good time.

The game we played was called Balderdash. The object of the game was someone had a word and the real definition. All other players needed to make up a believable definition to the word; the player with the real definition read everyone's definitions and all players chose the one they thought was the real definition. Everyone who chose the real definition got points and anyone whose definition was chosen received points. Grey, for reasons only known to him, made up definitions with sexual connotations for every word. It was embarrassing knowing it was *my* husband thinking up that kind of filth.

"What were you thinking?" I asked upon leaving my parent's house.

"What?" Grey asked innocently.

"How could you ruin the game like that?" By the third derogatory definition, everyone had had enough.

"Like what?"

"Are you kidding me?"

"I was having fun! Is that such a crime?"

"It was embarrassing! Not to mention disgusting." It infuriated me more when Grey laughed, and continued laughing whenever he saw me the rest of the night. We'd probably never be invited over to play games again, but Grey didn't care.

Because I didn't like going to bed angry, I got down on my knees and prayed for the negative feelings I was having toward my husband to go away. I knew I needed to pray more, but I'd always had a hard time with it. It seemed that I prayed more when things weren't going well, which seemed to be a lot lately. I knew I also needed to pray when life was good and let my Father in Heaven know I was grateful.

~~~~~~

A couple of nights later, we got into our worst fight yet over something that had caused me tons of grief since before our wedding...the military. I seriously couldn't stand it. Not only did they take Grey away for a month just two weeks after our wedding, they wanted him for another month. That wasn't counting the multiple weekends he'd already been gone.

He informed me he was leaving May fifth for his Annual Training in Arkansas. This could be a double stint, which meant he would go for the first two weeks, come home for a few days, and then be gone for two more weeks. We were supposed to find out before the unit left about whether they were required to do the second annual training.

"When did you find out you'd be gone for over a month?" I inquired.

"I've known about a week. Why?"

"Why am I only hearing about it now?"

Grey had the gumption to look innocent. "I just never thought to tell you. It's weeks away anyway." He shrugged like it was no big deal.

"Why do you have to go away anyway? With all your drill weekends *and* the entire month of October, you've been gone a lot." Didn't he get that whenever he was gone, not only did I worry about him coming home, but that he might not? Also, the temple situation was always and forever in the back of my mind.

~~~~~~

I was getting tired of everything in our trailer smelling like cigarette smoke; Grey had promised numerous times before we were married, and a few times since, that he would quit. I reiterated to him he had until he came back from A.T. I knew Grey hated ultimatums immensely, and I was pleasantly surprised when he said nothing but nodded his acknowledgment of what I was getting at.

May fifth crept up on me so quickly that I wasn't anywhere near ready when Grey left. No one knew whether there was a second training scheduled yet. The only thing I knew for certain was that Grey would be gone May fifth through May nineteenth. As always, I had no way of contacting Grey. All I could do was wait for him to call me—IF he called me.

The first week Grey was gone, I spent most of my time at both of my grandmas' houses. Both lived alone, but they loved it when the grandkids came to visit. When I wasn't doing that or working, I went to my parents' house. I wasn't surprised, really, when Grey didn't call the first week, but as the time grew closer and closer for his arrival and I still didn't hear anything, I began to worry. Maybe something had happened to him, or maybe he decided he didn't want me anymore.

The night before his return, the phone *finally* rang. He made some lame excuse about having to call his mom during the previous week and a half, because he didn't want to call me collect. Why then, I wondered, was he able to call now? Or why had he been able to call me from Boise when he went to school? He then launched into a commentary about some new friends he thought I'd like. *Probably more drinking and smoking pals.* "So, how are things at home?" Grey asked.

"Fine. Just working and spending time with my family. Do you know what time you'll be home tomorrow?"

"Uh...not sure, but hey, don't worry about picking me up. I'll catch a ride home with someone."

"No one lives this far out," I said as I wondered what was going on. Why didn't he want me to come get him from the armory?

I could hear hostility in Grey's voice when he said, "Just don't worry about it! I'll take care of myself. I gotta go. Duty calls. See ya tomorrow." Without so much as an *I love you* or *kiss my rosy-red behind,* the phone went dead. I didn't even have a chance to say good-bye.

~~~~~~

Grey returned home the next morning at five-thirty, waking me with all the commotion of bringing his baggage into the house. I was curious about who had brought him home but was afraid to ask. I was surprised when he came to my side of the bed, stroked my hair back and asked, "Hey, what would you think about meeting up with a couple of buddies from my unit tonight? They want to meet you since, apparently, you are attached to me."

"Sounds okay. Where?" Although I was groggy because of how early it was, I didn't care that he had woken me up or where we were going. I was totally elated my husband wanted to take me out!

"The Mango Tango in Salt Lake. They want to go hang out, dance and stuff."

"And get drunk," I added under my breath, but Grey heard it.

"Don't be all high and mighty, sweetheart. If I recall, you've been drunk a time or two," Grey sneered.

"Buzzed, not drunk. And it was only to piss RJ off. Didn't work, did it?"

"Still." A few minutes later Grey asked, "Are we in or out?"

I knew all too well that if I declined, he'd go without me, so I conceded. "Sure."

We met three of the other guys from the unit. I wanted so much to fit in that when one of Grey's friends offered me an Apple Pucker shot, I didn't refuse. I could be as cool as they were, couldn't I? I should've said, "Stop" but the Apple Puckers just kept on coming! Between Grey and his friends egging me on and my need to make him happy, I drank a lot, and fast.

When we got home, I was completely laid back, so much so, that everything, including our marriage, was better. "Maybe we should get you drunk more often. It makes *everything* better, if you get my drift." Grey waggled his eyebrows at me. I knew what he meant and could feel the knife twist in my heart as he put me down yet again.

"If you think that's the only way you're having sex with me, you're sadly mistaken." With that, I went to bed trying not to let his snide comment cause tears. Maybe he needed me drunk in order to find me attractive. Or maybe he liked that I was less inhibited when there was alcohol in my system. But I certainly wasn't giving in whenever it tickled his fancy.

~~~~~~

A few days after Grey got back from Annual Training, I transferred to a new department within the company I'd been with for over a year. My new position was customer service oriented. I oversaw taking prom orders (decorations, frames for pictures, keychains, pens, and anything else that could be kept as a keepsake) for schools all around the country. The position was better because not only did I get a raise, but I worked no later than five o'clock in the afternoon and no Saturdays.

As far as Grey was concerned, looking for employment had never been high on his list of things to do. Even after coming home from Arkansas, it was no different. It was his nonchalant attitude that caused the bishop to stop helping. He figured if he kept doing it, Grey would mooch as long as people would let him. Knowing I didn't bring home enough to make our house payment and meet our other bills, Grey and I decided to talk with the owner of the trailer. After a lengthy chat and an even lengthier silence, they foreclosed on the trailer, not only because we were too far behind, but because even if we didn't know they had sold it to us illegally, they knew I was smart enough to find out. They gave us two weeks to vacate.

Over the next ten days, I searched and searched for another place to live. Grey wasn't much help, but that didn't surprise me in the least. The one bedroom in an eight-apartment complex I found was perfect for us. It was smaller than the trailer and smelled like the mothballs in Grandma Kacie's basement, but the rent was cheaper than what we paid for the trailer because there wasn't any extra rent for the lot space.

With the help of Hank, Lynese, Grey's mom, and his sister, we were able to get everything packed and moved in one day. That was the easy part. Because I worked full-time, it took me almost two weeks to get everything put away and the place looking like a home.

~~~~~~

Our first Sunday in Grey's mom's ward (the local Church of Jesus Christ of Latter-day Saints congregation), I was introduced for what felt like the thousandth time, since the ward members had already met me on three or four other occasions. Right after church, the ward clerk asked if Grey and I had time to meet with the bishop. I wanted to say no but didn't.

"Are you two all moved in?" the bishop asked.

"Yes," Grey responded abruptly.

"Grey, how is the job-hunt going?"

"I go every couple days to Job Service and look at the classifieds all the time." Grey knew he wasn't being truthful but knew I wouldn't call him on it in front of the bishop. I rolled my eyes and tried not to let my total disbelief show.

"What are you doing besides that?"

"Working for Hank's dad." I swallowed a scoff at that news.

"Where do you stand on preparing to go through the temple?" The bishop knew I, at one point, had hoped to go through on our one-year anniversary.

"Bishop, I really don't see why going through the temple is so important," Grey replied. "I don't care. I know it's important to Hunter, but I just don't want to deal with it."

"Grey, being sealed for time and all eternity is the most important thing you can do for yourself and Hunter, not to mention for any children you may have. I want to see the two of you sealed on your first anniversary." Was he joking? Although I wanted to be sealed to Grey terribly, I seriously didn't think rushing into it was the answer.

As I listened to the bishop, I prayed that what he said might reach Grey. "Grey, are you still smoking?" This was the bishop's next question.

"Uh... Well..." Grey was going to lie. I could tell by the way he was hedging the question. "Not as much as I used to."

The bishop sat quietly for a few minutes, thinking over our situation. Then he said, "I'll tell you what… If you can quit and stay clean for the next four months, continue coming to church and paying your tithing, I will conduct a temple recommend interview at that point. Do you think that's a possibility?"

Grey noticed the hopeful look that crossed my face. "Maybe." At least he didn't turn the bishop down flat.

I still had several concerns about the stuff that had happened regarding Sheryl. I wanted to tell the bishop, this person who'd played Grey's father-figure his entire life. Maybe he could make Grey see the lines he'd crossed, something our previous bishop wasn't able to accomplish. Part of me thought what Grey did was cheating, but at the same time, they didn't have sex so was it? I brought it to the bishop's attention, but the moment Sheryl's name came out of my mouth, Grey jumped up as if he'd sat on something hot.

"When are you going to get the f*** over that?" he yelled at me, not caring whether anyone outside the office heard. He didn't even care that the bishop was sitting right there either. "I haven't been able to talk to her because YOU deleted everything, and my sister won't even let me near her computer because of you!"

The bishop looked at Grey and uttered sternly, "Sit down. Your wife has valid concerns and she deserves answers from you. You will not talk over her. You will not make her feel like she doesn't matter. And you will not use vulgar language inside this building. Ever!"

Grey sat down grudgingly at the bishop's request. As I watched him, I noticed he resembled a child who hadn't gotten his own way. "Grey, are you still in contact with Sheryl?" the bishop asked.

"No. Like I said, Hunter deleted my accounts and she made my sister promise to never let me near her computer." He glared at me like I had done something extremely horrible.

"Do you have any other concerns, Hunter?" The bishop directed this question at me. Boy, did I, but didn't think covering them now was a good idea.

"If he were truly not chatting with her, or anyone else for that matter, why does he get so angry when I want to talk about it?"

"Grey, do you have a response that question?"

"How can I be chatting when I don't have access to a computer?"

After a few more questions from the bishop with Grey swearing up and down he wasn't involved in any way with Sheryl, or anyone else for that matter, we left. I didn't think Grey was anywhere near done with our argument but was surprised when we got home and he said nothing. He spent the rest of the evening ignoring me, though. For me, it was spent pondering why I couldn't reach my sweetheart. I preferred his yelling to the deafening silence that threatened to engulf me.

~~~~~~

When Grey's birthday arrived in June, I wasn't sure what to do. I knew his family wasn't big on celebrating, or even noticing, birthdays, so Grey decided he wanted to go fishing with Hank. I was okay with it because I had a special night planned for later that evening. I was taken completely by surprise when, that morning, he asked if I wanted to go with him. "What happened to Hank?"

"Lynese won't let him come." I could hear the displeasure in his voice. "Man, that boy is f***in' whipped."

"Just because she has other plans?"

"No. Because he does whatever the hell she says, when she says. He has no balls. Boy, I'm glad you don't do that because you know full well I would rather leave than be bossed around like that."

I wasn't sure how to respond, so instead I asked, "When do you want to go?"

"As soon as you get your lazy ass out of bed and get dressed." Grey thought he was being funny, but I knew he *really* thought I was lazy. Heaven forbid if I wanted to sleep in on my day off. Besides that, I'd been feeling awfully tired the last few weeks and was nauseous all the time. I chalked it up to stress and work.

Although life had been pretty mellow since meeting with the bishop, I continued to hold my breath and tread lightly when Grey was around.

"Are you up yet?" Grey hollered from the living room.

"I'm up, I'm up," I mumbled. I seriously didn't feel good, but because Grey hardly ever initiated time together, I was determined to go, even if I was his second choice and felt like death.

~~~~~~

I'd never been down into Deer Creek Dam before. I had only seen it from the top. Of course, today had to be one of the hottest days we'd seen in a while. That, combined with the way I felt, made me hope Grey would make it a short fishing trip. It didn't surprise me that Grey let me navigate the very steep, rocky incline by myself. He didn't so much as bother offering his ass for me to hang onto, but instead whined that I was slowing him down.

We stood in the sweltering sun while I watched him lose lure after lure, but catch no fish. After about three hours (when all our water was gone and the sandwiches and snacks we brought were sad looking due to the heat) Grey was finally ready to leave. Hallelujah! However, coming down the trail was nothing compared to going up. We'd gone about twenty feet when I stopped.

"What the hell are you stopping for?" Grey's voice was gruff.

With a pale, sweaty face I replied, "Grey, I don't feel so good. I think I'm going to pass out."

"Oh, you're not gonna pass out. It's just hot. Now, come on!" His tone implied that he didn't believe me, but I stopped every few minutes during the half-mile hike back up to the car anyway. "Why the hell did I bring you? I should have known you would slow me up and make this a miserable trip," Grey muttered, thinking I couldn't hear him.

"I'm sorry," I whimpered.

~~~~~~

A few days after the fishing trip disaster, I was still feeling extremely under the weather. I thought about what *might* be making me sick. The doctors had explained to me that I would never carry a baby full-term because of the way my body was built and due to the stress pregnancy put on a woman if I tried, it could be fatal to me and/or the baby. I was new to the whole pregnancy thing — so much so that I wasn't aware a woman could cramp and be pregnant at the same time, but I was two weeks late. It stressed me out so much that I had to know. I couldn't wait and wonder any longer. On my lunch break from work, I bought a pregnancy test and, within less than the standard waiting time of a minute, I saw two distinct, little pink lines. My hands were shaking so badly I almost dropped the stick in the toilet. I couldn't stem the tears or the laughter that bubbled from me. I was so excited! I was going to be a mommy! I was so elated that I couldn't help telling everyone in the call center. This was after calling everyone I could think of, although I had no luck in reaching Grey to tell him the news.

When I arrived home, Grey was nowhere to be found. I spent the next two hours waiting for him. *Where could he be?* There I was with the biggest news of our lives and no one knew where to find Grey.

I was way too excited to let it dampen my spirits any. I met Grey at the door when I heard his truck. "Hi, honey." Grey looked at me with skepticism. "Will you do me one teensy, weensy favor?"

He knew something was up, but did as I asked and let me put a blindfold on him. "Okay, follow me." I guided him to the waiting couch.

"Are you going to tell me what this is all about?" Grey inquired, impatiently.

"All in good time. All in good time." I tried not to giggle but couldn't help myself. "Hold out your hand." I took the pregnancy test from my back pocket and placed it, face up, into his hand with the cap on the peed on end. I removed the blindfold, and, after a couple of minutes, it finally dawned on him what he was looking at.

He blurted, "Does this mean what I think it does?"

Not sure what his response would be I timidly answered, "Yes." The grin that broke out on Grey's face was something I hadn't seen in a long time; a genuine smile! "You're happy about it then?" I asked.

"Happy?" he replied. "Why would you ask that?" He acted as if he seriously didn't *know* he'd been a jerk the last eleven months.

Although it was close to nine o'clock at night, we decided to go give Grey's mom and sister the awesome news.

The Cheshire cat grin on Grey's face lingered even as we pulled back into our parking lot over an hour later. I debated whether to call my parents or wait until the next day. I'd been dreading the call since those two little lines showed up because I worried how my parents, especially my mom, would react, given how they felt about Grey. And how he felt about them.

I bit the bullet and dialed their number. "Hello?" my mom answered.

"Hi, Mom."

"Hunter, it's late. Is there something wrong?"

"No. I have news." I could hear her sharp intake of breath. "I'm pregnant!"

I couldn't hide my excitement, but when my mom responded with, "Oh," I was completely devastated. I hoped that she would at least *act* happy for us. She'd been happy when Reghan got pregnant for the first time. Why couldn't she be happy for me?

My mom's next question invoked tears. "Are you sure you can handle this?" She knew how badly I wanted to be a mom and what a miracle my getting pregnant was.

Even though I knew things weren't the greatest between Grey and me, I had no doubt about the baby. "Yes, Mom, I can. Grey and I are excited, and we want you and Dad to be happy for us." I then told her good-bye, hoping one day my parents might be happy for me.

The next day I called Grandma Marshall and Grandma Kacie. They both were excited but, at the same time, worried, given Grey's and my relationship. It was even harder to read my siblings' reactions. The only one I could get any sort of good vibe from was

Derek, but Derek had always given Grey the benefit of the doubt, and if he had negative things to say, he didn't say them to me.

~~~~~~

Although we were expecting a baby, I wasn't naive enough to believe things would miraculously get better between Grey and me. In August, the month before our first anniversary, Grey was still smoking, didn't care whether we would *ever* make it to the temple, and still had no "real" job, except the few hours a day he spent with Hank's dad doing whatever he did at the shop. I should have stuck to my guns when I gave him the smoking ultimatum before Annual Training, but we were expecting a baby and I couldn't do it on my own.

~~~~~~

Every now and again, sensing Grey would be more comfortable, the bishop asked us to drop by his house and fill him in on the goings on in our lives. He spoke more to Grey when he talked about the importance of having a job that would allow Grey to be the breadwinner. He did his best to help Grey understand why it was important, if possible, for mothers to nurture the children and take care of the home. He didn't bring up our plans for the temple. I figured he knew we weren't going to make it anytime soon. Not together anyway.

Because our family dynamics were changing, and even though Grey vetoed the idea whenever it was brought up, the bishop reluctantly asked if we would be willing to go to counseling. Knowing how rocky our marriage was, he thought it might help us get on track. Both the bishop and I were pleasantly surprised when Grey agreed to go.

~~~~~~

I was exceptionally nervous about counseling, especially marriage counseling, because there was no way to keep anything out of it. Everything would be open for all to see. I was not sure how Grey was feeling, but judging by his folded arms and the scowl on his face, I wondered if he felt the bishop and I had forced him into it.

Most of the first session was spent filling out paperwork; therefore, we didn't get into anything huge. Because the counselor wanted to get in as much time with us as she possibly could, she scheduled us once a week for the first month and a half. Our first *real* session was the next day at six o'clock, so I wouldn't have to take time off work.

That session was the same day as our first baby doctor appointment, which I went alone to because Grey claimed he couldn't get the time off (from Hank's dad, really?). As we sat across from the counselor, she could sense neither one of us wanted to talk. "How are you today?" she started.

Of course, Grey didn't want to answer, so I did, "I'm okay."

"Grey?" The counselor directed at him.

"Fine," was his monotone response.

We didn't get into deep stuff during the session, but the counselor gave us an assignment anyway. "I want the two of you to go for two walks together this week. You must hold hands and talk to each other. It doesn't matter about what, just talk."

When Grey and I were in the car afterwards I asked, "What do you think?"

"About what?"

"Us. Counseling. The doctor appointment you were too busy to come to."

"It'll be fine as long as you don't get hung up on the Sheryl business or going to the temple." Grey knew both subjects brought a lot of angst for me. As an afterthought, he asked, "By the way, how did the doctor appointment go?"

"I'm not making any promises," was my only response to the Sheryl conversation. Then, "Fine. The doctor says I'm at eight weeks." I wanted to drop the subject. Since Grey couldn't make the time to be there, why did I have to tell him anything?

"The baby's okay?"

"Yes." I handed him the sonogram picture.

"It doesn't look like a baby. Just looks like a blob," Grey scoffed.

"That's what a baby looks like at eight weeks," I answered, rolling my eyes.

~~~~~~

The next counseling session was nerve-wracking for me as I debated on what to say and what to keep quiet. The counselor asked me why we were there, so I dug into our story...

In the beginning, Grey acted like he was doing all he could to change, especially after I found myself unattached. I wanted so badly to be loved by a man that would see me: not the Cerebral Palsy; not the fat that engulfed my every curve; not the large butt, and not the fact that I couldn't do everything normally. I thought Grey was that guy, and he appeared to be working on his smoking and drinking issues, too. He hadn't flirted with any other girls, at least not while with me. But he began to treat me differently after our wedding. Three days after we married, Grey told me he was ashamed of me because of my Cerebral Palsy. And our relationship changed even more after he returned from Boise. Then there was Sheryl.

Without looking at Grey, knowing he was glaring at me, I told the counselor about that situation.

After I finished, the counselor asked Grey, "Do think your wife's concerns are valid?"

"I guess." Grey looked at the floor. I was surprised he hadn't blown up yet.

"Are you committed to her?" Grey didn't appreciate the committed question.

"Don't you mean am I cheating on her?" Grey scoffed. "The answer is no. I have *never* cheated on her."

"Sheryl wasn't cheating?" The counselor implored.

"How could I have slept with her when I've never even met her?" Grey was starting to lose control. I could tell it was only a matter of time before he began yelling. It didn't stop the counselor's line of questioning, however.

"So, you think that just because you never had sex with Sheryl, you were faithful to Hunter? What about the pictures?"

Glowering at me and through gritted teeth, Grey replied, "You told her about the pictures?! What the hell for? You promised you weren't going to bring any of that shit up! I thought we had dealt with this! Because of you, my sister won't even let me near her computer! I AM NOT going to let you ruin my f***in' life!"

The counselor was doing her best to calm him down during his tirade, but I knew from experience the best thing to do was to let him be.

"I had to tell her if she is going to help." I tried to sound strong, although my voice quivered. The counselor told me to look Grey in the eye and tell him how being told he was ashamed of me made me feel.

"Ever since you said that…" I looked directly at Grey, "…and maybe even before then, I've felt like *you* feel stuck with me, like I am not good enough for you, but there's nothing you can do about it and now that there's the baby, you *really* feel stuck."

The session ended there, but not before the counselor asked if we did the last assignment and gave another. Of course, we hadn't. There was no way I was going to get Grey to take a walk with me, much less hold my hand.

For homework we were both asked to jot down at least ten reasons why we loved each other. Grey was asked to come up with ways to express *his* love to me. I was almost 100% certain Grey wouldn't bother with any of the assignments.

That night there wasn't much talking in the Andrews house. When we arrived home, Grey sat out on the porch to smoke, swearing up a storm, knowing I could hear every hurtful thing he said, because he didn't bother to close the door. The phrase I heard before going into the bedroom was, "I should've taken her up on her damn offer to be with Sheryl."

As we got ready for bed that night—something we didn't do together often—I asked, "Do you really feel that way?"

Acting like he had no idea what I was talking about, Grey responded with, "What?"

"You really don't think I heard what you said while you were outside?"

"I have no idea what you're talking about."

"Yes, you do. Does 'I should have taken her up on her damn offer' ring any bells?"

"So you were eavesdropping?"

"It was kind of hard not to hear. You weren't exactly whispering. Do you?"

"Do I what?"

I was becoming frustrated. "You know what I'm talking about."

Grey didn't answer me, but promptly rolled over and pretended to sleep. I lay awake most of the night thinking about everything: my life, my marriage, the baby, the temple, and most of all, the love I had for the man lying next to me.

~~~~~~

Much to Grey's dismay, I decided to go back to college to finish my associate degree at Brigham Young University. Without talking much about it, I enrolled in the last two classes I needed to graduate, determined to complete it before the baby was born. Between work, school, doctor appointments, counseling, and stroking Grey's ego whenever he felt the need, I was busy all the time, which meant I was completely exhausted. Lucky for me, classes were only two nights a week.

My first night class happened to be on my birthday. I hoped Grey had remembered and planned something nice, but when I got home from class after nine o'clock that evening, I found him lying on the couch in his boxers. He was watching television, oblivious to me coming home or anything else for that matter. "Hey, babe." I bent down to kiss him. "How was your day?"

"Fine. Worked my ass off painting, though. I am so tired."

"I hear ya there." Although I didn't think he worked as hard as he thought, I wasn't about to start something. I didn't want to have to remind him of what the day was, but maybe the Happy Birthday balloon and cupcake I'd received at class might give the secret away.

Grey said nothing more and I, having way too much homework, took my balloon, cupcake, and books into our bedroom to study. When he finally came in a few hours later, Grey actually had the gall to ask me if it was my birthday. I couldn't hold back my emotions any longer. "YES! I would think you, of all people, would remember when my birthday is. I hinted at you several times and even waved the balloon in your face."

His answer didn't just hurt, I felt my heart breaking as well. "Birthdays are just another damn day."

"Are you serious? Yours haven't been *just another day* since we got together! Mine didn't feel like *just another day* last year."

"Well, they are." He didn't say anything else about it, but his comment stayed with me. I was even more determined that he wouldn't forget our anniversary! Or was that going to be an uneventful day as well?

~~~~~~

On September twentieth, one year after saying "I do" to the love of my life, I woke earlier than usual to make breakfast in bed for us, doing my best to make our day memorable. Breakfast consisted of sausage, pancakes, scrambled eggs, and orange juice for Grey and grapefruit and toast for me. I normally didn't eat breakfast, but since getting pregnant, I had to force myself to eat something. I tiptoed quietly into the bedroom and kissed him awake. His answer was, "What the hell do you think you're doing?"

"Happy anniversary, Honey!" Even though Grey didn't act excited, I couldn't contain my enthusiasm. I had my doubts that we would make it this long. Grey ate and ignored my comment, acting like I owed him breakfast in bed rather than seeing it as a symbol of my love for him.

I hoped Grey might have something up his sleeve for our anniversary, but with his track record, I wasn't necessarily holding my breath. I worked only half a day, knowing that, due to me being pregnant and tired all the time, it would take me longer than usual to get things done for the evening I'd planned.

Grey spent most of the day at the shop shooting the breeze with Hank and his dad. I never knew when he'd be home when he went over there and, because I didn't want a yelling match, I let him do what he wanted. He showed me more affection when I let him be. Oh, how I craved that attention!

That evening, after I made cube steak in mushroom gravy over mashed potatoes and Grey's favorite dessert of huckleberry-raspberry cheesecake, I waited and waited for Grey to come home. On my way home from work I had gone to Cal-Ranch and bought him a new pair of denim Wranglers and a cream colored, printed Henley shirt.

Around eight o'clock, Grey walked through the door. "Happy Anniversary," I said. The candlelight dinner I'd planned was ruined, but I wasn't going to let on that I was bothered by Grey's inconsideration.

"I thought we did all the anniversary crapola this morning." Grey sounded somewhat angry.

"Well...I..."

"Look Hunter, I'm not in the mood. All I want to do is take a shower and veg in front of the TV." He didn't comment on the dinner still sitting on the table. He did, however, notice the wrapped gift. "That mine?" He inclined his head toward the shiny paper.

Not bothering to hide the emotion in my voice, I choked out, "Yes," before the tears began to fall.

I could tell by his reaction that he hadn't given me a second thought on what was supposed to be a huge milestone in our marriage. What I really wanted to do was yell, scream, and throw things and demand he tell me why I meant so little to him. Instead, I whispered, "I love you, ya know" and left him to veg while I cleaned up dinner. I didn't bother with the dessert; I went to bed instead. Grey must've found it sometime in the night because, when I looked in the refrigerator the next morning, half of it was gone.

~~~~~~

I didn't want to talk about our anniversary at our next counseling session, but I'd been feeling horrible since that day and knew I had to talk about why it bothered me. Those feelings, added to the stress I had been under, were not good for me or the baby.

The counselor, as usual, started the session. "How are things?" I purposely didn't say anything.

When there was only silence the counselor turned to Grey. "Grey, the last time you were here we were talking about something that hurt Hunter badly. I had you do a homework assignment. Did you?"

"Nope," Grey answered, callously.

"Can you tell me why?"

"Didn't have time."

"You didn't have the time, or you didn't want to do it?" The counselor asked.

"I don't know! I just didn't do it, okay?"

"Will you do it for our next meeting?" The counselor knew it was a long shot.

"Yeah, sure."

The counselor then asked us, "Wasn't your first-year anniversary last week?"

When there was no response, she inquired, "Did you do anything?" The counselor could tell something was bothering me, so she directed the question to me.

"Yeah." I didn't know how much to tell for fear of the backlash from Grey. Before I knew it, however, I spilled the whole thing — from breakfast in bed to the candlelight dinner and the gifts I gave Grey.

"Why do you think Grey wasn't as excited as you about your anniversary?"

"I don't know."

"Some men don't look at these events like women do. They don't see them as huge milestones."

Does the counselor really believe that? I wondered. *Or was she just trying to smooth things over for Grey?*

Just then, Grey piped up with, "We're married. Why should we have to celebrate every year we're together? It's *just another day.*"

I couldn't hold back anymore. "Just like my birthday, right?"

"Oh, don't bring that up AGAIN!" Grey was steamed.

"Why not? Your birthday, we celebrate. Any day *you* deem important, we celebrate. Why should mine or even our anniversary be any different?"

The counselor added, "She has a valid point. Marriage is about compromise. Just because you, Grey, don't see these occasions as important doesn't mean Hunter feels the same way. You know, the few times we've met, that is one thing I've noticed. Grey, you expect your wife to be and do whatever you want her to. And Hunter, you do it without asking questions or making demands." She turned to Grey, "Did you celebrate occasions such as her birthday and Valentine's Day when you were dating?"

"Well, yeah."

"Why did you stop?"

"We're married. Those days aren't important anymore. What are you getting at?" Grey didn't like being put on the spot.

"When you were dating, you wanted her to see your best side. Am I right?"

"I'm still the same person," Grey retorted.

I tried not to scoff as I listened to the conversation.

"Hunter, did you complete your list?" the counselor asked. Of course I had. "Well, we are almost out of time. On top of the assignments I gave you, Grey..." she gave him a pointed look. "...I also want the two of you to work on compromising with each other, and I will see you next week."

~~~~~~

On Sunday, ten days after our anniversary, the bishop invited us to his home to see how counseling was going. Neither Grey nor I knew that he had not one, but two, ulterior motives. As we sat in his basement living room, I hoped he wouldn't ask about our anniversary. No such luck. I looked at Grey who gave me a look that screamed, "DON'T say a word." When the bishop asked about it, we both answered, "Fine."

Sensing there was more to it, but not wanting to make Grey angry, the bishop switched to Grey's job hunting. "Have you had any luck finding a job yet?"

When Grey's answer was "No," the bishop gave him the name and address of a cherry farm just outside of Salt Lake that was hiring warehouse workers. He explained he'd already spoken to the owner. He wanted Grey there at six-thirty the next morning.

"It's only for about a month, but you can bring in around two thousand dollars, or more. He also said if you do well, he may keep you full-time. Are you up for it?"

"Sure," Grey responded. I was so glad he had *something*. I hoped fervently he would keep it.

We, of course, discussed how counseling was going. Grey answered that everything was great! After a few minutes, the bishop asked Grey about his smoking. Grey announced he'd been cutting back. I wasn't with him all day, so I didn't know if he was being honest. In truth, I'd only seen him smoke once or twice when we were home.

"The reason I ask, Grey, is because I would really like to see the two of you go through the temple. I think if you do that and receive all the blessings that go along with it, you will find support you've never experienced. There is a temple preparation class which starts next Sunday, and I want the two of you to be there. It is a six-week class, so there is a big commitment, but I really think this would be good for the two of you, along with the counseling, of course."

I expected Grey to lose his temper the way he did whenever I brought up the temple. He didn't. His response surprised me, though. "Fine. If it will keep Hunter from nagging me, I'll go."

I did my best to ignore his response. I also sensed he was only telling the bishop what he wanted to hear and doing what the bishop wanted him to do because he had been Grey's father figure most of his life. Not to mention that he was the reason Grey finally had a job. No one wanted to be a disappointment to his or her parents. Not like I was.

~~~~~~

The following Sunday, an elderly couple held the class in their home. Being in their home felt more like Family Home Evening rather than a class, which was fine with me. I was somewhat surprised to see two other couples from our ward who looked to be around the same age as Grey and me. I knew from seeing them at church that they had both married young and had babies.

As the class began, we were asked to share a little about ourselves and what we hoped to learn from the class. One couple had been married for seventeen years and spent most of their marriage inactive, but had recently decided to "get their act together" so they could be a family forever; another couple married extremely young and the only way their parents would allow it was if they promised they would do whatever they could to stay active and to someday go to the temple. Gunner and Shaylie had been married almost a year; they had a four-month-old daughter named Michaela and wanted to be sealed on their one-year anniversary. Although all the couples were friendly, it was Gunner and Shaylie we connected with the most.

After class, Grey, Gunner, Shaylie, and I stood outside, talking and getting to know each other better. We women, of course, talked about Michaela and my pregnancy. The men talked about what they did for a living, hunting, and other manly things.

"So, what do ya think?" I asked as we were heading home.

"It's interesting," Grey responded.

"You really hit it off with Gunner."

"He's nice. You're not planning on doing coupley stuff with them, are you?"

"I was thinking we might. Maybe that's part of our problem. We don't go on dates and we never have anyone over. There have been several talks at church given about dating your spouse."

"Don't preach to me about what we *should* be doing. I'm taking this class, aren't I? You just said we don't do anything with anyone. What about Hank and Lynese? Have you forgotten them?"

"No, but don't you ever get sick of the same old, same old?"

"No." I could tell by Grey's response that I'd hit a nerve, so I left well enough alone.

~~~~~~

Over the next couple of weeks, Grey seemed to enjoy being the breadwinner. He was in a better mood and didn't snap at me as much, but unfortunately, the job didn't last. Grey called me at work one day. "Hey. What's up? You're not done with work yet, are you?" I asked.

"Uh, yeah. I got fired."

"What! What happened?"

"I sort of hit one of the bins with my truck and dented the truck all up," he replied defensively..

"Holy shit! Now what are we going to do? You've only been there two weeks!" I could feel anxiety rising like it tended to do every time I had to think about how we were going to raise this baby on pennies!

"They say I can come get my check the day after tomorrow."

Because I didn't want to discuss it any further for fear I might lose my temper, I used the excuse that I needed to get some work done and hung up.

CHAPTER SIX

I was so tired from a long day at work and school that I was totally unprepared when I walked in the door that October night. Grey was standing at the door with a HUGE grin on his face. Not only that, but he had dinner waiting from New York Burrito, one of his favorite take-out places in town. Because I didn't want to ruin his good mood, I didn't dare tell him New York Burrito gave me heartburn nor was I going to ask where he got the money for it since I paid the bills. It seemed odd to me that Grey had just enough money to keep his cigarette habit going and gas in his truck, and he ate out a lot, too. Did he get the money from his mom? Hank's dad? All the while I worked my tail off and was doing my best to finish school when all I wanted to do was sleep. We couldn't keep our bills current. That was where all my money went.

"Why the huge grin? You look like the cat that ate the canary." I couldn't help but laugh.

"I got a job interview!" Grey said in a sing-song voice.

I wasn't sure whether to be happy or scared. I'd been working on coming to terms with the fact that I wasn't going to be able to be the stay-at-home mommy I'd dreamed of since I was a little girl. "Where?" I asked, doing my best to sound enthusiastic.

"You know that call center they built over by the temple in Provo? Teton Landing Call Center?"

"The one that works with the cable companies?"

"Yep. I was looking in the paper today and saw that they are still hiring. I go in for an interview tomorrow. I thought I might drop you off at work, go to the interview, and stop to grab my check. I'll come get you before I go to the bank."

"That sounds okay."

~~~~~~

When Grey dropped me off the next day, I couldn't get rid of the sinking feeling that permanently made a home in my gut. I found myself worrying about Grey. *Did he get the job? Is he okay?* Oh, that terrible feeling would not go away.

"Hi, honey," I said when he pulled up after my shift. "How did the interview go?"

"You're gonna bitch at me." He looked a little pale.

"Whhaatt?" I was almost afraid to hear the story. I knew that no matter how much or little I might protest, I was going to find out what happened.

~~~~~~

After he'd dropped me off at work, Grey went home and got ready for his interview. Because the interview was in an office-like setting, he wore his black Wranglers, his white button-up shirt, and the hunter green tie with black swirling lines all through it that I'd given him for his birthday a few months before. He gave himself plenty of time to get there, but because he didn't care much for rules of the road, he pushed the speed limit until...he was caught. Just a few miles from his exit, he was pulled over by Utah State Police. As luck would have it, or wouldn't have it, when the cop ran Grey's driver's license, it came back that it had been suspended. When the policeman asked Grey about it, he told him he had no idea it had been suspended, but he REALLY needed to get to the job interview. For reasons only known to the policeman, he told Grey to go to his interview, then straight home. He told him not to stop anywhere else because if he got into any more trouble the police officer wouldn't vouch for him. Then he let Grey go with only a warning.

Grey went to the interview and everything seemed to go well. They explained that they would be calling in the next few days those they were going to hire. Grey thought for sure he would walk out with a job and was mad. He felt he deserved to know since he had made the trip down, so without heeding the policeman's warning he stopped at the warehouse to pick up his last check. It wasn't very big which made him angrier. And, to make matters worse, he was sure I would budget the money out and not even think of his "needs." Just because he was cutting back on smoking didn't mean he could go without it, Grey thought. He pulled out of the parking lot, not paying much attention to what was going on around him when, WHAM, he ran smack into another car with an elderly lady driver coming down the road. She wasn't driving extremely fast and Grey didn't see any damage to her car and very little to ours. After asking the lady if she was okay and exchanging insurance information, he left . . .

"You were in an accident?" I couldn't hold back the dread. This wasn't going well.

"Uh, yeah. But I told you, everything is taken care of."

"What's this garbage about you driving on a suspended license? Did you know? Where's the paperwork that says that?"

"I don't know and, how the f*** would I know?! Of course, *you* would think that!"

"That isn't nice." I wasn't going to let Grey know how bad the comment stung. I was one of the very few people that *did* believe in him.

When we arrived at the bank, I took his check and went into the bank.

I wasn't prepared for the sequence of events when I came out. There, standing against a police car, being patted down and put in handcuffs, was my husband. "What is going on?" I asked, trying to keep the shrill tone out of my voice.

"He's under arrest, ma'am," one officer replied.

"What for?" I was really trying to stay calm.

"Hit and run accident."

I looked at Grey. "I thought you said it was taken care of!"

Grey didn't say anything, and I started to panic. I wasn't calm when trying to get answers from either police officer, especially when I brought up the fact that I was four months pregnant. I was borderline hysterical. The officer's comment didn't help any either.

He said, "Lady, if you don't calm down, we'll book you right along with him! Now, if you will excuse us, we need to take him in."

Not knowing where else to go (I didn't want my parents to hear this, at least not yet), I somehow made it to my in-law's house. I wasn't sure how I arrived in one piece, as panicky as I was.

When I explained the situation to Grey's sister, she immediately called a bail bondsman who covered most of the cost. I had to come up with ten percent. I didn't have any idea where I was going to get it, but at that moment, I didn't care. All I knew was that I wanted my husband back.

We went to the police station where Grey was being held. After proving I was married to him, we found out the lady he hit called the police almost as soon as Grey had driven off, claiming she had been badly hurt. Whether she told them she had Grey's insurance information or not was anyone's guess. After paying the $85 that wasn't covered by the bail bondsman, I was able to take Grey home.

~~~~~~

There was so much more involved with Grey's situation than just driving on a suspended license; we were advised to retain an attorney. After meeting with the attorney, I felt better about the whole ordeal. He thought if we could prove Grey never received the letter stating his license was suspended, there was a good chance that particular issue would be dropped. As far as the hit and run, it appeared the woman didn't tell the officers she received all his information from Grey, nor was she hurt, so those charges had an even better chance of being dropped than the suspended license charge. After some digging and looking back through all certified mail that had been sent under Grey's name, the attorney found *that* certified letter was sent to Grey's mom's house and she'd signed for it. That was during the month Grey was in Boise and we were still transitioning all his mail to our address. Even after being shown a copy of her signature, his mom couldn't remember signing for it, much less remember what she did with it.

It didn't matter that he'd never received the letter, Grey still had several court appearances to make. Luckily, he only had to appear every month or so. I hoped it would all be over by the time the baby was born. Going to court with him was too stressful on me. Having a baby to tote around would make it that much harder.

~~~~~~

Grey's job interview had almost been forgotten with the hubbub surrounding his arrest. I usually wasn't home early, especially not on a school night, but I was working on homework for my class when Grey answered the phone. "Hello."

"May I speak to Grey Andrews, please?"

"This is he."

"Grey, this is Mandy from TLCC (Teton Landing Call Center)."

"Yeah?"

"We want to offer you a position with us. Are you able to start on Monday?"

Not even thinking to talk to me about the driving situation first, he immediately replied, "Yes!"

Part of me was excited that he had a job—a job he got entirely on his own. But having to drive him wasn't something I was looking forward to. Oh well, at least he had a job!

"Please tell me I'm hearing this correctly." It was all I could do not to squeal.

"Yes. You heard right," Grey answered, but he seemed to have lost the enthusiasm he had when he was talking to the manager.

I couldn't help it, I squealed! I gave Grey a huge hug. Come hell or high water I would do whatever I could to support him in this position.

"I am so proud of you!" Grey acted like he didn't know what to do with that comment. "What about transportation?" I didn't want to put a damper on a good thing, but it was something we needed to hammer out in the next four days.

"You're off at four every day, right?" Grey asked.

"Yeah. So, I can come get you, take you to work by five o'clock, and pick you at ten. It even works around my school schedule since class is at seven o'clock and I'm done by nine in the evening."

It was a ton of running around for me, but what else could I do? We needed money to raise the baby I carried. We were not only trying to save money for our baby, but maybe with the new job Grey could get some child support paid off too. He hadn't been paying it because work had been so sporadic and the pay minuscule. I paid what I could because I couldn't stand the idea of him *ever* going to jail again.

"What about counseling?" I questioned, knowing he'd rather forgo the whole thing.

"We aren't going to be able to do that..." Grey tried getting out of it. Counseling was important, especially if we were going to make *us* work.

"Let's see what your boss says on Monday, then we'll take it from there. We also need to figure out your drill weekends since you can't drive yourself."

"I'll take care of it. That's none of your f***in' business anyway." Grey was being nasty. He acted like *he* was making all the sacrifices for everything to run smoothly. I was afraid I was going to have to deal with him staying at the armory in Orem every month instead of coming home. It would help save gas, but that didn't mean I had to like it. Boy, I hoped I would survive the next several months! Who knew when or if Grey would get his license back?

~~~~~~

Grey's first day at work went well. He cold-called residents who already had cable and tried to up-sell them on digital. When he wasn't doing that, he took incoming calls for people who already knew they wanted to upgrade. I'd been praying he would not only find a job but keep it as well. Hopefully, this was it!

After talking with his manager and explaining the situation, she allowed him to take Wednesday nights off to continue with our counseling sessions. Grey wasn't too happy about it, but what could he say? He couldn't drive.

~~~~~~

During the whole mess with Grey's license and finding a job, we continued not only counseling, but temple preparation as well. By the fourth week of class, which happened to be the last week in October, I was getting more and more frustrated with the whole temple situation. Even with taking the classes and getting ready for our new addition, Grey *still* didn't see the importance of being a forever family. After class, I finally pressed the issue. "Are you just going through the motions because the bishop told you to or is this leading somewhere?"

"I want to go, I do. I just don't see why it's so important."

"Grey, it's called living the gospel. You aren't supposed to understand all of it. If you did, you wouldn't still be on the earth. You are only asked to have faith, keep the commandments, get baptized, go to the temple, and keep the covenants you make there.

Heavenly Father knows all our faults and imperfections. That's why there's repentance."

"Oh, I don't know." He had continued smoking, but the bishop held onto the hope he would quit if we set a temple date. I had my doubts, but he *was* the bishop. "It's just too hard," Grey whined.

"It isn't supposed to be easy. I know the thought of no smoking scares you, but I have faith that you can do it. If you don't do it for you, or even me, do it for our baby. I really want to go before the baby's born. This baby is the reason being sealed as a family is crucial to returning to our Heavenly Father. You know that."

Grey was silent for several minutes, then he said, "Okay. If it will shut you up, we'll go before the baby gets here. But I still don't get why being together forever is all that important." He wasn't happy about it, but at least he'd set a goal.

I was so excited that his remark didn't even bother me. I reached over (as far as I could, being five months pregnant) and kissed him passionately. It was something we hardly engaged in anymore but surprised me by allowing me the honor. I couldn't remember when I had been so happy—not since RJ.

~~~~~~

In November, two weeks before temple preparation ended, Shaylie and Gunner came to class delighted to tell everyone they were going through the temple the weekend after we finished classes. We found out through the grapevine that Hank and Lynese would be going through the temple just before Christmas. Why Grey didn't know about that was a mystery to me. He and Hank talked about everything! Maybe he did know but didn't want to hear any more from me about it.

Grey and I were doing well enough, and I didn't want to jinx it. He'd not committed to a date yet, and it bothered me. It wasn't like he didn't know how badly I wanted this. How badly I'd *always* wanted this. Ever since I was a little girl, my dream had always been to someday be sealed to my soul mate in the temple.

I was happy for our friends, but I was also struggling with the fact that, although Grey had stated we could go before the baby was born, he hadn't committed. With only two weeks left of class, I wanted a date set, so after class I once again broached the subject.

"Grey, can we set a date yet? We are almost at five months and the closer we get to our due date, the harder it will be for me to go through."

Grey sat quietly for a minute then replied, "Fine, set the damn date!" but he didn't appear happy at all. I wondered if he was only doing it to appease me. I set the date as soon as I was able to call the temple a few days later. When I told Grey our sealing date was set for January 15, 2001, he looked scared. Because I was so excited, I couldn't wait to tell everyone. Of course, Grey's mom was as happy as I was. She'd never thought she would see her son take this step. My parents were another story all together. When I let them in on the plan, the reception I received was anything but warm. I wasn't entirely sure they wanted to be there. As I talked with my parents, I wondered if I would ever again do anything they would be pleased with, especially my mom. Grandma Kacie made it known to everyone that she would be there to support me, no matter what.

~~~~~~

On Tuesday, November 12, 2000, I had my five-month checkup. It was the first appointment Grey had been to. This was the fun appointment, though. We got to find out whether our baby was a boy or a girl. I figured that was the only reason he came along, but at least he was there. When the nurse called for us, she asked, "So, this is daddy, huh? Nice to meet you."

"Yeah, you too." Grey seemed immensely uncomfortable.

After checking my vital signs, temperature and weight, the doctor entered the room. "So, are we going to find out the sex of this little guy today?" I wanted the sex of the baby (or flavor as my mom called it) to be a surprise, but Grey didn't like surprises. Since we were working on compromising with each other, I decided to let him have this one.

"Let's see," the doctor said as he rolled the jelly-covered Doppler over my bulging belly. "It looks like a boy, and he's not modest at all!" He chuckled.

Grey chose that moment to open his mouth. He exclaimed, "Yep, just like his daddy!"

I was so embarrassed, I wanted to die! My face turned beet red and I couldn't wipe the goop off my stomach fast enough. I wanted to get out of there, but no such luck.

After I changed, the doctor explained to us that, because of my physical condition, they would monitor me every two weeks from this point until the birth. They didn't know how my body would respond to labor, so they wanted to make sure we were all ready for even an unforeseeable outcome. I absolutely wanted a natural birth with no drugs and the doctor was okay with it, barring any complications. A cesarean could be a real possibility, however. He recommended Grey come with me to the rest of my appointments because they didn't know what was going to take place. "You are handling the pregnancy better than we expected."

I was so ecstatic I could hardly contain myself, but Grey looked like he was going to puke. "What are you thinking?" I asked as we headed home.

"How are we going to take care of two f***in' kids?" He just had to mention his daughter. "You realize you can't quit your job, don't you?" Grey knew how badly I wanted to be a stay-at-home mom.

I didn't answer, but yes, I was aware of that. I wished I had the guts to tell him I shouldn't have to pay for the fact that he didn't wait until he was married before dickey-dunking. Not only that, but he should be the breadwinner, not me! Why did he have to put such a damper on the day?

We only had an hour before I needed to take Grey to work. Oh, I hated that trip, especially the bigger my belly got. We called everyone we could think of with the news. *"We are having a **boy**!"* My mom was concerned about the whole labor thing. I explained to her what the doctor said and assured her I'd prayed about it and had a good feeling about how things would turn out.

~~~~~~

The next day was our six-week mark since counseling had begun and decision time as far as how much more counseling we'd do. The first thing the counselor asked was, "Do you feel counseling is helping the two of you?"

In all honesty there hadn't been any real improvement in the way Grey treated me. I thought that my being pregnant and the high-risk nature of it might cause him to change his actions toward me, but not even that had an effect. The only difference I noticed was the way I reacted to him, and that was because I chose to alter it. Whenever he got mad, I let him rant until he was done, which usually ended with him storming out of the house.

When it came to the club and dancing, there wasn't any use fighting that issue because it was futile to argue. He did what he wanted, when he wanted anyway. He would say things like, "You f***in' knew I danced before you married me" and "I don't ask for much, damn it; just one night, that's all!"

Renegade was a local dance club that offered Thursday night country dancing. They'd been closed for several months for renovations, but much to my dismay, they were back open for business. Luckily though, Grey seldom went since working at TLCC required him to work Thursday nights.

Grey was the first to respond to the counselor's question. "Yep. I think it's helped a lot."

Curious as to how he felt counseling helped, the counselor asked, "Oh, how so?" She knew Grey hadn't put any effort in changing his behaviors. She even wondered if he'd really quit smoking and was no longer using the Internet to meet women.

He knew he hadn't quit smoking or any of the things that bothered me. He made it look that way just to shut me up. And, because I wanted to have faith my husband had changed, at least to some degree, I chose to believe in him.

"We don't fight as much as we used to." We didn't because he got his way ninety percent of the time. "And we are going through the temple in January." Grey responded with an impish grin, almost like he came up with the plan by himself.

The counselor was shocked, to say the least. "Are you ready for that?"

"We want to be sealed before the baby gets here, and we're almost done with our temple preparation classes," I responded.

"Well, that's good, I guess." The counselor wasn't very convincing. As it turned out, that was our last session. The bishop didn't feel comfortable paying for it when Grey hadn't done any of the homework assignments and didn't put any effort into it. I should've been surprised, but I wasn't.

Before we left, the counselor wanted to talk to me privately. "I think, for your own wellbeing as well as the baby's, you need to continue individual counseling."

"Why?" I wondered if the counselor honestly cared what happened to me, or the baby. Once we left the office, we were no longer her concern.

"I didn't want to say this in front of Grey, but I don't think he has any intention of changing anything. He uses people as long as he needs them and then discards them."

"He won't do that to me or the baby. I know he has issues, but we love each other. We'll be okay." Even as I was saying it, I could feel doubt creeping in.

"What about the baby? What happens if, after the baby's born, Grey can't handle the crying or changing diapers, and he takes it out on the defenseless child?"

I wanted to get out of there. So I said, "I'll think about it." I thanked her and left, knowing I had a whole lot to think about. The only thing that mattered was the baby.

~~~~~~

Thanksgiving came faster for me than ever. Maybe it was because I was having a baby and had more to worry about: the baby, Grey and his court dates, and Grey keeping a job, not to mention the things the counselor said. There was so much that needed my attention, I wouldn't be the least bit surprised if I went into preterm labor.

Grey's first court date was the Monday before Thanksgiving. The judge explained the reasons his driver's license was suspended. It boiled down to child support. Even when Grey tried to squeeze in a conversation about terminating his right, the judge bulldozed over him. He told Grey, in no uncertain terms, he'd better set up a payment plan and stick to it or it might be a long time before he would get his license back and he could possibly serve jail time.

Of course, Grey had a lot to say afterward, mostly about the judge. We hadn't even left the courthouse when he said, "What kind of dumbass judge was that?"

"What are you talking about? He told you why your license was suspended and told you what you need to do to get it back."

"Yeah, but he was more concerned about the child support than anything else. He wouldn't listen when I tried telling him I want nothing to do with the baby. You were there. Weren't you paying any f***in' attention?"

"Yes, I heard everything the judge said and, although I don't like being a step-mom (I hated that word), I see what he means. You made the baby, and she's your responsibility."

Grey's response didn't surprise me, but it did sting. "You don't have to be a bitch about it."

124

What?! I thought I handled the fact that he'd had a baby with another woman, and hadn't bothered telling me, considerably well. *Why does he call me such names whenever I don't agree with whatever he is talking about?* I wanted to ask him, but I was afraid of his answer so, as usual, I acted like nothing was wrong.

The idea of Grey going to jail made me sick, literally. I would continue to do what I'd done since the whole thing started. I'd take care of what payments I could, if only to keep him out of jail.

~~~~~~

One day, during the first week in December, not ten minutes after getting home from taking Grey to work, he called. He'd been fired. Again! "Are you serious?" I was completely pissed.

"Hunter, I don't need this shit right now. Just come get me." Grey sounded like he blamed me. What were we going to do for money? I didn't work full-time anymore—not that I could as far along as I was anyway. Over the next several days, I pushed Grey to get another job, sometimes even calling places for him that I thought might work. He didn't seem at all worried, nor did he act like he really cared whether he worked at all. Somehow, he was hired for a position at a cabinet and door manufacturing place in Lehi. The pay wasn't as good as TLCC, but at least it was something, and I wouldn't be driving as much as I had when running him to and from TLCC.

~~~~~~

On December 16th, I graduated with my Associate Degree in General Education from BYU. Part of me wanted to walk with the rest of the students, but a bigger part didn't feel like waddling across the stage in front of thousands of people. I'd do it when I got my bachelor's—whenever that might be. I wanted so badly for Grey to tell me how proud he was of me, but nothing was ever mentioned. I wasn't exactly nice about how nonchalant he acted either.

"You really don't give a shit, do you?" I asked. My parents had taken us to dinner to celebrate and we'd just gotten home.

"About what?" he asked innocently.

"You know very well what!" I exclaimed.

"Your diploma? It's not like you got a bachelor's degree or anything. What do you want, a medal?"

How could he be so inconsiderate? I didn't want to say something that might set him off, so even though there was snow and it was freezing outside, I put on my coat and went for a walk. Grey didn't care that I was leaving. He parked himself in front of the TV and didn't say another word.

While walking, I thought about the concerns the counselor had brought to my attention. *Was she right? Was I headed into a disaster or would going through the temple finally open those baby-blues?* I wanted badly to be sealed, especially for the sake of the baby, so much so that I quickly pushed those thoughts away and focused on the good things. Grey had a job, he was paying his child support, sort of, and we made it through most days without too many disagreements.

Grey said nothing to me as I climbed into bed that night. What did I expect? An apology? The counselor's words crept in and sleep was a long time coming.

~~~~~~

Christmas, like Thanksgiving, was the same except, for some reason, Grey decided to go with my dad, brothers, and brothers-in-law to get Christmas trees up Provo Canyon. Other than getting our tree, Grey took no part in the pre-Christmas festivities, leaving me to decorate our tree and our apartment—alone. I enjoyed doing it most of the time, plastering Christmasy window clings to the front windows, a Merry Christmas door cover to the front door, and little silver bells that jingled every time someone opened a door in the house. This year, though, it was harder, and I wished my husband would help me. He barely said anything when I asked what he thought of the Christmas feel to our little apartment.

Although I was almost six months pregnant, caroling and candy making were a lot harder, but those were still the highlight of the season for me. Opening gifts on Christmas Day brought feelings of amazement to me because, by this time next year, Grey and I would be parents! Knowing this gave Christmas a whole new meaning. No longer would it only be about Grey and me, but it would be about this amazing gift Heavenly Father had entrusted us with.

I watched my husband as he opened his gifts, almost greedily. Did he realize what a blessing he had been given? I doubted he saw it the same way I did.

~~~~~~

On New Year's Eve, we all ended up at my mom and dad's house playing The Farming Game. The decision to play The Farming Game was almost unanimous. Almost, because Grey wanted to play Balderdash. That request was quickly shot down — by everyone! No one, least of all me, was in the mood for a replay of the last time we played games together. It had taken my parents that long to get up the nerve to invite us again. For some reason, Grey took it in stride and was having a good time anyway. We ate tons of finger foods and drank apple cider until I felt like I was going to pop. After going to the bathroom for the fifth time in the first two hours, I stopped counting and enjoyed the festivities.

We were having so much fun that we almost forgot to ring in 2001. The night didn't end at midnight for us, however, and the game continued. Two o'clock in the morning found Reghan's husband doing his dangdest to still beat the pants off everyone else. It was a good thing no one had to work the next day!

As Grey and I crawled into bed that night, I couldn't help but say a prayer of thanks that we'd had such a good day together. And like many times before, I prayed the good days would continue. For the first time in a long time, I drifted off with a smile on my lips.

~~~~~~

The Sunday after New Year's, Grey and I received our temple recommends. Nervous didn't begin to describe my feelings. Although I knew a little of what to expect, it didn't stop the anxiety.

As I sat across from the bishop, answering question after question, I couldn't help but wonder how Grey would handle his interview. I still had concerns about whether he had quit smoking or not. When I voiced them to the bishop, he didn't seem at all apprehensive about giving Grey his recommend. I tried not to let it bother me.

It didn't take long before Grey came out holding the same slip of paper I had. There was part of me that expected him to not get it. Before going home, we scheduled a meeting with the Stake President the following Tuesday.

Meeting with the Stake President should have been more nerve-wracking than meeting with the bishop had been, but it wasn't. It was easier for me. Maybe it was because I wasn't talking to Grey's father figure. Instead, I was just another member needing a temple recommend interview.

Grey, on the other hand, was more afraid. While we waited, he blurted, "Do we have to do this?"

"What? What do you mean do we *have* to do this?" My heart started racing.

"I'm not sure I'm ready for this. I'm not even sure I want to do this."

Before I had a chance to take his question in or respond, I was called in for my interview. A few minutes later, Grey went in. He must've gotten over his apprehension because, when he emerged, both of us had signed recommends.

For my own peace of mind, I prayed that night whether going through the temple was the correct course of action for us to take. I received an overwhelming calmness as I listened for a response. That calmness stayed with me through the next several days. I knew, even if no one in my family could be there, I was doing the right thing.

~~~~~~

The only person in my family that could be or wanted to be there was Grandma Kacie. The night before, however, she ended up in the hospital due to congestive heart failure and water retention. I was adamant that we needed to see her before the next day. I knew she couldn't be at the temple, but I needed to talk with her beforehand anyway.

"Grey, we need to go see Grandma Kacie." I'd just gotten off the phone with my mom.

"What for?" He didn't act like it was a big deal that she was in the hospital again.

"Didn't you hear any of that?"

"Yeah. Your grandma's in the hospital. And?" He sounded so callous and I wasn't sure where it was coming from. Grandma Kacie had always been good to Grey.

"We need to go see her."

"What for? She's okay, isn't she?"

"No. She's retaining a lot of water and the doctors aren't sure what is going to happen. I need to see her!" I left Grey home, not wanting to make him come with me, and I didn't want to start an argument.

~~~~~~

"Oh, Grandma. I wish you could be there." I could feel the tears as they slipped down my cheeks.

"I will be, in spirit." She did her best to comfort me, but she wasn't looking well.

"I just wish Mom and Dad would come."

"I wish that too, but, Sweetheart, they have their reasons. Besides that, you aren't doing this for them anyway. You are doing this for you and Grey."

"I know. It's just hard." I stayed until Grandma fell asleep. For some reason, the enthusiasm I had was all but gone. Throughout the rest of the evening, I second-guessed my decision.

The next morning, Grey and I, along with our escorts (the people walking us through each step of the temple process), had to be at the Provo Utah Temple by eight o'clock.

Being seven months pregnant made the entire day difficult for me to do what I needed from start to finish without someone to help. It would've been hard with Cerebral Palsy alone but being pregnant added a level of difficulty I wasn't prepared for.

The whole experience put me on a spiritual high. I felt like no matter what, if Grey and I continued feeling the way we did at that moment, if we continued to attend our church meetings, pay our tithing, and remembered and followed the covenants we made that day in the temple, we would be okay.

Afterward, I wanted to go see Grandma Kacie, so we stopped at the hospital on our way home. I'd promised her I would tell her how things went. I figured my mom would be there and I didn't know if I could act all happy-go-lucky in front of them if my dad was there too, because I was hurt that they weren't there for me on my important day. My mom did ask how our sealing went before leaving the room, but I was almost certain it was because Grey was there.

~~~~~~

Almost immediately, after the spiritual high wore off, Grey went back to being his "loving" self. Marriage was hard, but life with Grey was near impossible! I'd never been more grateful that he had a job than I was then because at least he had something to take up his time other than hanging out at Hank's dad's shop. I needed time without the put downs, yelling matches, threats, etc., and his job provided that. It seemed since our sealing, Grey got louder, meaner, and cruder. If that was at all possible. The name-calling was at an all-time high. His favorite names to call me were bitch and cunt, especially if he was looking to knock me down a few pegs. The F bombs had come to be a regular part of his vocabulary as well. What happened to the man who came out of the temple with me that day?

CHAPTER SEVEN

On January twenty-seventh, my mom and Reghan surprised me with a baby shower. Knowing Grey and I didn't have money, they provided everything for my baby: onesies, clothes, diapers, blankets—most everything the baby could possibly need! Reghan was letting me borrow her bassinet because she wouldn't need it for several months. I wanted to let my sister and Mom know how much I loved and appreciated what they'd done, regardless of how they felt about Grey, but I couldn't find the words. Hopefully, the tears streaming down my face would convey some of that to them.

~~~~~~

I found myself getting more and more anxious as my due date got closer and closer. April twelfth was coming too fast. One day in mid-February while at work, I wasn't feeling quite right and all I could do was cry. I called Grey, but he wouldn't pick up his phone.

Next, I called my mom. Mom not only had seven kids of her own, but had delivered a couple. "Mom?" I couldn't talk without crying.

"Hunter, what's wrong?" she asked, concern thick in her voice.

"I don't know. My stomach hurts and I don't feel good."

"Did you call Grey?"

"Yes, but he doesn't answer."

My mom was angry, but she tried to hide it because she didn't want to upset me more than I already was. "Have you called the doctor?"

"No."

"Call the doctor. Tell them what you told me and call me back."

I called and told the nurse how I was feeling. She thought I might be experiencing preterm labor. She recommended I go home and rest. Having someone to monitor contractions wouldn't be a bad idea either. I was scared to death when I called my mom back. It was WAY too early! I couldn't have the baby yet!

"I thought that's what it might be," my mom replied. She could tell I was losing it. "Honey, you'll be okay." I wondered if she believed that or if she only said it to calm me down.

"I don't want to go home alone." I was still in tears. "What if I have him now?" I was nearly hysterical.

"You'll come over here. You're at work and we are closer than your place. Besides that, you need someone to monitor you." Mom then said something she'd been telling me my whole life, "Don't borrow trouble. Everything will be fine."

"Okay. I'll be there in a few minutes."

"Are you sure you're okay to drive?"

"Yeah."

When I arrived at their house, my parents took turns monitoring my contractions. The contractions were sporadic and unable to be timed accurately, at least not at the beginning. If I didn't start feeling better or things got worse in the next few hours, my mom would take me to the doctor.

When I finally reached Grey, he didn't sound at all concerned when I explained to him what was going on. When most husbands—at least the ones I knew—heard their wives might be in labor, they dropped everything. Grey didn't do that. He told me to "keep him posted."

That, of course, not only hurt me, but pissed my dad off. He took the phone from me and proceeded to rip Grey a new one. "THAT is your wife! YOU should be here helping track her contractions, holding her hand, and anything else she wants you to do! Get your ass over here, now!"

"I f***in' can't! She doesn't need me, she has you!" Grey hung up.

My dad was so livid he couldn't think straight! "That kid just told me he seriously didn't care that he made a baby! Nor does he care what happens to his wife or child!" My dad told my mom, thinking I was out of ear shot. No such luck; I heard every word.

I was in so much pain, though, that I didn't have time to be hurt or even angry at my husband's callous behavior.

~~~~~~

After several hours of steady contractions, my mom took me to the doctor while my dad went to find Grey. "…whether he wants to leave or not," my dad quipped.

While waiting for the doctor, I became extremely dizzy and lightheaded and felt for sure I was going to pass out. My blood pressure was extremely high at 159/109. The doctors were able to bring it down and, thankfully, stop my contractions, but they put me on bed rest for the remainder of my pregnancy.

Being on bed rest was going to make getting Grey to work a lot more difficult. As luck would have it (someone was watching over us), one of the guys Grey worked with, after finding out the situation, took Grey to and from work.

I couldn't stand being on bed rest, but between my mom, Reghan, and Shaylie being around all the time, it was bearable. Not only that, but since Grey didn't have a current license, he was dependent on other people to take him places: to get smokes—he claimed he wasn't smoking, but I had my suspicions, and a functioning nose—to go dancing, to get to work, or whatever, his activities were limited. The nice thing for me was that they all knew I hated him going to the club, so no one would take him. The only person I worried who might was Hank.

~~~~~~

In April, two months after being put on bed rest, my real contractions started out of the blue and, because I was close enough to my due date, the doctor didn't stop them.

My mom was unable to be there because two weeks ago, my parents had to make a trip to Michigan to look at a golf course. They figured I wouldn't go into labor while they were gone, but the baby had other ideas.

By nine o'clock in the morning, I was in so much pain I doubted I was going to make it. I'd given up on natural childbirth at that point. I finally gave in and asked the nurse for medication. That was a huge mistake, because all the Demerol did was make me sound drunk. I could barely form a coherent thought, much less a sentence.

As the hours dragged and the contractions became increasingly worse, I found myself watching Grey, hoping he would take part in the birth of his son. Each time my parents called, he would tell them I was fine, and the contractions weren't too bad. Mom, of course, knew differently but she also knew the side effects of Demerol, so she told Grey to let me know they were coming as fast as they could. He didn't bother doing any of the things the nurses suggested might help me: rubbing my back, talking to me instead of flirting with the nurses, getting ice chips, and things of that nature. He complained most about what was on television and how bored he was.

During one particularly bad contraction, the management from *West End,* the government housing we'd applied for eight months earlier, called asking if we were still interested in an apartment.

Instead of answering the question himself, Grey asked me what I wanted to do.

"Can't you take care of that?! I'm a little busy here!" I was pissed because he seriously wanted me to take care of everything! The manager wanted us moved in by the third week in April. That meant I would barely be out of the hospital and would have to pack our apartment up. Grey, after several minutes of hemming and hawing, finally told her we'd take it.

~~~~~~

At one o'clock that afternoon, I was far enough along that I could have an epidural. The nurse explained to Grey he needed to stand in front of me and talk me through the breathing exercises we learned in Lamaze. After explaining each step, the anesthesiologist began inserting the needle into my back. Grey almost passed out as soon as he saw the needle. The nurse sat him down and finished helping me.

I felt bad that my husband couldn't deal with this part, but there was a part of me that wanted to call him out, thinking he purposely pulled the passing out card, so he wouldn't have to do anything.

I was able to relax a lot easier after the epidural and, in response, my body decided it was time to have a baby. Resting as much as I could as I listened to Grey laugh at whatever show he was watching, I wondered what I was doing. Grey didn't love me. I wasn't even sure he loved the baby, or that he even wanted him. I'd hoped that going through the temple would wake Grey up some, but all it did was make him worse. I knew I deserved this punishment because I had chosen Grey, but the baby didn't. This baby deserved a daddy that loved him and wanted him as much as I did. This dilemma haunted me even as things started moving faster.

Because my mom wasn't there, I demanded Reghan be in the delivery room whether Grey was okay with it or not. If his reaction to delivery was anything like the epidural, I wanted someone I knew could be my strength. Reghan arrived at the hospital around two-thirty that afternoon.

Not long after she got there, Grey said, "Oh, it's damn good to see you. Now that you're here, I'll go wait in the hall. Come get me when the baby's born."I

I couldn't believe my ears, and Reghan was livid! It might have been because she was pregnant and her hormones were raging, but more than likely it was the inconsiderate word vomit that gushed from Grey's mouth.

Reghan grabbed Grey by the throat and seethed through clenched teeth, "I don't think so! YOU got her into this, and YOU will get her out!"

At four fifteen in the afternoon on April 6, 2001, Tyler James Andrews made his entrance into the world. Almost immediately, the doctors took the baby away. "Is he okay?" I asked anyone who would listen. I had heard him cry, but I had yet to get a glimpse of the little person I so desperately wanted.

"He's not breathing well," Reghan replied.

"Why? What's wrong? If anything happens to my baby..."

I found it a bit peculiar that it was my sister answering my questions and not my husband. In fact, I didn't know where he was! After Tyler came out, Grey disappeared. Reghan said, "The umbilical cord was wrapped around his neck. They didn't realize he was distressed until just before he crowned. That's why they used the suction cup to help him come out."

"Where is he?" The nurses were working on him as they weighed and measured him. He weighed six pounds and was twenty-two inches long.

A nurse from the neonatal unit came in at that point and explained that, because of how tight the umbilical cord was, they wanted to put Tyler on oxygen for a little while.

Grey finally made an appearance by the side of my bed after Tyler was taken to the NICU. He kissed me, which came as a shock, but I'd take it. Whatever I could get. Soon after, though, Grey left to get food—so he claimed.

I couldn't stop thinking about my little boy as I tried to stop the shaking that started during delivery. The nurses explained it was due to the trauma of birth and, if they could keep me warm, it should stop. Reghan had to go back to work not long after I showered and settled in. I didn't want her to leave because it was all a bit overwhelming. Even for me.

Before leaving, Reghan had some intensely colorful words for Grey because he ditched me and our baby. It was probably a good thing he wasn't around.

When Tyler was brought to me four hours after his birth with a clean bill of health, I was thrilled! I'd been so worried, but he was there with me and I could hold my tiny little boy! Where was Grey? Didn't he realize he was missing an important moment? Did he care?

I didn't want to think about it as I held and cooed over the tiny little person God had entrusted to my care. I couldn't believe I was a mom! I'd waited for this moment my entire life! I looked at him in awe. How marvelous was it Heavenly Father chose *me* to be his mommy? It was hard to relinquish Tyler to the family and friends who came to see the new arrival.

Mom and Dad made it back from Michigan in less than thirty hours. They didn't take the time to go home before coming to the hospital to see their new grandson. They didn't have to ask what the baby's name was because I'd had two or three combinations chosen even before I was married, but my favorite had always been Tyler James.

~~~~~~

My parents had only been there a few minutes when the hospital room phone rang. It was Grey. He was calling from the police station. According to him, he'd gone to get something to eat and, as he was pulling back into the hospital parking lot, a police officer pulled him over and arrested him. Apparently, they'd had a bench warrant for him since the end of December.

"What the hell?" I asked my husband.

"I don't know. I thought we were all done with this shit."

"Yeah. Me too."

"Do you think your parents can come bail me out? I don't want to stay the night in this hell hole." He didn't act concerned about me or the baby. Didn't even ask!

"Seriously?" I knew my parents didn't have the five-hundred dollars to bail him out and I didn't want to ask. It wasn't their problem and, because of the way he treated them, I would expect them to turn him down flat without thinking twice.

"Just ask." Grey was getting angry. I did. I was surprised they didn't turn him down but said if they had the funds they would. Grey wasn't happy but ended up spending the night in a jail cell.

My mom stayed at the hospital with me while my dad, instead of being at home in their own bed, spent the entire night chasing down Grey's attorney. My mom spent most of the night up with Tyler. He didn't want to sleep or eat, just cry. Even though I knew I needed to rest, I couldn't get more than an hour here and there; I was too worried about Tyler, Grey, and my parents.

Mom and I talked a lot throughout the night as we waited to hear from my dad. One moment, as I was holding Tyler, who was thankfully asleep, we looked at his tiny little face as he grinned. I stated, "Mom, I am holding a future General Authority."

"I think so too." There was something about my little boy that was special. We stared at him for a long while in silence, a comforting feeling engulfing the room.

We talked about the move to our new apartment. Since things were so crazy when my parents arrived, there hadn't been time to tell them the news.

"You know you aren't packing, right?" she gave me the 'you know I won't stand for it' look.

"We have to be ready to move into the new apartment in a little over two weeks."

"Grey will have to do it. If he can't do it by himself, maybe members from your ward can help."

"You think I should supervise, right?" I couldn't help but giggle because she and I both knew I didn't delegate well. Just like my mom, if I wanted something done right, I had to do it myself. I knew my mom was right, though, and promised that was all I would do—supervise and delegate.

Just then, my mom got quiet and somewhat serious, again. I hated it when she got that way because, more times than not, it was something about Grey, and it usually wasn't nice or helpful. The next conversation changed the way I looked at the issues between Grey and my family. Mom said, "Last Sunday, we found a ward in Detroit to attend and, during Sunday school, we watched the movie *The Prodigal Son.*"

"That's a really good movie."

"I had never seen it, but you know the part where the kid comes back, and he's changed and all that?"

"Yeah."

"Well, typically you would think I would be thinking of your brothers, but that's not who came to mind. It was Grey."

"Grey? Why?"

"Look at his family. The way he was raised. All he really wants is to be a part of a family. At least that's the reason I hope he acts the way he does and not just because he's a bonafide jerk. I decided from that point on, we are going to be better where he's concerned." I started to cry as I hugged my mom, and, of course, baby Tyler thought he should join in.

Although Tyler was given a clean bill of health, the doctor wanted to keep us an extra day because Tyler was having a hard time with nursing.

When Tyler and I were finally released, it was decided that we, including Grey, would stay with my parents while we packed our apartment up for the move. That decision, of course, I made on my own because my husband was still sitting in jail. It had taken my dad most of the night, but he found the attorney who explained it wasn't Grey's fault he was arrested, but the attorney's receptionist. She never made the correct changes to the schedule. Due to this mix-up, our attorney paid Grey's bail *and* gave us back the partial deposit we'd given him when the whole thing started.

~~~~~~

"It's not fair that *you* should get all the time off work when it took both of us to make the damn kid and get him here." Grey pouted as I drove him to work a few days after Tyler was born.

"Are you for real?" I asked, completely in awe of his logic.

"Well, yeah. I've been there the whole time. I don't get much sleep because the kid has to eat every two f***in' hours. And you expect me to function well enough to hold down a damn job? Where are the father's rights?"

"Let me get this straight... You think that just because you stood by me while having the baby—not wanting to be there, I might add—and you've lost a little sleep, you should have the six-weeks off, too?"

"Hell yeah."

"Hhhmmm. Did your insides feel like they were being ripped out? Did you have to deal with horrendous contractions? Did you spend nine months with each month becoming increasingly uncomfortable?" I shook my head.

"Well, no. But I had to listen to you bitch about everything."

I was so grateful we were at the shop by then that I didn't even bother responding with a comment. Nor did he strain himself to give me a hug or kiss.

I was still mulling over that ludicrous conversation in my mind when, not a half hour after dropping him off, Grey wanted me to come get him. The story he spun for me was that the owner decided to let all employees go because none of them were working out. Neither I, nor anyone else who heard the story, believed it.

Grey wasn't at all interested in getting another job. He was content to mooch off my parents, to simply sit around watching "Maury Povich." Two days after losing his job and after countless hours of watching him ogle talk shows while eating my parents out of house and home—forget helping me take care of Tyler—I confronted him. "Get off your ass and look for a job." I yanked the remote from his hand and turned the television off.

"What the f*** for? You'll be going back soon, and besides, we are moving into government housing so if I don't want a damn job, I don't need one. Besides, rent won't be that bad." He actually thought that was a good idea!

"No, see, THAT is where you're wrong. I've decided that I want to stay home and raise Tyler. I will go back for two weeks to get my insurance payout, but then it's your turn."

"What the hell are you talking about? We agreed that you would go back to work after your maternity leave was up." I could tell I'd hit a nerve.

"No. *You* decided that. Not me." I didn't say anymore on the subject because Grey needed to realize how serious I was. And I meant what I said.

~~~~~~

The day after Tyler's one-week check-up, Grey and I signed lease papers for our new apartment. The manager didn't know, at that point when the move-in date would be because the old tenant's

142

belongings were still in it. However, she wanted us ready to move in no later than the third week in April. That gave us two weeks to get everything packed.

Grey seriously hated being the one to pack everything, and he had no qualms about complaining about it. "I don't get why you are allowed to sit on your ass and tell me what and where things go."

Our last move had been a huge mess because nothing was organized. This time I made sure every box had a room labeled on it and everything was packed nicely, instead of being thrown around. It would make unpacking much easier. It was obvious by his mannerisms that Grey thought it was all unnecessary.

"Sweetheart, I *did* just give birth and I'm supposed to take it easy for the first six weeks. That's what the doctor said. I want unpacking to be easier this time around as well. If you recall, there was a lot of throwing stuff wherever there was room when we moved here."

"This f***in' sucks!" Grey boomed, and then I heard words like "lazy whore," and "stupid bitch" come out of his mouth. I pretended not to hear any of it because I didn't want a fight on my hands. Not with Tyler around. Trying to make it easier for him and wanting to keep the peace, I labeled boxes for Grey and put them into their respective rooms.

~~~~~~

My parents ended up dealing with Grey's laziness for three weeks instead of one. I wasn't happy about the whole situation because I felt like we'd put my parents out enough. Not only did my husband take liberties with their stuff, but he didn't help with the baby either. When he did hold Tyler, he was forever being told to hold his head or "Grey, don't bonk his head against the ceiling. That can cause brain damage."

Grey's response to that was, "He needs to be damn strong. The kid needs to learn to hold his f***in' head up," or something equally

143

stupid. While we were at my parents' home, we made sure Grey only held the baby while sitting down, which wasn't often since he didn't have much to do with the baby.

~~~~~~

Finally, moving day arrived! The management had, once and for all, decided what the issues were with our apartment. What those were we weren't made privy to, but I didn't care. I was tired of mooching off my parents and needed a place of my own.

Grey expected me to help him load our belongings in the horse trailer Hank let us borrow. My mom put a stop to that quick. "She isn't moving anything, Grey." There went the 'mom look' again.

"Why the hell not? She's fine." Grey responded with contempt.

"In case you've forgotten, she just had *your* baby and she isn't to do anything besides care for Tyler and herself for six weeks. You know that!" I couldn't believe my mom had reiterated exactly what I'd been telling him, almost word for word!

My mom suggested to Grey that he get some of the young men from our ward to assist in moving all the boxes. Grey, of course, wanted to play the martyr and didn't heed her suggestion. In fact, he continued to expect me to help. I didn't. He finally asked Hank, and with only the two of them, it took longer than it would have had he taken my mom's advice.

Grey wasn't at all happy with me when he returned to my parents' house that night; he also acted like Tyler was a nuisance. Of course, the baby was crying, and Grey was in such a bad mood that he wouldn't pick Tyler up when I asked. Instead he said things like, "Why do I have to get the damn baby? I just got done moving all our f***in' stuff." More grumbling followed, but with the baby crying it was easy to tune him out. I hoped my parents didn't hear all the chaos.

The next day my mom and sister came to the apartment to help put things in order, to make it look like a home. Thankfully, Grey wasn't there. I didn't know where he was, but sometimes it was easier when he was gone. They hadn't seen the place yet, so I gave them both the tour.

It was a two story, townhome-style apartment. When you walked into the front door, you entered the living room; from there, there was a small hallway with a half bathroom off to the left; at the end of the hallway was a tiny kitchen and dining area. Upstairs there were two bedrooms and a full bathroom. This was the nicest place Grey and I have lived since we were married eighteen months before.

As we unpacked my mom asked, "Are you worried about having Tyler here at night?"

"Not really. I wanted to show you, even at your house, I can do this by myself. That's why I didn't ask for too much help, even at night. I'll be okay. I'm thinking Grey won't be much help, if any at all." I wasn't surprised when I found out later that night that I was right.

~~~~~~

One week before I was supposed to return to work, I repeated that it was imperative Grey have a job before my two weeks were up. Somewhere. Anywhere. Grey still wasn't happy, but at that moment, I didn't care. I felt like the only way to wake Grey up was to give him no choice. "You can't tell me what the f*** to do!" He sounded like a kid who'd been caught doing something naughty.

"I'm not telling you what to do. I'm telling you how it's going to be." I was tired of being the one making the money and paying bills. I'd explained this to him before, but it appeared he needed to hear it again.

"What are you gonna do if I don't get a damn job? Quit still?" I could tell he was angry, because his nostrils flared like they did when he was mad about something or was on the defensive.

"Yep." I put emphasis on the P.

"You can't do that, bitch! Someone has to make the f***in' money around here!" Grey yelled as he turned and, without warning, punched the pantry door. He stormed out of the apartment, slamming the door.

To say I was shocked was an understatement. I'd become used to the threats that Grey levelled about finding someone else, the admission that he regretted marrying me, the profane words that were a common occurrence, and even the name-calling, but this was something new. He'd never punched anything before.

I was so shaken by Grey's outburst that I started panicking. Even though he was gone, the anxiety continued full force! I'd suffered from panic attacks for most of my life, but since marrying Grey, they came more and more often. I was grateful, at least, that Tyler was asleep upstairs and completely unaware.

It was after two o'clock in the morning when Grey returned. He tried talking his way out of the frightening experience, but I didn't want to hear it. I found myself wondering what would be next. Worse yet, who? Would he escalate to hitting me or take his anger out on the baby? The counselor's fears came back to haunt me.

Grey tried to tell me he'd never been with anyone that made him take responsibility and that was why he lost his temper. He claimed he'd never done anything like that before and promised never to do it again. Because we were sealed together forever, I let the matter drop, hoping against hope I wasn't going to regret my actions.

~~~~~~

On May 17, 2001, I returned to work. It was one of the hardest days of my life because, although I only worked four hours, I still had to leave my baby. I tried not to cry, but a few tears slipped out anyway. Of course, Grey made fun of me, doing his best to make me feel bad! Grey had gotten his driver's license back and used *finding a job* as an excuse to take me to work. He didn't let up the whole way there. By the time we got there I had never been so glad to see the building even though I was leaving my baby with the sitter Reghan used for her children. At least I could escape from the taunting for a little while.

~~~~~~

Those two weeks I had to work felt like a lifetime. On my last day, I didn't even have the "I'm going to miss this" kind of feeling I thought I might after working there for three years.

I loved staying at home with Tyler. Every day he accomplished something new and, had I kept working, I would have missed out on all Tyler's milestones. Although he was only a couple months old, I did my best to put him on a routine, so his naps and bedtime were at the same times every day.

Grey, of course, wondered what I did all day, because he thought taking care of a baby was easy-peazy. One day his arrogance showed just enough for me to see he thought all I did during my day was sleep, watch soap operas, and eat bon-bons. "No wife of mine is going to be that f***in' lazy," he proclaimed. "If you can do that, you can damn well work." He couldn't get over the fact that I wasn't letting him off the hook regarding working.

"You sincerely believe all I do is watch soap operas, sleep, and eat bon-bons, huh?" It was ludicrous, I tried my hardest not to laugh, but I couldn't stop the snort that escaped.

"Why are you laughing at me, damn it? It isn't funny," Grey pouted.

"I'm sorry." I replied, although I wasn't. "I don't think you understand what comes with taking care of a baby 24/7. Not only the baby, but the house in general. How do you think the house stays clean or your laundry gets done? Or better yet, who do you think cooks your meals? Who gets up with Tyler when he needs to eat? Who changes his diapers? May I remind you that he's over two months old, and you haven't changed one single solitary diaper?" I wanted to tell him we could change places if he was so inclined, but he most likely *would* watch soaps and eat bon-bons. And, my house would fall apart. "You *are* right about one thing, though."

"I am?" Grey face registered shock. Like I'd never told him he was right before. "About?"

"The soap operas. I do have them on for adult conversation while I clean."

"Yeah right. See, that proves you don't do a damn thing all day."

Grey wanted to continue the petty little fight, but I wasn't giving in. Tyler, sweet little boy that he was, chose that moment to wake up and want food. This was my out, thankfully. I kissed my husband on the cheek, smiled, and went upstairs to take care of the baby.

~~~~~~

For me, Grey getting his license back in August was a blessing in some ways, but in others, it caused more grief and heartache. Not only had the clubbing every Thursday night started again, but he made sure I was well aware he was staying at the armory every drill weekend, and there was nothing I could do to stop him. Most weekends he came home smelling like cigarette smoke and alcohol, which made discussing anything about drill almost impossible without a yelling match. This proved he didn't quit at the bishop's request. The thought that we were sealed under false pretenses made me sick to my stomach.

~~~~~~

One particular weekend was an M5 meaning Grey needed to be at the armory on Friday night and would stay until the end of drill on Sunday. As before, Grey couldn't or wouldn't understand why it bothered me when he was gone an entire weekend. At least with it being an M5, I didn't have to worry about what he might be doing after drill each night. M5's were all military, which meant no partying. I was hoping it might be a peaceful weekend for Tyler and me as I kissed Grey good-bye at the door. Friday evening went off without a hitch. Out came my bon-bons—Cookies and Cream Ice Cream—and chick flick watching commenced after getting Tyler settled, at least for the next few hours anyway.

Saturday morning, as I was putting on my makeup with Tyler in his swing nearby, the telephone rang. "Hello?"

"Is this Grey Andrews' wife?" The girl on the other end sounded scared.

"Yes. Who's this?" My gut clenched. This wasn't good.

"You don't know me, but I work at Payless here in town. I thought you might want to know that I saw Grey in here the other night, and he wasn't alone. There was a girl with him. A very pretty girl." She emphasized pretty. I was getting nervous. "They made no effort to hide they were into each other. I don't want to cause any trouble, but, if it were me, I'd want to know." The girl hung up before I could ask her any more questions.

How did the girl get our number? It was unlisted. Not my biggest concern, however. No, I needed to worry about the girl who was all over my husband in public. I was exceptionally disturbed by the news, but couldn't do anything about it until Grey came home. It bothered me so badly that, although Tyler slept well, I didn't. I should've been sleeping when he did, not worrying about Grey's extra-curricular activities. It was almost dawn when I finally drifted off to sleep, only to be awakened an hour later by a starving Tyler.

On Sunday, I debated going to church. Would it do any good to pretend I was okay when I wasn't? I knew my mother-in-law would love to see Tyler, but I didn't want to run the risk of anyone asking questions I wasn't prepared to answer. We lived in a small town. *What if others had seen him as well?*

I waited all day, mulling over in my mind what I should say to Grey. It was after ten o'clock that evening when he finally walked in the door. Tyler was in bed, thankfully, asleep. Even though I was mad and anxious about the call, I gave him a hug and kiss. Of course, his answer was, "Hunter, I'm f***in' tired. All I want to do is shower and go to bed."

"We need to talk."

"Are you f***in' kidding me? Now?"

"Yes, now." I took a deep breath and forged ahead. "I received a most interesting phone call yesterday."

"And?" Grey had no patience. "Come on, spit it out already!"

"One of the cashiers at Payless called and told me she saw you the other night, at the store, playing tonsil hockey with some girl."

"Really? What's the cashier's name?" The patronizing tone in his voice made me cringe. How did he possess the ability to make me feel so stupid?

"She didn't tell me."

"Convenient. Did she tell you what day she saw me?"

"No."

"I will tell you this once, then I don't want it brought up again, like all my other transgressions you love bringing up. I was nowhere near Payless…much less with another girl. Don't you think I learned my lesson with Sheryl? You bitched and moaned about her for so long that I'm not stupid enough to see someone else or be seen by anyone." He didn't say anything else but went straight into the bathroom. I should've known Grey would have an answer for this. He had an answer for everything he did. The arrogant way he handled the conversation, and many others, made me doubt myself as a woman and a person.

The conversation about the Payless girl, as I called her, widened the already huge rift between my husband and me. Although I tried to forget and act as if everything was okay, Grey continued being Grey. He didn't see the importance of being home at night with his family, much less talking to his wife when he was

150

home. Grey didn't seem to understand that I needed the adult conversation and I needed him to *want* to be at home.

I grew up being told, "If you don't do what you can to turn your husband on, someone else will." I spent every day refreshing my make-up before Grey came home, making sure every hair was in place, not wearing baggy t-shirts, but putting on something flattering. After Tyler, though, it was as if he found me even more repulsive than before. It didn't stop him from getting his own needs met, insisting intimacy be in the dark with a wham, bam, thank you, ma'am air to it. Always in a hurry. To combat the feeling that my husband didn't find me attractive, but only used me as a whore, I found comfort and solace by continuing to write in my journals. How much I wrote and how deep I got with each entry depended daily on Grey.

~~~~~~

After spending several months hanging out with Hank at his dad's shop, Grey, with my help, got a position working on trucks for a local construction company. We'd been dependent on the help of others—mostly his mom—during the months Grey had been unemployed, but he was ecstatic about the position because it was pretty much the same stuff he did with the Reserves. Once again, as I had many, many times during the eighteen months we'd been married, I prayed that he would keep this job. I was beginning to wonder if I would ever feel at ease when it came to money and bills.

A few weeks after starting the job, Grey showed up at home in the middle of the day. His excuse was that there wasn't much for him to do so they let him go early, but he had used company time to take breaks whenever he felt the need and had also used the cell phone the company provided to make personal calls—personal calls that were not to me.

CHAPTER EIGHT

September 11, 2001 was the beginning of HUGE changes in the nation and the Andrews family. A little after nine in the morning, Grey called and asked if I'd been watching the news. When I told him no, he demanded I turn on the television. I caught a little of what was said by the reporters—things like, "airplane hit the Pentagon" and "two planes flew into the World Trade Center" and "terrorist attacks" and "Flight 93 down"—as Grey hurriedly explained what was happening.

I remained glued to the television until I couldn't stand it anymore. I found myself fielding calls from almost every member of both families as they checked in to see about deployment. My biggest fears were manifesting themselves. From the moment Grey told me he had re-enlisted in the Army National Guard, I feared there would come a day when he would be gone for months at a time, or possibly years.

~~~~~~

As the days and weeks went by, I waited in fear for the call that didn't come. The nation as a whole was on high alert, as there was talk of war, capture, and putting a stop to terrorism. The only thing that changed was the freeze that was put on all military, meaning that, if a soldier's time was up during the frozen period, they weren't discharged.

Grey was scheduled to be discharged in December 2001, but due to the recent terrorist attacks, he wasn't. Instead, he switched from being a diesel mechanic to working a petroleum pipeline, which meant more time away for training, as well as another two-year commitment, at least. Grey went to drill exactly as he had been the last two years, but because he was training in a new area, his annual training would be longer. He would go in two-week increments, twice during the Spring or Summer so he was gone a month total, and continue the one weekend a month he was already doing..

Finding out the reservists were usually the last of the military to be called up was an immense relief to me. After talking to Grey's commander, we found out their current unit was nowhere near ready for deployment. That eased my mind somewhat, but it didn't stop the fear and anxiety whenever the phone rang.

Our second anniversary came during this time of turmoil. Having a baby and not a lot of money, I managed to buy Grey a card and the new Neil McCoy CD he'd been after. I also decided to make a special dinner for the two of us to enjoy by candlelight after Tyler was down for the night. Once again, Grey did nothing. He did, however, want to know if he got a gift. Giving him the benefit of the doubt (something I did a lot), I blamed his ambivalence on the attacks that happened ten days before.

~~~~~~

I had hoped that being sealed in the temple and welcoming Tyler into our home might make my husband grow up, at least a little. However, once again, when it came to Grey, I was wrong. He still had the job with the construction company, but as time and the month of November wore on, he got sent home early a lot. By the fifth time he came home early since starting the job in August, I wasn't handling it well, especially when Grey avoided answering why.

Without Grey's knowledge, I decided to get some answers. Luckily, Grey's boss was in his office that day. The shop smelled of gas and an almost fiery smell. Thankfully, I didn't have to wait in the shop area, but inside the secretary's office. I'd never met Grey's boss before, but as he reached out to shake my hand and by the look on his face, I got the feeling that he wasn't going to tell me anything good. "Hello, Mrs. Andrews."

"Hello." My palms were sweaty, so I had to wipe them on my jeans before shaking his hand.

"What can I do for you today?"

"Well, as you know, Grey has been sent home early quite often. I need to know why."

"Have you asked him?"

"Oh, yeah. There's never a real answer, though. Just his typical, 'I don't know.'"

"You probably came out here without telling him, huh?"

"Yes. I need to know what's going on, and he isn't going to tell me the truth."

"Normally I don't do this, but because what he's been up to not only affects his job performance, but potentially your marriage, I feel you should know."

The blood rushed in my ears. Somehow, even before he told me anything, I knew what I was about to hear was true.

"You are aware that he has been given a company cell phone?"

"Yes."

"Company policy states that it is supposed to be used for company or emergency purposes only."

"Okay."

"Grey seems to think he can use it to call anyone he wants."

"Meaning?" I asked.

155

"I pay the bills for all cell phones my employees use. He uses it to call numbers I'm not familiar with. I know your home number, so I know he isn't calling you."

"Do you know who he's calling?"

"I don't. All the bill shows me is numbers. That's not the only reason he's been sent home."

"There's more?"

"He takes several breaks throughout his eight-hour shift when he's only allowed two fifteen minute breaks and one thirty-minute break. I've told him not to smoke on the premises where there is gasoline because it's hazardous, but he has yet to heed my warnings."

"What did you just say?" I asked. I wanted to make sure I heard him correctly.

"About the breaks? He looked confused.

"No. Did you just say he's been smoking?"

"Uuhhh...Yes. Didn't you know?"

"No. I've suspected it but didn't know for sure."

"I am so sorry. I never would've brought that up if I was aware you didn't know."

"It's okay. Thank you for telling me." I walked, half hurt and half angry, to my car.

~~~~~~

I wasn't exactly sure how I was going to bring up the phone calls and smoking thing with Grey. He would, for sure, be pissed that I went to his boss in the first place. So much so that he would make his issues my fault, regardless. He was home when I got there and, because it was kind of like ripping off a Band-Aid real fast, I delved right in. "Grey... we need to talk."

"Again?" He didn't seem at all enthused about talking to me. No shocker there. "What now?"

156

"I had a very interesting conversation with your boss today."

"You what?!" His nostrils were flaring like they did when he was infuriated.

"Since you won't give me a straight answer when you get sent home early, I went to ask him."

"That is none of your f***in' business!"

"It is when it affects not only my livelihood, but also my son's." My heart was racing, but I was not backing down.

"Whatever he said, it's not true!"

"So, you don't use your cell phone to make personal calls? Not to me, I might add."

"So?" Grey didn't bother making excuses. "I'm allowed to on my damned breaks."

"That's not what he said. What about taking breaks several times throughout the day?" I paused for a second. "What about your many smoking breaks?"

"He told you I'm smoking?!" Grey was furious.

"He just echoed what I already suspected."

"That's all he told you?"

"Is there more?" When Grey said nothing, I kept going. "I have one more question."

"What?" He didn't want to continue. "If I answer, will you shut up?"

"Did you ever quit smoking?"

"Guess you'll never know, huh?" he replied snidely before turning back to the TV show I had interrupted when I came in.

That night I prayed harder than ever before that my sweetheart had only made a small lapse in judgment, instead of what I feared had been going on all along—that he had lied to the bishop just to get his recommend to shut me up, as he so eloquently liked putting it.

~~~~~~

As our third Thanksgiving drew near, Grey wanted to only make an appearance at my parents' house instead of hanging out there, as we'd done in the past. That, of course, caused a huge fight.

"Why don't you want to go over there?"

"Because that's all we ever do. On every holiday! We spend every damned one with your family." Grey replied.

"We do that because your family doesn't think holidays are important and all we do at your mom's is sit and watch *Xena: Warrior Princess.*"

"My mom doesn't get to see Tyler much." Grey was pulling out the big guns now.

"That's my fault?"

"You're with him all the time. You could get off your lazy ass and take him over."

"I'm with him all the time because even when you're home, you're not home. You've either got your ear to that stupid cell phone you have for work or you're glued to the television. You hardly acknowledge the baby. And you can just as easily go over there any day, or your mom can come here."

Thanksgiving was one battle I won. Grey finally gave in and we had Thanksgiving, and Christmas for that matter, with my parents, much the same as we had the previous two years. Tyler was too little to care about all the festivities of either holiday, but I took a lot of pictures anyway. It was quite a riot to watch the nine-month old eat a chocolate sucker and the mess that ensued! When we made candy, he, along with his cousin, thought they needed to help. They made a huge mess! But with all the pictures I'd taken, he would be teased by his Mommy forever. The way this child saw the holidays in the future weighed heavily on mine and Grey's shoulders. His knowing the true meaning was our responsibility, and I was determined that he would know…with or without Grey's help.

~~~~~~

By the grace of God, Grey had managed to keep the
construction job—by far the longest job he had kept—so for
Valentine's Day 2002, which happened to be on Thursday that year,
I wanted to go to *Renegade* and dance with my husband. I debated
whether to tell him but was almost certain he would veto the idea
and go alone. Buying a Valentine's Day card, I made a coupon to
put on the inside that read: **Good for dancing at Renegade with
your wife on Valentine's Day!** I put the card together and left it in
his lunchbox where I was sure he'd see it when he went to lunch.

I waited anxiously all day to find out whether he got it or not.
When he came in the door that evening, he didn't say anything
except, "What's for dinner?"

"I thought we could go out. I already have a sitter for Tyler."

"I'm going dancing," Grey replied.

Excitedly I asked, "Oh, so you got my card huh?"

"Yep.

"So? Let's go. We can drop Tyler off at Mom and Dad's, grab a
bite, and then go dancing."

"No."

"No? You just said you wanna go dancing."

"Yeah. Without you." The finality of his words cut me deeply.
I'd tried so hard to overlook his smoking, although we'd been
through the temple. I'd overlooked the cell phone usage, as well as
the "Payless Girl" and, then there was Sheryl. Oh yeah, let's not
forget that he was ashamed of me. And he couldn't be bothered to
take me dancing?

"Why not me?" I wasn't going to let this go.

"You know as well as I do how ridiculous you look when you
dance. And you know I don't dance left handed. Besides, dancing
with you is embarrassing. Makes you look like a retarded cunt." He

didn't say anything else, just showered and left. There was nothing left for me to say. That name he called me threw me for a loop.

After calling my mom and lying through my teeth that I was not feeling well—with Grey's words still reverberating in my head—I spent the rest of the evening watching movies Grey wouldn't watch with me. It wasn't a complete lie because hearing the words, "Makes you look like a retarded cunt," made me literally sick to my stomach. Tyler's little antics helped me keep my cool enough that the tears didn't fall until Tyler was in bed and I was sitting alone in the living room, writing in my journal. I let the tears wash over me and spill onto the pages as I scribbled furiously. I'd married Grey for better or worse, and we were sealed forever. I couldn't see how my life with Grey could get any worse. The saying "You made your bed, now you have to lie in it" ran through my head. I may have, but Tyler didn't deserve any of it.

~~~~~~

One March evening just before Tyler turned eleven months old, we were at my parents' house for pizza and a movie. Grandma Kacie was living with them because she had gone through hip surgery several weeks earlier, and not too many days after getting out of the hospital, she fell and broke her other hip. When she developed bed sores while in the nursing home, my parents decided to move her in with them. She would have to live with someone who could care for her for the next two or three months and then she would be able to move back to her apartment. Tyler loved spending time with his grandparents and great-grandma, so much so that a lot of my days were spent there while Grey was at work. That day was no different. It was my mom's idea to order pizza and watch a movie. Although Grandma Kacie wasn't too fond of pizza, she went along with it. I called Grey, told him the plans for the evening; if he wanted dinner, he needed to come over after he finished for the day.

As we were eating pizza, watching *Dr. Doolittle,* and chatting, Tyler stood up by the couch—something he'd been doing for quite some time, so I wasn't paying too much attention. All of a sudden, Tyler started baby stepping from the couch to the entertainment center. "Oh my gosh!" I kind of whispered and hissed at the same time so I wouldn't startle Tyler. "He's walking!" We watched a couple more seconds until Tyler plopped on his bottom.

"You guys are in for it now!" I could see the pure glee in my mom's eyes. I didn't doubt she was right, though. Grey and I were in serious trouble with a toddling little boy on our hands.

~~~~~~

Tyler's first birthday came all too quickly for me. It seemed like only yesterday I was delivering him, and there he was saying a few words, walking, and becoming a toddler.

Because it was his first birthday, I decided I wanted as much of his extended family there as possible. Of course, Grey wasn't interested in planning the party. Because of the way he'd been acting, there were days that I felt like a single parent, and more times than not, I felt like I had two children instead of one. I swore there were days they tried to out whine each other.

Reghan had begun making birthday cakes for her kids' birthdays so I asked if she would make a *Thomas the Train* cake for Tyler. All of Tyler's grandparents were present, both of his great-grandmas, and lots of aunts, uncles, and cousins from both sides. After singing Happy Birthday to him—which he thought was loud—Tyler's older cousins wanted badly to help him open presents. He was more interested in the bags and noisy paper than the presents themselves, and he happily shook the tissue paper around, making tons of noise. His cousins became enthralled with the bags and paper as well. It was funny, the things that could hold little children's attention.

When cake time came, instead of digging in and making a big mess I'd hoped to get a picture of, Tyler gingerly touched the frosting and looked at me like, "What am I supposed to do with this?" The look on his face was so cute that I had to take the picture before I could get him to eat his cake, if only to use as leverage when he grew up!

~~~~~~

From the moment Tyler took those first steps at my mom and dad's, I knew my life would never be the same. He did his dangdest to maneuver the stairs, which scared the daylights out of me. He even tried to run like the big kids. That scared me that much worse!

One day, not long after his first birthday, Tyler was toddling from the living room and down the short hallway. Suddenly, I heard a blood-curdling scream! My heart nearly stopped at that moment.

Instead of staying on the carpeted area in the short hallway that connected the living room and kitchen, which he usually did, Tyler had gone into the kitchen and slipped on the linoleum. I heard the blood curdling scream from the living room. I got there and watched in horror as his eye connected with the corner of the cabinet, unable to stop it. There was blood running down his face and he was crying so much that he was shaking and breathing in little gasps! I did the first thing that came to mind. I grabbed a cold, wet cloth and put pressure on the wound. At the same time, with Tyler screaming at the top of his lungs, I called Grey. I explained what had happened and that I needed him to come home so we could take Tyler to the doctor. He was using my car because his truck wasn't registered, leaving me with no transportation.

Grey asked, "Is he unconscious?"

"No."

"Is he breathing?"

"Yes!" I couldn't believe him..

"Then what the hell do I need to come home for?!" he replied impatiently.

"I can't tell whether he needs stitches or not. And you have my car!" After waiting for Grey's response, I spit out, "Never mind. I'll just call someone who cares."

Without giving him a chance to respond, I hung up and called my mom. She didn't hesitate to drop everything and come over, even though she was in class. She wasn't surprised by Grey's response either. Pissed, but not surprised. Because super glue was often used to close wounds like Tyler's, I didn't want those kinds of chemicals in my baby's body, and stitches were painful, my mom brought her old fallback—steri-strips. I remembered using those many times growing up because going to the doctor wasn't always an option.

Tyler was steri-stripped, cleaned up, given Tylenol, and playing as if nothing was out of the ordinary when Grey walked in the door. He wasn't happy that my mom was there, but what could he do? Remove the steri-strips? He stomped around and groused but didn't show his true self. There was no way he would let my mom see his real temper, especially since she knew how he'd left me hanging.

We must've been accident prone, or at least pain prone in our house because, not three days after Tyler's spill, Grey came in the door during his lunch hour. I could tell there was something wrong even before I saw his face. "Hey, are you okay? You look like you're about to throw up."

Tyler was so excited to see his daddy that he ran at him with arms widespread. Grey was so out of it that he yelled at the little boy, "HEY! Watch it!" Of course that made the baby cry, which only made Grey angrier. "I'm going upstairs."

After calming Tyler, I went upstairs to talk to Grey. "Did you take some Ibuprofen?" Grey was pale and didn't look well, but that didn't stop him from being belligerent and rude to me.

"What do you take me for? A dumbass? Of course I did!" I did my best to remember that he was in pain so I wouldn't snap back.

Over the next week, Grey didn't attempt work. He complained about his neck and head hurting too much to do anything but sleep. It didn't stop him from taking smoke breaks, though. His excuse? Smoking made his head hurt less. He'd told me over and over that he was going to quit, but with the terrorist attacks, he was anxious, and smoking helped calm his nerves.

Even as he lay in pain, I wondered why I put up with all the degradation. The only answer I had was that I loved him.

After two days of listening to Grey complain about his neck and head, I made him go to a chiropractor. Did I know where the money was coming from? No, but I couldn't listen to him anymore!

If he wasn't whining that he hurt, Grey whined that the baby or the television was too loud, or it was too hot or cold. He complained I didn't take care of him well enough—that I didn't bring him what he wanted to eat or drink whenever he demanded. Did he remember or even care that I was tending to a baby's needs, and the needs of our child came first?

Four days and two chiropractic visits later, Grey was as good as new. He had pinched a nerve in his neck, which caused the neck and headache pain. Although he was cleared to go back to work after the first visit, Grey milked his time off for all it was worth, running me ragged in the process. I was happy when Monday morning arrived, and I got to kick him out the door! Sometimes he was more difficult than the baby!

CHAPTER NINE

With the decent tax return we received, and after much discussion and rule setting—mostly for Grey's benefit—in June, we decided to buy a computer. That way we could stop mooching off other people when we needed something.

Grey was more excited about having the computer than I was. I had mixed feelings about it because I felt that, although Grey hadn't been chatting with other women, at least not that I was aware of, Sheryl would always be in the forefront of anything involving a computer. I had to learn to trust him and this was the best way I could think of to do it. Besides, he'd wanted one for a long time and I was a sucker when it came to making Grey happy.

It took Grey what felt like an eternity to choose the computer he wanted. I'd tried to get him to bring my dad because he was a computer genius when it came to specs and what not. Of course, Grey nixed that idea really fast.

After finally picking out the computer, Grey decided he was hungry, so without asking whether I was, and knowing I always had snacks and stuff for Tyler no matter where we went, he stopped at McDonalds. By the time Grey was finished, it was rush hour, and the traffic was horrible. I sincerely hated rush hour and Grey knew it. I didn't like feeling as if I was boxed in between cars. That's exactly what happened when we arrived at the corner of Janican Road and Highway 20, with Grey at the wheel. There was a red vehicle in front of us, a ditch on one side, and a large green 4x4 behind us.

I was extremely exhausted due to being up with Tyler the last few nights, not to mention having a whiny husband. Tyler wasn't only teething, but he was still fussy because of the gash above his right eye. I was pretty sure he continued to have a headache.

Because the baby was content, and Grey was driving—maybe I should've been more afraid for that reason alone—I decided to try and ignore the boxed in feeling and sleep. Hopefully, closing my eyes would make the claustrophobic feeling dissipate. Not long after laying the seat back and making sure the seat belt was fastened correctly, I heard, "You'd better brace yourself!" I'd been out of it long enough that I had no idea what Grey meant. It didn't take long before I felt more than heard, the crunch of metal on metal as the 4 x 4 smashed into the back of our car. It felt like I was above my body, watching as I whipped back and forth. Somehow, even with my seatbelt on and the seat laid back, my head still managed to smash into the windshield.

My first coherent thought was Tyler. I could hear him crying as I tried to clear the dizzying fuzz from my head. When I was finally steady enough to go to him, what greeted me made me angry! The truck hit us so hard that it loosened the seat belt and tipped Tyler's car seat over.

I was not calm by any means but tried to keep my voice level. "What in the hell were you thinking?!"

"I'm really sorry. When I saw the guy in front of you move, I thought you would too."

"How would you feel if it were you in my shoes with a baby in the back seat, damn it?!" Of course, I was still angry, but Grey... Wait, where was Grey? There I was, holding a screaming baby and dealing with the nincompoop who hit us, and he had the balls to sit in the car like nothing had happened? He didn't even bother moving it off the road until the police arrived.

As the police talked with the guy who hit us, and Grey—he finally decided to make his presence known—I sat in the front seat of our car holding Tyler who was calm and content, playing with my earrings. When the policeman came to get my version of the accident, I explained that I was almost asleep when Grey warned me, seconds before the truck hit. He asked whether the baby or I were hurt. Having been in a couple of car accidents prior to this one, I was aware that sometimes pain and injuries didn't manifest until hours after the adrenaline wore off. There didn't seem to be any injuries, but we were going to get checked out anyway, just to be sure. The police let us leave as soon as they had our statements.

Although it was getting late, I wanted to stop at Mom and Dad's to fill them in. The biggest questions everyone had was how Grey knew we would be hit and why he was the only member of the family with time to brace himself. I, of course, didn't have any answers. Not long after we arrived, my entire body started to ache—so badly that I couldn't hold back the tears.

After putting Tyler to bed a couple hours later, I took Ibuprofen and tried using a heating pad, especially between my shoulder blades. It didn't do anything to help, and Grey's degrading comments didn't help matters either.

"Shut the f*** up! I'm trying to sleep! Some of us have to work tomorrow! Don't be such a damn cry baby!"

"Oh, leave me alone! I didn't call you names and all that shit when your nerve was pinched, did I?"

"Uh. Difference, you're not hurt. You're just being bitchy." He thought I was playing it up just to get sympathy from him. He didn't have a clue what that word meant!

~~~~~~

Tyler and I ended up going to the same chiropractor Grey did. X-rays were taken, and the chiropractor worked on Tyler just to make sure he was okay. He tried lessening my pain over the next few weeks, to no avail. If anything, my pain worsened the more he tried to fix it. I also went to my regular doctor, who prescribed pain medication, hoping to lessen the pain to the point that whatever was wrong would fix itself. The pain medication barely touched it and the doctor told me I was just going to have to live with it. Because we had no insurance, I couldn't get a second opinion, so the pain continued. Having Cerebral Palsy didn't help the pain either. If anything, it made it worse.

As my pain got progressively worse, taking care of Tyler was about all I could manage. It was so bad that I didn't have the will to argue with Grey over how much time he spent on the computer. The rules we set went right out the window once it was set up. He was on the stupid thing almost continually. He opened a new email address for himself with a password I was not allowed to know, and he had a messenger account as well. He said he "needed his privacy." This was where the trust came in. When he said he wasn't chatting with anymore Sheryls, I needed to believe him. That's what he said every time I asked why he hated it when I watched him on the computer.

~~~~~~

One September evening, just after our third anniversary— which once again, Grey didn't see the point in celebrating— I let curiosity get the better of me. Grey had been on the computer all day, so, after putting Tyler to bed, I stood far enough away that he couldn't tell I was looking at the same thing he was. I was so horrified by what I saw I didn't realize I had gasped until Grey turned around—quickly getting out of the page he had up.

"What the f*** are you doing?" he yelled. There were pictures of nude and scantily clothed women and girls; some looked as if they were teenagers.

"I could ask you the same damn thing, you jackass!" I countered.

Grey knew he'd been caught. "You're f***in' spying on me? I've told you a thousand times not to watch when I'm on the damn computer!"

"Now I know why!" I tried to keep my voice down because I didn't want to wake the baby. "How long have you been into porn?" If I was honest with myself, I knew how long. At least as far back as Sheryl, anyway.

"THAT is none of your damn business!" Grey didn't care whether he woke Tyler up or not. He wasn't the one who took care of him anyway. It was almost as if he wanted to wake him up. Nor did he act like it mattered if the neighbors heard.

"Yes, it is! Being your wife and eternal companion makes it my business!"

"Oh! I knew you would throw all that temple shit at me someday! I never should have f***in' agreed to it!"

"Are you serious? I cannot believe you just said that!"

"Well, now you know!" With that he headed for the door.

"Where are you going?"

"None of your business!" When I tried to stop him from leaving the kitchen by blocking his way out, Grey raised his fist like he was going to hit me. But almost as a second thought, he punched a hole in the kitchen wall. I backed out of his way. I didn't want him to know how frightened I was as I willed the tears away.

As I stared at the hole in the wall, I was well aware Tyler or I might be next. I had only seen him this angry once before, and that time he only bloodied his knuckles. Not five minutes after Grey slammed the door, there was a knock.

To say I was surprised when I answered the door would be a fib. I'd felt for some time the police would eventually be called to our house, especially now that we lived in a place you couldn't use the bathroom without someone knowing about it. Anyone could've called them.

"Ma'am, is everything okay?"

Even though I was shaky, I answered, "Yes."

"Your neighbor called in a domestic disturbance. Said they were concerned with all the yelling that was going on. You're married to Grey Andrews?"

"Yes." The look that crossed between the police officers was strange. I wondered if they knew something I didn't. "He just left."

"We saw him. We can track him down if you want to press charges." The police officer looked at the hole in the wall with concern. "Did he hit you?"

"No, he didn't." I thought about pressing charges, but I didn't want to anger Grey any more than I already had.

~~~~~~

The next morning, the manager called us to her office. "The police were called to your apartment last night." It wasn't a question. "You do know it states in the lease that domestic disturbance is grounds for eviction." Again, not a question.

"It was my fault. I promise it won't happen again. Please let us stay." Why I was taking the blame, I didn't know, except I didn't want to move again. And at that point, I would do anything not to have to endure Grey's wrath.

I should've known better because, as we were walking home, Grey grumbled, "Thanks to your bitching at me, we have to watch ourselves now. The f***in' neighbors will be onto us."

"I didn't call the cops!" This didn't help. "I took the blame, too, damn it! Does that mean nothing to you? We could be going home to pack if I hadn't talked fast." Nothing I said made him understand, so I left it alone, letting him think what he wanted to.

~~~~~~

The beginning of October brought a pretty big change for my family. Because Grandma Marshall was older and her health was declining, it had become impossible for her to live alone any longer. Two weeks before her ninety-fourth birthday, my parents decided she should move in with them. It wasn't an impromptu decision. As far back as I could remember they'd said that, when the time came, neither grandma would live anywhere but with them.

I spent a lot of time with both Grandma Marshall and Grandma Kacie, who had been able to move back to her apartment in May, helping my mom in any way I could. Being a stay-at-home mom allowed me to be of greater assistance. On more days than not, after Grey left for work in his truck that wasn't registered; he didn't seem to care that it was illegal, I packed Tyler up in the rented Monte Carlo I drove as my car was being fixed, and did what was needed: laundry, assisting with bathing, grocery shopping or just spending time with them. Grey, of course, simply thought I was slacking in my "wifely" duties.

~~~~~~

Grandma Marshall's birthday was on the thirteenth. Grey knew I hated going to family events alone. Mostly because when he wasn't there, I got bombarded with questions. About our marriage, about his smoking and drinking, and anything else they wanted to ask.

I hated that it sounded like I was begging. "Grey, please. Come with me."

"What the hell for?" he was indignant.

"Because she has never said a bad thing about you, and who knows how many more birthdays we'll get to share with her."

"So? Who the f*** cares?"

"So? You're kidding me, right?"

"What do I get out of it?" There it was, the ultimate question. Grey never did anything unless he benefited from it.

"Are you serious? You care more about what you want than my grandma?"

In the end, Grey went, but not until I promised to let him go dancing for the next month without saying a word.

~~~~~~

Grandma steadily went downhill following her birthday. For the most part, she was lucid, but there were days when she was in so much pain, she slept a lot. Some days she knew where she was and others, she didn't. Every day Tyler and I were with her—I made it a point to be around her as much as possible. I realized the likelihood that he would remember her was slim; he was only seventeen months old, but I had to try. For reasons I couldn't put into words, it was as if I needed him to remember her.

~~~~~~

Since I didn't know what was wrong with my back, and because the other driver's insurance company didn't want to pay for any of my medical needs, I hired a personal injury attorney in November. I hoped he might be able to get them to at least cover my medical bills for a while, so I could get a second opinion. I met with him, but he didn't have real great news for me.

"Hunter, since we don't know what caused your pain, I can't ask the insurance company to cover anything."

"Are you serious? I wasn't in pain before that car accident."

"Yes, but you told the police officer that you weren't hurt." That wasn't exactly what the police report said, but he was an attorney, so I didn't correct him.

"So, what now? Are you telling me the same thing the doctor and chiropractor did? I'm "just going to have to live with this"?"

"We can go for a settlement, but I'm afraid you'll be disappointed."

"All I want is for him to take care of my bills, so I can find out why I'm in so much pain and do something to alleviate it."

"I'll see what I can do. You'll need to get all the documentation you have on it: the police report, the chiropractor notes, the doctor's notes, and statements or information from anyone else that can shed some light on the difference in your abilities before the accident. This won't be a fast or easy fix. It will eat up a lot of my time, and I fear the outcome won't be what you want."

"I have to try. Thank you." Over the next few weeks I got everything together the attorney needed, including statements from my parents, Grey, the bishop, and even our home teachers; they could all attest to the change in my ability to take care of every day chores.

~~~~~~

November 23, 2002 was a rough day for Grandma Marshall. She'd been in so much pain that my mom had to keep her sedated pretty much all the time. I spent the day sitting next to her bed, talking to her even though she was asleep, spelling my mom, and playing with Tyler when I needed a break. Tyler and I arrived home quite late. Of course, Grey was pissed off that he had to fend for himself when it came to dinner. I didn't really care. I had more important things to worry about now, and besides, he was a big boy. He could fix himself something to eat for one night. I found myself thinking about Grandma Marshall while I gave Tyler a bath, read a story, sang, and put him to bed. He was barely old enough to care whether he had a nightly story, but I'd been reading and singing to him since before he was born. As I sang "I Am a Child of

God" to him, stroking his blonde hair, I couldn't help but think things were about to change.

And change they did. The phone rang just as I closed Tyler's door. "It's your mother." Grey grumbled. I hated the way he said her name like it left a bad taste in his mouth.

"Mom, is everything okay?" She didn't call this late unless... "Grandma's gone, isn't she?" I wasn't asking.

"Yes. She passed away just after you went home. I was sitting next to her. I felt it wouldn't be long and I didn't want her to be alone."

"Mom, she knew you cared and loved her. Even though it took you over twenty years to reach sainthood." We both laughed through the tears. "Is Dad okay?"

"Not really, but he will be."

To say the remainder of the night was restless for me was an understatement. The tears that started as I was singing to my little boy didn't dissipate. Grey wasn't any help either. It would've been nice if he would have shown some empathy. Instead, he said things like, "She was old, so what the big assed deal?" and "I hate it when you turn on the f***in' tears!" It wasn't because it hurt him to see my tears, but because he thought crying was weak.

~~~~~~

Over the next few days, my parents made plans for Grandma Marshall's funeral. Because her home was in Park City, and that was where most of her friends were, the funeral would be held in her church building there. My parents decided at the last minute to have a viewing the night before the funeral as well as one the morning of. The one request my Grandma had was that my dad sing at her funeral. I didn't know how he was going to do that, but it was for his mom, so I knew he would sing his best.

Thanksgiving Day was a somber affair, to say the least. We had the usual: turkey, ham, broccoli salad, Waldorf salad—one of Grandma Marshall's favorites—and mashed potatoes and gravy.

The day, however, just didn't feel right; Grandma Marshall wasn't there, and everyone felt it. We did our best to make it memorable anyway, knowing she was with Grandpa Marshall who died twenty-one years before. Telling stories about Grandma Marshall helped ease the heartache a little as we remembered her as she was. It didn't help either that Derek and Dylanie, my sister-in-law, weren't there, and no one knew whether they would make it to the funeral.

~~~~~~

I made it very clear to Grey that, because he wasn't coming to support me for the viewing the night before the funeral, the least he could do was watch Tyler. Everything was going to be an emotional upheaval, and chasing Tyler around, especially with the pain I was in, wouldn't be easy.

He agreed, although I had to twist his arm. He waited, however, until just before Reghan came to get me to drop a bomb. "Oh, by the way, I'm going with Hank to pick up Lynese's Christmas present. We have to take his pickup, so I can't watch Tyler."

"What?!" Was he serious? "When did this come up?"

"Oh, a few days ago. I just forgot to tell you." He didn't act the least bit sorry.

"Are you kidding me?!" I was sure Reghan heard at least some of the extremely heated conversation, because she didn't wait for me to open the door but walked into World War III—at least as close as it could get when Grey paid more attention to whatever he was doing on the computer than talking to me. I hated that thing! I had since we bought it.

"Fine. I'll take him with me. Since I'm not as important as Hank and Lynese." I quickly packed a diaper bag for Tyler and, because Reghan didn't need to hear any more, I asked her to take him to the car.

She did hear Grey quip, "Oh, get the f*** over yourself, Hunter," before she walked out.

"You don't care that this is hard on me, do you?" I wanted to swear at him, but didn't. Instead, I didn't give him a chance to respond before turning to leave. Not before he got one more dig in though.

"Get the hell out before you make me do something you'll regret!" And, under his breath, "Geesh, f***in' cunt!" Of course, he didn't see the hurt that crossed my face.

Derek came home from Georgia, where he and Dylanie lived with their one-year-old daughter. Knowing Reghan had witnessed Grey's angry outburst, I figured it was only a matter of time before Derek and my parents heard about it. While guests came to pay their respects and talk with my parents, Derek and I sat on the couch—thankfully, Reghan was chasing Tyler around—and talked. Because we talked a lot on the phone, in texts, and by email, Derek was painfully aware of how lousy things were between Grey and me. Derek had always given Grey the benefit of the doubt, but he'd gone too far this time.

"Hunter, you need to give Grey a taste of his own medicine," Derek said.

"What are you talking about?" I was afraid I knew exactly what he meant.

"He told you to 'Get the hell out,' right?"

"Yeah."

"Come stay at Mom and Dad's with me. I'm only going to be here until tomorrow night anyway."

I wondered if it would do any good, but I was such an emotional mess that I was grateful to let someone else take the reins. It was settled. After the viewing, Derek, Reghan, and I went back to

176

my house. Derek took down Tyler's crib while I packed a bag for us and wrote Grey a note. The note read:

Dear Grey,

You told me to "Get the hell out" before I left for Grandma's viewing, so that's exactly what I'm doing. When you decide you want to talk, I'll be at Mom and Dad's.

I love you!
Hunter

It took me longer than usual to get Tyler calmed down enough to sleep. Not even singing his favorite song "I Am a Child of God" helped. It was almost as if he could sense the turmoil between Grey and me.

~~~~~~

The morning of Grandma's funeral was a sunny one, but with a lot of snow. As I got Tyler and myself ready, my thoughts turned to my husband. I wondered what he might be doing and whether he had even bothered to go home the night before.

During the viewing, Derek was a tremendous help with Tyler as we took turns keeping him busy. As I watched Derek play with Tyler, I couldn't help but think that he had to be missing his baby girl. I wished Grey would show the same care and love to Tyler and me. I didn't want to go to Grandma Marshall's funeral alone; I really needed him there with me. I decided that, although it was probably a stupid idea, I wanted him to, at the very least, go with me to the graveside service. "Grey?" I was almost in tears as I called him.

"What the hell do you want?" I could tell I woke him up.

"I know you're mad at me, but I need you."

"What the f*** for? Your family's there." The way he said it made me cringe.

"Come on," I choked on the tears that threatened, "you know that of everyone in my family, Grandma Marshall was one of the ones who gave you the benefit of the doubt. If you won't do it for me, do it for her."

"The funeral has already started, hasn't it?"

"Almost. I know you can't get here for that, but will you go to the graveside with me?"

"Fine, whatever. But my truck doesn't have enough gas to get to the cemetery."

"Meet us at Mom and Dad's around one o'clock. We'll stop and pick you up."

"Whatever."

Before I could tell him I loved him, the dial tone beeped loudly in my ear. My mom and dad weren't happy that we needed to pick Grey up, but in order to make Grandma's funeral as peaceful as possible, they didn't comment. The funeral itself was peaceful and calming. It was as if Grandma was there, giving her approval.

We waited almost forty-five minutes for Grey to show up at my parents' house, but he didn't. I called him but got no answer. Once again, I ended up alone. The graveside service was harder on me than the actual funeral. This was the last thing I was going to get to do for my grandma. I was also having a hard time accepting the fact that Grey didn't love or care about me enough to go through it with me.

~~~~~~

It was late afternoon by the time we returned to my parents' house. I was hurting over my grandma, and even more so that Grey thought so little of me that he would make me go through this without his support. If I was honest with myself, I would acknowledge that, in all the time I'd been with him, he had never supported me, so why would he today? I decided that, because Derek was leaving the next morning, I wanted to go with the rest of my family to take him to Salt Lake where my parents had booked a couple of motel rooms for the night. But first, I had a few things my husband needed to hear. I would've invited him, but he needed time to think over what I was about to say.

Leaving Tyler in his grandparents' care, I went to my apartment, not bothering to call first. Grey was on the computer— surprise, surprise—and as soon as he heard me walk in, he quickly turned it off. "What are you doing here? Where's Tyler?"

"Uumm. I live here, and Tyler is at my parents' house. We need to talk."

"So, what the hell do you want?"

"You know why I left last night, don't you?"

"Yeah. You were pissed at me."

"No. You told me right after we found out Grandma died that you would watch Tyler so I could go to her viewing, and you'd give me that time since you weren't going with me."

"So?"

"We haven't been on the same page about anything for some time now, if ever. You act like going through the temple was my idea and my idea alone. You still smoke, you still drink, you have "friends" you chat with on the Internet, and I just found out you have a pornography addiction. What else is going on with you that I don't know about? Not to mention that on more days than not, you act like I'm a huge bitch and I only care about myself."

"You know I don't like being told what to do! You know I don't like you watching over my shoulder like I need a damn babysitter! As far as my drinking and smoking, that is my business! What the f*** do you know about it anyway?"

"You don't see your role as the patriarch of this family as important. Being a forever family wasn't in the cards for you, was it? Do you even want to be a family?" I asked, afraid of what his answer would be.

Grey didn't say anything, so I forged ahead before I lost my nerve. "This is what I'm going to do. "I am going with my parents, Derek, and Reghan to Salt Lake to spend time with Derek before he leaves in the morning. When I come back tomorrow, it is up to you whether I bring everything back here and stay or pack what's left. I love you and want to be with you, but I can't take the walking on eggshells, the internet shit, your smoking and drinking, the name calling, and the way you belittle me. That doesn't even include the issues I have with sex. You know what you need to do." I gave him a hug and a kiss, neither of which he returned, and left.

~~~~~~

The time we spent with Derek was something we all needed. We talked about Grandma Marshall, telling stories about when we were growing up and when Dad was a kid. We also spent time playing in the hot tub and swimming pool.

Reghan and I left soon after Derek got on the shuttle to the airport the next morning. I was extremely nervous and more than a little anxious to go home. Tyler fell asleep during the ride home; neither he nor his mommy had slept well the night before. When we arrived at my place, Reghan offered to carry Tyler into the house because of the pain that was my never-ending companion.

When Reghan was gone, I planted myself on the coffee table in front of the couch where Grey slept. I woke him up by saying, "Am I staying or going?"

Groggily, Grey slowly opened his eyes, stretched and replied, "Staying."

"You know what that means, right?"

"Yes."

The next day, Grey went to the doctor, presumably to get help with his smoking and drinking. He was put on Wellbutrin that was not only an antidepressant, but also worked on the addiction centers in the brain. It helped him to get a better handle on his addictions.

As the next several weeks wore on, as far as I could tell, Grey didn't chat as much. In fact, when we were home, he rarely used the computer. I made it a point to take him at his word that he was changing for the better. He took me dancing when he went, which was few and far between anymore. I didn't think much of it when, instead of dancing with me, he continued dancing with other girls, but he made sure they asked me if I was okay with it beforehand. It didn't dawn on me that him prancing all those prettier girls, who could dance, in front of me was just as destructive to my self-esteem as all the other things Grey had been known to do.

~~~~~~

Christmas was a little easier to handle than Thanksgiving had been, even though we felt Grandma Marshall's absence acutely. Derek and his family came to visit, making it more manageable. We hadn't seen Dylanie since they were married almost three years before, and were seeing the baby for the first time. We spent the time together playing games at Mom and Dad's, making Christmas candy, and caroling. I only hoped the new Grey would stay present while they were there.

CHAPTER TEN

The year 2003 began with everything falling into place, or so it seemed. Although Grey still had issues with my parents, from my vantage point it looked as if he was letting those roll off him like water off a duck's back.

We spent New Year's Eve with Shaylie and Gunner. Shaylie noticed a difference in Grey. We hadn't seen them in several months because they had moved to Salt Lake, and we didn't have the time to get together as much.

"Is it just me or is Grey different?" she asked me.

"I told you about the ultimatum, right?"

"Well, yeah, but I didn't think he would take it this seriously. I don't think I've ever seen him this affectionate with you."

"I couldn't take it anymore."

"I'm glad he's decided to take you seriously. I know you were having a hard time."

We played Life, a new game that we got for Christmas. This time Grey didn't demand we play *his* choice. As I watched him interact with Tyler and Michaela, Shaylie and Gunner's daughter, I started to think that maybe things would be good between us.

We played one round of Life, then Phase 10, and then topped the night off with a game played with UNO cards called Spaz. I ended up teaching the other adults how to play it and we all burst out laughing because of how silly we looked. Because we'd played the games so late and the kids were already asleep, Shaylie and Gunner slept on our air mattress when we finally called it quits at four o'clock in the morning.

~~~~~~

One evening in late January, Grey received a phone call — the phone call I'd been dreading since September 2001. He was told he needed to be prepared for possible deployment. They would let him know within the next seventy-two hours. Grey looked at me as he hung up the phone. Without being told, I knew who the call was from. I dropped the spoon I was stirring homemade chicken and noodles with, ran to the bathroom, and promptly threw up.

"Why now?" I started to cry.

"We don't know what's going to happen yet." Even though he didn't think I could see it, Grey was excited. "Don't count your chickens before they hatch. Isn't that what your mom says?"

The next morning, just before ten, the phone rang. I could feel the fear gnawing at my gut as I waited to hear the news. Grey and twenty others from his petroleum pipeline unit were being called as "fillers" for a company out of Maryland. We needed to be at the armory at one o'clock that afternoon to learn the specifics.

I immediately called my parents to see if they could watch Tyler and to let them know what was going on. They sounded concerned about it. Whether it was only for Tyler and me, or for Grey as well, I didn't know. It was nice to know they were willing to help, even though Grey had never given them any reason to.

We dropped Tyler off with my parents at noon and arrived at the armory about fifteen minutes early. During the briefing, we learned the selected reservists would be leaving early Monday morning, only forty-eight hours away. The next few hours were spent going over paperwork — such as making sure power of attorney was current so the significant others could sign legal papers and things of that nature.

183

They explained that a Family Readiness Group was being formed to assist those of us who were on the home front. If we needed something while our soldiers were away, we were supposed to go through the chain of command with any concerns. That meant we should contact the head of the FRG before anyone else.

The question on everyone's mind was how long our soldiers would be gone. Unfortunately, no one knew the length of time, nor did they know if our soldiers would even go overseas. They could just as easily be sent home. It was all dependent on the government.

While waiting to go over paperwork, I couldn't help but worry that everything Grey and I had been working toward since I gave him the ultimatum in November would ultimately be for nothing.

Grey must've sensed my uneasiness, because he leaned over, put his arm around me, and whispered, "Don't worry. Nothing will change. We're going to be okay."

I would hang onto the words *nothing will change* during his time away. I couldn't, however, help noticing the excitement in Grey's voice.

It was after six o'clock in the evening by the time Grey and I picked Tyler up. We filled my parents in about what was happening. My mom, knowing I wouldn't say anything in front of Grey or Tyler, took me in the kitchen to find out how I was holding up. I was well aware my family didn't believe Grey was changing, but I needed my mom and any support I could get.

My mom said, "Honey, you've known this was a possibility, especially after September eleventh. You need to dry your tears, fix your make-up, and act as if nothing is out of the ordinary. He doesn't need to watch you fall apart."

That's exactly what I did, too. For the next forty-eight hours, as we packed everything on Grey's list, visited family and friends, got addresses of those he wanted to correspond with while he was gone. When I dropped him off at the armory on Monday morning, I didn't shed one single tear. As we said our good-byes, though, I clung to him for dear life. He hugged Tyler; the twenty month old had no idea what was going on.

I made a vow then and there that, even with Grey away, Tyler would know who his daddy was, even if only through pictures and sparse phone calls. Although Grey and my parents didn't see eye to eye, they told him they would take care of his family, but he needed to care for himself and come home. Then, without a single backward glance, Grey picked up his bags and walked away.

~~~~~~

One good thing about Grey being deployed was the insurance the family received during active duty. That made it possible for me to get a second opinion about my pain. Little did I know that not only was Grey going to be gone a long time, I was headed down yet another long road with my pain issues.

After looking at the x-rays and getting an MRI, the doctor found that not only did I have severe arthritis in my lower back, but the Scoliosis that was found when I was a kid continued causing problems. Oh, and then there were the four herniated discs! They put me on a regimen of pain medication, along with depression and anti-anxiety medication that helped enough I could take care of Tyler, who was a rambunctious almost two year old.

Since taking care of Tyler was nearly impossible even with medication—not to mention I had just sent my husband to unknown whereabouts for an eternity—I applied for disability. Disability wasn't an easy feat to conquer and after three denials, I gave up on it. Grey made enough that we could catch up on our bills and save quite a bit if I stuck to a budget.

~~~~~~

The unit Grey was filling in for spent from February to April in Maryland, training for a mission that might or might not happen. I only spoke with Grey a few times during that period. He insisted it was because he didn't have enough time to call me and everyone else he wanted to keep in touch with. As far as I knew, the only way they could correspond with family was through phone or letters. That wasn't exactly the truth, but I didn't know that.

The unit, consisting of over three hundred members, finally left for Kuwait on April 3, 2003. Grey called me from the airport, just after midnight my time. "Hey, babe!" He hadn't called me that in a long time.

"Where are you?" I hadn't gone to sleep yet, which at that moment, was a good thing.

"At the airport."

"You're finally going over, huh?"

"Yeah. Didn't think it was ever gonna happen."

"Are you scared?"

"Hell no! This is the bomb!" Then he asked, "How's Tyler?"

"He's no worse for wear. I can't believe you're going to miss his birthday."

"I know. But you'll record it and send me lots of pictures?"

"Of course."

"Well, we are boarding so I'd better get off here."

"Okay. I love you. Be safe."

"Yeah. Me too," was Grey's last response to me. Well, me too was better than nothing, wasn't it? It didn't hurt any less, though. At least he was wearing his wedding ring—something he hadn't done since just after our wedding.

~~~~~~

I worried almost continuously that the unit wouldn't make it to Iraq, but two days after I talked to Grey, I received a phone call from Grey's lieutenant's wife. They had arrived safely in Kuwait. She also gave me a different address to send care packages to. Then she told me I that his time away, six-month rotation didn't start until they landed on foreign soil.

I sent Grey a letter a week and emailed him every few days, sometimes every day depending on how lonely I felt. After using the chain of command and getting nowhere, it became apparent that if the families left behind needed help, we had to contact the unit in Maryland. The head of the FRG there happened to be Grey's Lieutenant's wife (the same one I had forged a rapport with) and, because I didn't have the time or ambition to chase answers, I emailed or called her whenever I had questions.

~~~~~~

Tyler turned two just after Grey left the states. Trying to make up for the fact that his daddy wasn't there, I threw a huge party for him. Mom called me earlier in the day to tell me she wasn't sure she was going to make it and that I needed to make sure Grandma Kacie got there.

Come to find out, Mom and Grandma Kacie had gotten into a little tiff the night before and that was the reason Mom didn't know if she would be there. Grandma told my mom, "If you keep up with how you treat Grey, you're going to lose your daughter. Regardless of how you might feel about him, he is her choice and you don't want to alienate her." It made my mom angry; maybe because she knew that, on some level, what Grandma said had merit.

I took tons of pictures to send to Grey and had Hank videotape the party so Grey could watch it when he got back. I hoped Tyler didn't feel Grey's absence too badly, but as I watched as his face lit up as he opened his presents, I couldn't help but shed a few tears. His daddy was missing out!

~~~~~~

Not knowing whether Grey would be home in time for his birthday in June, and knowing it took several weeks for him to receive packages, in May I had my mom take glamour shots of me for him. It was something I'd wanted to do for a long time, but never had the guts to do. The pictures turned out pretty good. There were five or six I liked that I put in a portfolio to send him. Along with that, I sent more pictures of Tyler, as well as some of both Tyler and me, and candy he couldn't get (some Idaho Spud bars and Pixie Stix). I only hoped I gave it enough time to get to him. At the same time, I started a cell phone plan so there would always be a way Grey could reach me.

~~~~~~

By the middle of May, I hadn't talked to Grey at all, but I'd gotten two letters (It took about six weeks' turnaround time for letters). In the first one, Grey said they should be home by mid-July because they were in Iraq but had yet to do anything besides "a whole lot of nothing." The second letter said they might even be home by Grey's birthday, which was in less than a month.

The next part of the letter shocked me. He said when he came home, I couldn't smother him; he might need to move out to get acclimated back into civilian life but didn't want a separation or divorce. What did he think moving out was? He then contradicted himself and said he couldn't wait to come home. *But he didn't know if he wanted to stay? Seriously?*

At the end of both letters he did something he'd never done before—inside of a heart he wrote GA + HA—I smiled through the tears that started to fall. I couldn't understand why he thought he wanted more time away from us, but at the same time claimed he loved me.

~~~~~~

As June arrived, Grandma Kacie's heart was acting up. It wasn't totally unexpected because she had congestive heart failure. However, she was also diagnosed with diabetes and immediately put on an insulin regimen, which was a shock to us. The day of her release from the hospital, we were thrown for another loop—she had colon cancer. They performed emergency surgery, taking all the cancer and her gallbladder. Luckily, it hadn't spread. She spent the next three weeks in the hospital.

She ended up moving in with my parents after being released because at her post-op appointment, the doctor told her he wanted to begin chemotherapy and radiation. They wanted to make sure they had removed all the cancer.

Grandma really didn't want to go through the treatments because she knew both would make her sick. And she was already extremely tired. After talking with my parents, Grandma Kacie made the final decision she wasn't having chemotherapy or radiation, nor did she want to be on insulin. She didn't even want to continue the medications she'd been taking for several years for her heart. My grandma was dying! It was yet another hard dose of reality to swallow.

She was taken off all her medications except the ones to keep her comfortable. I spent a lot of time at my parents' house because my dad worked out of town during the week and my mom had been taking the prerequisite classes to get into the nursing program at Brigham Young University.

~~~~~~

We celebrated Grandma's eighty-third birthday on May twenty-fifth. Tyler helped his grandma bake the cake and helped

Great-Grandma Kacie frost it with more chocolate frosting than anyone knew what to do with. And because Grandma couldn't blow out too many candles alone, we put three on it and let Tyler help her.

It seemed as if Grandma knew her time was limited. Grandma's birthday was more of a somber affair, although we tried not to be down. Reghan and her family came, and we had a weenie roast in Mom and Dad's backyard—something Grandma Kacie loved, and something Tyler had never done before.

The boys, who were four, two, and two and a half had a blast. They thought it was great fun to watch the adults light the hot dogs on fire. They liked their marshmallows burnt to a crisp, too. And they ate them that way!

As I watched the goings on around me—the boys chasing each other around the back yard, filling up on sugar and hot dogs, and loving on Grandma, Grandpa and Great-Grandma, I felt as if something was going to change again, and soon! Something or someone pushed me to take pictures of that night, especially ones with Grandma Kacie.

~~~~~~

Watching my grandma's health quickly decline, I couldn't help but wish my sweetheart was there to go through it with me. As Grandma worsened, she began to have conversations, and what looked like parties, with people only she could see and hear. She could no longer leave her bed. Walking by her door or even being in her room, we could hear her laughing and talking. We liked to think she was talking to family and friends who'd passed.

July thirteenth would forever be engraved in my mind because Grandma and I had a conversation I would never forget. When I arrived at my mom's that day, something nudged me to Grandma's room where I spent most of the day; Tyler was playing with the purple duck he so loved, on the floor, blissfully unaware of what was going on around him. Grandma seemed more herself than usual. Most of the time she wasn't aware of too much, but that day she wanted to talk to me. She told me how much she loved Tyler and how special he was (I lifted him up, so she could kiss him). Then she looked at me with absolute seriousness and said, "I'm going home."

"Grandma, you are home," I replied.

"No." Her voice firm. "I'm going *home*, to Heavenly Father." It was as if she knew her time on this earth was nearing its end. I kissed her forehead and hugged her gently.

That conversation played in my mind a lot throughout the rest of the night and even into the next morning.

~~~~~~

My dad called me around noon the next day and asked if I'd spoken with my mom. He'd been trying to get a hold of her, to no avail. "I haven't, but I'm headed over in a few minutes and I'll have her call you. She probably had a long night."

"Okay. Thanks, hon."

When I arrived, all was quiet except for Grandma's labored breathing. After checking on Grandma who was sleeping soundly, I quietly went to wake my mom who had been up most of the night. Grandma had been in extreme pain, and my mom hadn't left her until almost dawn.

After wiping the sleep from her eyes, my mom went into Grandma's room. Suddenly I heard a frantic, "Hunter!"

The picture that accosted me wasn't something I was likely to forget. Grandma was lying on the bed. Not breathing. Not moving. Nothing. She wasn't there. It was as if she waited until my mom wasn't alone to take her last breath. We thought the breathing I'd heard as I came into the house may have been Grandma's last breath.

Not long after the funeral home came for Grandma, Dad got home, and I left. I needed to be alone. To grieve for the wonderful woman my grandmother was, and hold onto my boy, the special boy that she'd loved so much.

I discovered the instructions on how to make a Red Cross call, so they could let Grey know what had happened. I hoped they'd let him come home, although Grandma Kacie wasn't technically his family.

~~~~~~

We had Grandma Kacie's viewing the night before her funeral on July 18, 2003, not eight months after losing my other beloved grandma. I began having a hard time letting Tyler out of my sight, even for a little bit. Oh, how I wished Grey was here! He hadn't called me yet either, which made handling this alone that much harder. Yes, my family was there, but everyone had someone to help them through, and I didn't.

The viewing prior to the funeral was long, and Tyler wasn't helping matters. Why he'd picked today to be a stinker was beyond me. He didn't want to stay where I seated him, nor did he want to be quiet, especially during the family prayer. It amazed me, though, because just as we followed the casket into the chapel, he quieted down and stayed that way. Through the whole funeral he quietly colored with Reghan's boys, ate snacks with them, and was his usual, sweet self.

Watching them while talks were given, I couldn't help but shed a tear. Those little boys wouldn't know her. Grandma had one request. My dad sang a moving rendition of "Will There Be Pine Trees in Heaven." Of course, it made me cry more.

Grandma Kacie's graveside service brought a flow of tears that, no matter how I tried, I couldn't stop. Once again, I was standing at the graveside service for yet another cherished member of my family. This, too, was the last thing I could do for Grandma Kacie, just as it was the last thing I could do for Grandma Marshall.

After the funeral and the dinner, I took Tyler home for a much-needed nap. I should've stayed at Mom and Dad's, but I didn't want to encroach on their grieving process. That evening, I was awakened from a fitful slumber. My grandmother stood at the end of my bed, saying nothing. Just as quickly as she appeared, she was gone. To this day, I like to think she was checking on me, to make sure I would be okay.

~~~~~~

It took Mom and I a few days to get up the *umph* to touch Grandma's room or her apartment. Even after she'd moved in with my parents, her apartment was kept as if she lived there. We knew we had to tackle it sooner or later, but it would be there tomorrow, next week, or even next month. We were in no hurry.

~~~~~~

A week after the funeral, I finally heard from Grey. He said the only reason he was calling was to tell me that because Grandma Kacie wasn't blood related to him, the military wouldn't let him come home.

"Did you get the Red Cross call right away?" I asked.

"Yeah. The same day you called."

"Then why are you just now letting me know? That was two weeks ago. It would've been nice if you had told me before the funeral." He could tell I wasn't in a good mood. Mom and I had spent the last two days cleaning Grandma's apartment, deciding what to keep and what to give away. Knowing that Grey's mom didn't have nice clothes or jewelry, my mom and I made a joint decision to give her some of Grandma's things.

"Some of the guys get to go home for two-week furloughs."
He'd completely dodged my question.

"Do you?" I asked hopefully.

"Uuhhh, no," he hesitated.

"Why not?" My mood wasn't getting any better. In fact, I wanted to scream! With everything else I'd been dealing with, that was not something I wanted to hear.

"Well, anyone whose wives are due or have had a baby get first out. The rest of our names were put into a hat and the ones that get drawn, get to go."

"Has your name been drawn?"

"Not yet. I don't think it will."

"Why?"

"I kind of got pissed the other day and punched my commander, so I'm out."

"What?! Why the hell did you do that? Seeing Tyler and me isn't important to you?"

"Of course, it is. Don't get pissy with me or I'm getting off."

"Then why would you go and do that with something like seeing your family on the table?"

"I was mad, okay? Can we drop it? It's done, and I can't come home. That's f***in' it."

The old Grey, the one I'd spent the last several months hoping wouldn't come back, was showing. I could tell by the way he talked to me.

"Look, I gotta go. I just wanted to let you know I'm not coming home until our deployment is over." He didn't say good-bye or anything.

~~~~~~

My mom didn't get into the nursing program at BYU so, after looking at colleges in Georgia, and with a huge push from my dad, in September, they decided to move. I had a hard time with this because I didn't want to be left alone. Reghan was around, but she had her family. She didn't need to be taking care of her big sister, too. I wasn't aware that my predicament was a big part of the reason my mom didn't want to leave. Although she was excited to be closer to Derek and his family, she'd just lost her mom and didn't know if this was what she wanted to do. They'd promised Grey they would take care of us, and she couldn't see how that was possible, with them living thousands of miles away.

~~~~~~

A couple of days before Grey's and my fourth anniversary — I'd sent him a care package a few weeks before — I received an email from the head of the FRG in Maryland. It read:

> **Hunter,**
>
> **How are you and Tyler? I'm sorry about your grandmother. I just received word that the soldiers will be home sometime in April 2004. Please let me know if you have any questions.**
>
> **Averie Hamilton**

Armed with this new information, I decided to go with my parents to Georgia. There was no way I could talk to Grey about any of it, but I was sure he wouldn't want me spending the holidays alone. At least, I hoped that was what he'd think.

I began planning for our move. Because storing our two vehicles for the unforeseeable future was going to be expensive, I sold both my car and Grey's truck, put everything else in storage, and cleaned my apartment.

~~~~~~

Leaving was harder than I thought it would be. I knew I'd be back in six months but saying goodbye to Reghan stunk! My mom had the hardest time of all. Too many changes, too fast. We finally hit the road on October twenty-fifth; I still hadn't told Grey, and the letter I'd recently sent wouldn't get to him until after we were in Georgia. Tyler, my mom, and I took their car and my dad drove their Ford Explorer with the U-Haul trailer hitched to the back.

Having to keep a two-and-a-half year old occupied in a car that was stuffed to the hilt all day and into the night was utterly exhausting. My mom bought Tyler *Piglet's Big Movie* because Piglet was his favorite character; she also bought him a *Bob the Builder* DVD and we had several Disney cartoons. We made a rule that, because he could play with toys and color during the day, he wasn't allowed to watch DVD's until naptime and after dark.

As if losing both grandmas, having Grey deployed, *and* keeping a two-year-old on an even keel wasn't stressful enough for both my mom and me, two days into our trip we watched, horrified, as my dad drove the Explorer up a hill against severe winds; the U-Haul fishtailed to the point that he had a hard time keeping it and the Explorer from going over the edge. Being right behind him, we watched in dread as he fought to stay in control and on the road. I had never heard my mom plead with Heavenly Father so hard; telling him one more loss was too much and to *please* keep Dad safe. Our prayers were answered almost immediately when the wind all but stopped and my dad was able to correct himself. Through tears my mom thanked God extensively for keeping my dad from going over the cliff. Hopefully, that would be the worst thing we had to face on the trip.

~~~~~~

My mom and I had a lot of time to talk. We talked about everything. We shared the sorrows and struggles I felt about losing my brother Mitch twenty years ago.

When I was seven, my two-year-old brother, Mitch, drowned on his birthday. I was watching him that day when my older brother, Wes was supposed to be. Mom told Wes he was in charge before she left for work that night. Wes told me to play with Mitch and when I got tired to take him in the house where Grandma Kacie was. There was a canal on the opposite side of the fence that ran the length of our front yard. There were missing boards that my dad had asked the landlord to repair, and the landlord said they would take care of it—and they did, after Mitch died. The paramedics who found him figured Mitch must've crawled through where the missing boards were, slipped, hit his head (he had bruising on his forehead) and fell in. Even though I was only seven, I blamed myself for Mitch's death. For many, many years I struggled with the idea that I let him die.

"But I let him get away from me," I told her one day while talking about that long-ago day.

"You were a little girl. You should never have been in that kind of situation. I want you to know that I have *never* blamed you," Mom said.

"Ya know, when I think back on that day, I see Mitch's face clear as day. When I said to him, 'Mitch, get over here,' he looked at me as if he wasn't there; like there was someone from the other side either with him or calling him. Do you think if he hadn't drowned, he would've lived?"

"I don't know. I don't think Heavenly Father takes those he doesn't need for more important work," my mom replied.

We also talked about Grey and how I hoped the changes he was making prior to deployment were still there.

My mom said, sincerely, "I hope so." She doubted it but didn't tell me that. Surprisingly she added, "When he gets back, if he is in a place that he is able to attend the temple, your dad and I will surely be there." Then she said something I would never forget. "Hunter, maybe the reason you married Grey is because *you* are God's instrument in saving him."

~~~~~~

Living in a motel with a two-year-old was tough! Too small a space with too many people! My dad quickly found a job with a local construction company in the area where they were looking to buy their house. Mom spent her time getting ready to start nursing classes in January of 2004. She had a few prerequisites she needed to complete before then, so Tyler and I spent most of our time at the motel by ourselves. It was warm enough still that we spent our afternoons before nap time swimming and playing in the pool.

After staying in our first motel, my parents decided that switching scenery was a good idea, so we stayed no more than a week or two in each place. I was getting tired of keeping Tyler busy all day with only a few things to do. The next couple places we stayed, we made sure there was a playground nearby to give Tyler and me a break. Something different to do. Getting onto a schedule helped the monotony some, but I found myself writing letters to Grey daily and compiling them to send once a week.

~~~~~~

Grey must have gotten his anniversary care package which told him where we were because he sent a letter for me to Derek's house. He talked, once again, about needing his space, going to school, what was going on in Iraq, or at least what he could tell me. To say he was okay with me moving was a misconception. He thought I should have stayed in Springville, and he didn't care if I was alone for Thanksgiving and Christmas. He seemed angrier that I sold his pickup than anything else. Even after I explained why I did it, he didn't care! I could feel him slipping back to his old self—the one he'd been working to change when he got called up.

Along with the not so sweet letter he sent to me, he sent one he wanted mailed to Hank. Why did he not mail it himself? I wondered. Then I read, "DO NOT READ THIS! MAIL TO HANK!

Don't read it? Is he kidding? After I read it, I wished I hadn't! In it, he all but admitted to having sex with anyone who would give it up! He claimed that having sex in the ass wasn't really cheating! I hurriedly, but shakily, wrote Hank and Lynese's address on another envelope, put the letter in and sealed it. After sending it off, I did my level best to forget what was written in that letter. For the most part it worked.

~~~~~~

Wanting to get Grey's Christmas package to him by Christmas, my mom, Dylanie, and I made him a flannel blanket. My mom took pictures of Tyler and me and framed the best one. I wrote and framed a poem for Grey; it explained all the love I felt for him as well as what I needed and wanted from him. Tyler colored some Christmas pictures for him. I sent it the second week in November, hoping he would get it before Christmas.

~~~~~~

A week before Thanksgiving, my parents finally found their house. Moving in was hard, but at the same time, a relief. Tyler and I shared a room even though there were three bedrooms. This was a new and strange place for him, and I didn't want to change too much, too fast. Since I'd sold his crib before leaving Utah, I bought him a toddler bed. It didn't do much good though, because he continued trying to sleep in my bed. Every night found him in my bed, and every night I put him in his several times. I did my best to make the room "ours," putting the television I brought on top of the dresser and having a stash of Disney movies Tyler liked to watch. I also put pictures of us on the walls, so he saw Grey's face every day.

While I was hanging the pictures, Tyler came over and pointed to the one of our family. "That's Daddy," he said matter-of-factly.

"Yes, sweetie, that's Daddy." Tears were forming in the corner of my eyes. I'd been praying the whole time Tyler wouldn't forget Grey, and it appeared he hadn't.

"Mommy, are you sad?"

"Yes. Mommy's kind of sad."

"Why?"

"Because I miss Daddy. I wish he was here with us. That's all."

"Don't cry, Mommy."

To change the subject, I asked, "Hey, since everything is almost moved in, how about we watch *Treasure Planet* before bed?" That was something Tyler got to do occasionally, if I was having a downer day, like now, or if he had been exceptionally good.

"Yaaayyyy!" he squealed, "that's my favorite!" Tyler might only be two-and-a-half, but he talked like he was much older. He'd been that way since he said his first word, "bebe," at nine months.

After his bath, we snuggled together on my bed and watched the movie, eating teddy grahams, red licorice, and sunflower seeds. I didn't want missing Grey to mar the time I had with Tyler. I only wished Grey was there to share it with us.

~~~~~~

It had been a year since Grandma Marshall passed away and only a few months since Grandma Kacie. If that wasn't tough enough, having Reghan and her family in Utah made it that much more difficult. The added challenge of my sweetheart being thousands of miles away didn't help either.

Along with Derek, Delaynie, and their daughter, we had the traditional Thanksgiving. Derek didn't have to call my mom, me, or Reghan to get the dressing recipe for the broccoli salad he loved because Mom and I were there. I just had to tease him about it, if only to make a funny, because we didn't do serious in my family well.

"Hey, Derek, how are you going to make the sauce? You don't have to call anyone."

"Ha, ha. You're here. You'll just have to tell me."

"Or not. You should know it by heart by now."

We bantered back and forth like that for the rest of the day. After dinner we ate too much pie, watched *How the Grinch Stole Christmas*—something we did every Thanksgiving Day—and played games. The kids got along famously and had, in the short time we'd been there, become wonderful friends.

Much to my disappointment, Grey didn't call. With the letters he'd written recently about what he wanted or didn't want, I didn't know why I was expecting it. It would've been nice to hear his voice though.

~~~~~~

My parents had been discussing when they might make a trip back to Utah, even before we left Utah. With Thanksgiving being so rough, they decided that, because Derek and Delaynie were spending Christmas with her family, we would go home a few days before Christmas and spend it with Reghan.

It took us several days to find cheap enough plane tickets for the four of us and, as the day to leave grew closer, I became more anxious. I'd never flown in an airplane, so I wasn't sure what to expect. Mom and Dad both assured me it was no big deal. The night before we left, we had Christmas dinner and presents at Derek and Dylanie's house, since we wouldn't be there for on Christmas day. Of course, I had my ever-present friend—the camera—with me, taking pictures of everyone and everything. I was afraid Grey would miss something vital if I didn't.

Because I gave him such a hard time at Thanksgiving, I expected Derek to tease me unmercifully about how scared I was to fly.

"It's not that bad," he said instead. "You might actually like it."

"What? You're not gonna give me a hard time?" I was quite surprised.

"Nah. You have enough stuff to deal with. Besides, I think everyone is nervous the first time they fly. I know I was when I went on my mission."

For some reason, Derek's reassuring words made me feel much better.

~~~~~~

Derek was the kind of person I wanted to be—always kind to others, giving people the benefit of the doubt even if they didn't deserve it, and loving everyone, no matter what. No matter what Grey said or did, Derek loved him because I loved him.

~~~~~~

The next morning, December twenty-first, we arrived at the Savannah Hilton Head International Airport two hours prior to take off, as per the instructions on our itinerary. Getting Tyler up at five o'clock in the morning was no easy task, and boy, was he cranky! Luckily, we had a layover in St. Louis, Missouri. We got our bags checked in without a problem and waited to board the plane. Tyler was in such an awful mood I didn't have time to worry. Some might say that was a good thing.

Flying wasn't so bad. The worst part for me was the take off. I didn't realize I was holding my breath until my mom leaned over and said, "Hunter, you can breathe now. We're in the air." It felt almost like we were in a car.

"I didn't know I was holding my breath."

"See. It's not too bad, right?"

"No it's not." I felt kind of sheepish for being such a scaredy-cat.

Tyler even stopped being a stinker, which made the flight pleasant. We arrived in Missouri at nine forty-five. and decided to eat while we waited for our connecting flight. Of course, Tyler's favorite place on earth was McDonald's, so we went there for breakfast. Our layover ended up being almost three hours instead of thirty-five minutes, due to plane issues.

~~~~~~

I had never been so excited to see Salt Lake City International Airport as we stepped off the airplane and headed to the baggage terminal. Mom and I waited with Tyler as my dad got the rental car squared way.

Because we were three hours late getting home, and since Tyler had been awake since early that morning, it took no time at all for the lull and warmth of the car to put him to sleep. I only wished it was longer than thirty minutes to Springville because it was in no way long enough. And waking Tyler up was never a good idea.

Because Reghan's house wasn't big enough to accommodate everybody, my parents, Tyler, and I stayed at the Cotton Tree Inn not far from Reghan's house. This allowed for hot tubbing and swimming for the kids, giving them more to do.

I purposely didn't tell my mother-in-law we were coming home for Christmas because I wanted to surprise her. I was literally shocked that Grey's brother hadn't spilled his guts.

On Christmas Eve, Tyler and I showed up on her doorstep. The tears that welled up in her eyes almost did me in. "Oooohhh. Ohh my!"

"Hi, Grandma Andrews." Tyler squealed. He giggled as she held on tightly to him. "Grandma. . . Grandma, I can't breathe." She let go and he scampered off her lap and chased her dogs, Brinley and Sakota around the small living room. "Come here, you silly doggies." Tyler desperately tried catching one of them. It was funny to watch because they were twice his size.

"Tyler, leave the poor doggies alone." I tried not to laugh.

"Oh. He's fine. He can't hurt them dogs none. Besides, they need the exercise." Grey's mom laughed.

We talked for a long time about Tyler, Grey, and my marriage to her son. My mother-in-law sounded almost as concerned as I was when I told her his demands upon returning home. "You're not going to give it to him, are you?"

"I don't know. I try not to think too much about that right now."

"I don't think you should."

"We'll cross that bridge when we come to it, I guess." I couldn't help the worry that niggled at the back of my mind. She didn't usually voice her opinion, especially not about my marriage to her son.

~~~~~~

Christmas Day was a difficult day for me because Mom and Dad had each other and Reghan had her little family. I was stuck there, without my sweetheart, and there wasn't even a guarantee he'd call. As I watched Tyler open his gifts, I couldn't stop the tears as they fell. I became angry all over again that Grey had joined the National Guard Reserves without asking how I felt about it. I understood we weren't married yet when he made the decision, but we were engaged.

Reghan must've sensed I wasn't doing well because she came over to me and set a box in my lap. "What's this?"

"Open it and find out." Reghan pushed.

What I found made me cry harder. Inside was an amethyst and silver-plated ring. "What's this for?" I asked.

"I wanted to get something just for you. This has got to be hard on you, and I want you to know that I love you." We both burst into tears.

"Thank you." I gave her a hug. The rest of the day was a little easier. But...Grey didn't call. Again.

Over the next few days, I split my time between Reghan and her family, all of Grey's family, Shaylie and Gunner; and I even spent some time with Hank and Lynese. I wondered if Tyler and I should stay or go back to Georgia for the next few months. Neither decision was easy and not being able to talk to Grey about it didn't help.

~~~~~~

Grey emailed me in January, just after we returned to Georgia from Utah. It was the first email I'd received from him since he got to Iraq. He instructed me to set up a messenger account. Because they were on the home stretch of their deployment, he was allowed two half-hour calls per week and at least an hour every other day of chat time, sometimes longer.

Each time we chatted, Grey repeated that when he returned, he wanted the first two weeks to do whatever he wanted, whenever he wanted to do it, with no questions asked. He declared it was the only way he would come home to me and Tyler without moving out.

I explained in one chat session his coming home was like a do over for us. We were debt free. I wasn't going to bring his or our past into the newness of being a family again. I hated talking about his space so much that I did everything in my power to steer clear of that subject. I was aware that he might have a rough time acclimating back into civilian life, but because he was in a unit that had nothing to do with the front lines, his commanders thought the soldiers wouldn't have any adjustment issues. Not huge ones anyway.

The way Grey's chat sessions and emails came across, it sounded like he wanted to go back to smoking, drinking, no job stability, dancing without me, chatting, pornography, and other things of that nature. I would do whatever I had to in order to make sure that didn't happen!

He also demanded to know how much money I'd been able to save while he was away. I didn't want to tell him that between getting out from under all our creditors and making sure Grey's child support didn't lapse there wasn't a lot in savings, not to mention, whenever he was allowed rest and relaxation days, the sums of money that came out were exorbitant. His response was, "What have I been over here working my ass off for?!" I was certain that if we had been talking on the phone, he would be yelling at me. He had no desire to understand how hard it had been for me to keep from having to file bankruptcy. Grey really thought he made a lot of money on active duty? I wished I could show him how much he really didn't make.

CHAPTER ELEVEN

The night before Tyler and I were to return to Springville for good, Derek, his family, Dad, Tyler, and I went to my mom's Nursing Open House to support her in her new endeavor. Tyler and I could've flown home sooner, but I genuinely wanted to be there for my mom. She had been through a lot during the last several years and I wanted to show her I cared and loved her despite our differences. My mom was so proud of her family that she took the three grandkids who were there and pictures of all the others and showed them off to everyone. Seeing my mom smile was something I didn't see often, and it was nice. Maybe spending time with Derek and his family wouldn't be a bad thing after all.

February 7, 2004 dawned bright and sunny in Georgia. It didn't take me long to pack the few items I was taking back to Utah. Because Tyler and I weren't scheduled to fly out until five-thirty that evening and we were pretty much ready to go, I decided to see if Grey was in the chat room. He was. His first couple lines read: *The higher-ups have extended our stay in Kuwait another fourteen days. That means we won't be state side until April first.*

I told him it was no big deal, although it was to me. However, I felt that I had to hide how I really felt so I didn't set him off or make him angry. Little did he know that I already knew he wouldn't be home until April, but I was still let down because I knew those dates could change.

~~~~~~

Flying with Tyler alone wasn't as bad as I thought it would be. We had an hour layover in St. Louis, Missouri just like the last time, so we spent the layover eating dinner at the same McDonald's. I was super grateful, however, when we landed in Salt Lake City with a few minutes to spare. Hank and Lynese were waiting for us as Tyler and I came through the terminal at ten-thirty that night. Unfortunately, it took us until almost one o'clock in the morning to get our luggage.

~~~~~~

Hank and Lynese were in the process of packing because they had decided on a whim to move to Dallas, Texas. I didn't think Hank had said anything to Grey, and I was totally not looking forward to that conversation. We talked about it during the drive to their house where Tyler and I would stay for the next two nights. "What made you guys decide to leave?" I asked.

"Hank needs new surroundings," Lynese responded.

"That's the only reason you're moving?"

"I don't want him working for his dad forever." I noticed Hank wasn't saying anything. It made me wonder if he was up for the move.

"That's it?"

"Yep."

"You're going without a job?" I was skeptical.

"We'll get jobs pretty fast down there." Again, Hank said nothing.

"Have you talked to Grey, yet?" I asked Hank, but again, Lynese answered.

Finally, Hank opened his mouth, "No."

"You haven't said anything? When are you planning on telling him? After you're gone?"

"I'll email him tomorrow, after church," Hank responded.

"Can't you wait until he gets back? He really misses you guys."

"No. Hank needs to get out of here." Lynese again.

Nothing more was said on the subject as we pulled into their driveway. After putting a sleepy Tyler to bed, I took a bath, trying to get the grime of the day off my skin and to help me relax.

I was still in awe that I had flown alone with my toddler and no major mishaps had taken place. After getting dressed, I called my parents. Although they were two hours ahead of me, I didn't want them to worry. I talked to them for a few minutes then turned the television on to get my mind off all I had to do in the next few weeks. But my honey was coming home! That made it all worth it!

~~~~~~

Monday morning, Reghan and I met with the manager of the brand-new apartment complex she'd found for us to sign the lease and get the keys. As I walked through the apartment, getting an idea as to where I wanted furniture to go, I couldn't get over the fact that we would be the first to live there. The living room and kitchen could be seen from the front door. The Berber carpet was a nice bluish-gray color—a bit scratchy, but extremely good for hiding stains, if you asked me. There was a space for our washer and dryer just off the kitchen and the bedrooms at the back were small, but I didn't care. The walls were a light tan color and the linoleum was browns and tans. My denim colored and earthy furniture would fit nicely with the color scheme. That was only the beginning of *Tornado Hunter!*

Within the first week of being home, everything was moved in and put away. As far as vehicles went, Reghan had been looking at cars for me and knew what I liked. I wanted a car that said sporty, but at the same time, a mom could be seen driving it. It didn't take long for me to find just the right car; a deep purple Pontiac Grand Am SE sedan. I had Grey's power of attorney so, after talking price, I gave the salesman the down payment and drove away.

Moving into the new apartment and getting a car were my two major items of business to get done before Grey came back. Boy, I'd given myself WAY too much time!

Once our internet and cable were installed, I chatted with Grey daily. I still didn't know when he was coming home for sure and he wasn't offering any news. The only thing he told me was that he didn't just want space; he still wasn't sure he wanted to come home to me at all! Sure, he wanted to come home to Utah, just not me.

How was I supposed to react to that piece of information? Like I hadn't been alone, dealing with real life while he was gone? I literally begged him not to make any rash decisions, but to wait until he got home. It scared me that he acted and sounded as if he really wanted out.

~~~~~~

Grey called me twice over the next few weeks. The first call had "unknown" on the caller ID; I argued with myself whether to answer. I wasn't big on answering calls I didn't know, but it was a good thing I had. We talked for over an hour. "Just wanted to let you know that we are in Kuwait right now and should be back in the states in the next few weeks."

"Do you know when, yet?" I could only hope they had a date set.

"Nope."

"Honey, are you okay?" Something was bothering him, and I was pretty sure that it had to do with Hank and Lynese. They had decided to move 1,200 miles away to Dallas, Texas, and Grey was having a difficult time with it.

"I'm f***in' fine," he groused.

Secretly, I was glad they were gone, but there was no way I was telling Grey. Having them gone might give Grey and me the fresh start we desperately needed. "Is it because Hank left?"

"Couldn't they have waited a few f***in' days until I got home? Did you even ask them to wait?" I didn't appreciate the accusatory tone in his voice.

Why Grey thought I had any pull when it came to Hank, I would never know, but I had talked to them and Lynese was adamant they leave when they did.

"Yes, Grey. I tried to get them to wait, but you have no idea when you're even going to be state side. What did you expect them to do?"

"You just don't get it. Hank is my best friend. When will I see him again? Now, I don't know what the hell I'm going to do."

Hearing him say that hurt. "You have Tyler and me."

The response I received was a scoff, followed by a hurried, "I gotta go."

~~~~~~

Normally, I didn't read the paper, but because Grey needed a job when he got back, I went and picked one up. What I read on the front page caught me off guard; it was an article about Grey. Having an article written about him wasn't what bothered me. The lies that were printed did. As far as I could tell, there was a woman who claimed she adopted soldiers who "didn't have families," sending them care packages and what not. And for some unknown reason, she printed a story about my husband:

Local Soldier Stranded Overseas with No Family

Grey Andrews is a local soldier, filling in for a unit out of Maryland. I have interviewed Sergeant Andrews and was made painfully aware that this twenty-seven-year-old from Springville, Utah, has been overseas for several months with no one to care whether he makes it home safely. Sergeant Andrews explained to me during our phone interview that he is single and unattached, does not have children or any other family, locally or otherwise. It is because of this, and, after falling absolutely in love with this soldier, I have chosen to adopt him and see that he gets care packages and letters on a regular basis.

Grey called not long after I read the article, so my emotions were still higher than a kite. Of course, when I asked Grey about the article and why he would tell a virtual stranger complete lies, he had the nerve to say, "Well, I don't feel married. Okay?"

I was mad about the article and didn't do anything to soften it. "First, you need space, which I am willing to give you. Second, you want to move out for a few weeks to get used to civilian life? Third, you don't feel married?" Gritting my teeth so I wouldn't cry I quietly reiterated, "I will tell you again, like I've always told you, I love you no matter what. But you are asking a helluva lot from me!"

He responded with, "So?" and hung up, saying nothing else.

I might have been hurt because Grey was undoubtedly choosing single life over his family, but I was also extremely stubborn and was not giving up on us. After I finished reading the offensive piece and hashing it out with my husband, I called the paper and demanded a retraction. I explained that they probably should investigate thoroughly before printing a story. I let them know that Grey not only had a mother and siblings, but was married and had kids! The newspaper apologized profusely and promised a retraction, but the damage had already been done. Those who'd seen the article and knew Grey and I were married couldn't fathom why anyone would do that! Others asked why in the world I stayed. Once again, the only answers I had were I didn't know why he did it and I loved him.

~~~~~~

By the middle of March, I began to wonder if I would ever see Grey again. He called on the fifteenth. He'd been stateside for more than two hours so why had he waited so long to call me? It was noon in Utah, making it two o'clock in the afternoon in Maryland. Although part of me wanted answers, I was more than ecstatic he was on home soil, so I pushed those thoughts aside.

"Do you know when you'll be home yet?" I couldn't hide the eagerness in my voice.

"We'll fly into Salt Lake on April first. It'll be late, so I might just stay in Salt Lake that night."

"Uuhh, no. I'll come get you. You've been gone a long time and I don't want to be away from you any longer than I have to."

"Fine, whatever." Then he said, "Can I ask you a question?"

"What?"

I was astounded by the question he blurted out. "Did you get fat?"

"What?" Was he really asking me that?

"While I've been gone, have you bothered to lose the damn baby fat?"

The short answer was my weight did the same thing over the past fifteen months that it had done my entire life. It fluctuated. "Does that matter?" I asked in disbelief.

"Yes, it does. You know how I feel about that issue. We even talked about it before we got married. That you would only gain weight if you got pregnant and then lose it as quickly as possible. While I was home, if I recall, you didn't do a damned thing to lose it. Remember?"

"Yes, I remember." I was in total and utter shock that, after being gone for over a year, Grey cared more about my weight than anything else.

I'd been working on losing the baby weight, wanting to be skinny and beautiful for Grey, but didn't have much luck in getting rid of *the baby pooch*. "Not yet. It's a work in progress."

"All I have to say is, you better not look like a fat assed cow when I get home."

My cheeks were getting hot and I could feel my temper rise. Along with that temper, though, was the *not enoughness* I felt when Grey threw negative comments at me. I began to fear the old Grey was the one I'd be picking up in a few weeks. Not knowing how to answer—and perhaps more honestly being afraid to answer—I told him I needed to take care of Tyler and quickly hung up the phone. I could only hope that he'd be okay with the baby weight I continued to possess.

Why did he have to be so mean? Once again, I fought with my inner demons. Maybe he was right. Maybe we needed to be apart. On the other hand, maybe being home with Tyler and me would help Grey return to where he was before deployment. I tried not to dwell on the negatives of our relationship, only the positives. At least he was coming home. Right?

~~~~~~

That night I offered to watch Reghan's boys, ages four and two, so she and her husband could go out. I wasn't about to begrudge that to anyone, not after being alone for so long. Getting three little boys ready for bed was a hassle and a half. After they were all ready, they climbed on Tyler's bed for a story. Of course, the youngest couldn't quite get up by himself so I picked him up and, because my back hurt and I didn't have my weight distributed evenly, I stepped backward on my right ankle (which also happened to be my "bad" one), trying to catch myself. I heard a pop and crunch and hit the floor. Luckily, Tyler's bed was close enough I at least had somewhere soft for my nephew to land when I dropped him. So much for a story.

Man, it hurt to move, much less walk! I limped into the living room and situated the boys with a movie, not wanting to frighten them. I was NOT going to call Reghan. I would survive until they finished their date.

When she came to get the boys and saw how swollen and purple my ankle was, Reghan insisted I go to the Emergency Room. Luckily Tyler was still up. It was after midnight when we arrived. By the time all x-rays were finished, and I spoke with the doctor, I was exhausted! It was only a nasty sprain according to the ER doctor. I needed to ice it several times a day whether it hurt to put ice on it or not. He then explained that I needed to walk as normally as I could. If it wasn't better in a week I needed to follow up with my regular doctor.

I only lasted about three days before I went to my regular doctor. He took another x-ray. Lo and behold, there was a hairline fracture that the other x-ray hadn't shown. The doctor wrapped it and told me, in no uncertain terms that I was not to put any weight on it for at least two weeks. He was completely flabbergasted that any doctor would tell me to put weight on an ankle as purple and swollen as mine.

I couldn't fathom how I was going to take care of Tyler, not to mention getting everything ready for Grey's homecoming! Even if I hurt like hell, I had no choice.

Luckily, Reghan was a great help where Tyler was concerned. The boys loved playing together, and I found myself calling her daily over the next few days. More times than not, she took Tyler to her house, so I could either rest or focus on Grey's homecoming.

~~~~~~

Although Grey was a douchebag to me, nor would he decide what he wanted, I wanted to do something special to welcome my sweetheart home, for that was how I still saw him. He was the only one in our area who'd left at the beginning of the war. The other families from the unit were putting up banners and fliers by the armory, but as far as welcoming Grey home, it was all on me. After speaking with the head of the Chamber of Commerce, they gave the okay to put banners up provided I stayed inside city limits. It didn't leave many places to put them. Springville wasn't that big. The Chamber put a Welcome Home sign on the digital billboard in the middle of town that read: *Welcome Home, Sergeant Andrews.* The banners I had made read:

Reservist Grey Andrews Returns.
Welcome Back from Iraq, Sergeant Andrews.
I'm Happy My Daddy Is Coming Home!

I hung a banner at the entrance to the apartment complex, one just coming off the exit into town, and the other at the Maverick gas station in town. Of course, due to my broken foot, I needed tons of assistance to hang them up. Luckily, our new ward provided us a couple of very nice home teachers, and the stake missionaries helped as well. We got it done with a day to spare.

~~~~~~

After fifteen months of being apart, the day to pick my sweetheart up finally arrived. That April day crawled slowly as I did my best to stay busy, waiting for time to leave. Tyler seemed to sense something was about to change because he was a little more irritable than usual. Maybe it had to do with the fact that he would be up way past his bedtime. Or maybe my little boy could feel that life as he knew it was over.

Picking up Grey's mom at nine o'clock that evening, I was completely nervous! Why was I so nervous? I'd been married to this man for four and a half years. It could've been because I hadn't seen him in so long, or it could be the fact that he made it a point to let me know what his intentions were when he returned at every turn.

We made the thirty minute drive to Salt Lake City International Airport. Although there was still another thirty minutes before the soldiers landed, there were swarms and swarms of people waiting to greet them. A few minutes before ten o'clock, the commander gathered all the families together and allowed us to wait on the tarmac for the soldiers to deplane. Of course, they were the last off. As each soldier stepped off the plane, I waited with butterflies in my stomach to see Grey's face.

Tyler saw Grey before I did and the next thing I knew, he broke away from me and, while running as fast as his little legs could carry him, he yelled, "Daddy, Daddy, Daddy, Daddy!" while jumping at Grey. The look Tyler gave Grey was priceless! If only Grey would remember this moment.

As the group entered through the double doors, we were saluted by the American Legion and other National Guard members decked out in their dress uniforms. We only stayed for about fifteen minutes, giving Grey enough time to greet and talk with everyone he wanted to. As far as his response to me, he gave me nothing, not even a hug, when he saw me. He'd been gone fifteen long months and nothing? *Was he for real?* Did he seriously think this had been a walk in the park for me?

The ride home was a little disconcerting for me. Grey was distant, more so than I expected. I tried holding his hand, but he jerked it away. I had spent the last several months hoping we could pick up where we left things, but the way he responded to me now made it harder and harder to hold onto that hope. I sensed there was something Grey wasn't telling me. Not even sure I wanted to know, I asked anyway. "Is there someone else?"

Hesitating ever so slightly, Grey answered, "F***, no!"

"Then what's the matter? I thought you would have at least been happy to see me."

"I'm just tired."

"Oh." I wasn't sure what else to say.

It was late by the time we took Grey's mom home and got to ours. Having put Tyler in his pajamas before leaving to get Grey and then stopping to "potty" him before leaving the airport, it took no time at all to put the already sleeping boy in his bed. I looked for Grey and was greeted by a huge mess instead of my husband. Grey brought his bags into the house and dropped everything in the middle of the living room floor. I found him outside, smoking. Oh, great! Of course, I wasn't going to say anything about it because I didn't want his first night back to end with an argument, seeing as how it started off so stellar!

"Hey." I sat next to him.

Immediately, Grey moved away from me. It was as if he thought he might catch a disease or something. "Hi," he said once he was a safe distance away. "What are you doing out here? Shouldn't you be in bed?"

I hated how, in one sentence, Grey could make me feel like I was nothing more than a nuisance to him.

"It's okay. I can wait," I replied.

"I DON'T WANT YOU TO WAIT! DAMN IT! LEAVE ME ALONE! I told you I wanted two weeks f***in' to myself with no questions asked! STARTING NOW!" he yelled, not caring who heard. None of these people knew him, and he didn't care what they thought anyway.

Without saying another word, I somberly stood up and left. Once in our bedroom, I crammed the new deep red nightie into my bottom drawer under everything else that was in it; I guess I wouldn't be needing it anytime soon. I didn't bother to wipe away the hot tears as they slipped down my cheeks. I didn't see Grey the rest of the night. He decided sleeping on the living room couch was preferable to sleeping with me.

This was not how I imagined his homecoming night to be! I cried hot tears into my pillow for a long time. I don't know what time it was when I finally fell into a fitful slumber.

~~~~~~

Grey decided his two-week hiatus should start the next day. He didn't acknowledge anything family related, not even Tyler's third birthday, which was a mere five days away. I tried talking to Grey about it. "What do you think we should do for Tyler's birthday?"

"It's this weekend? Sunday?" Like he didn't know.

"Yes. I thought about doing a family party with a Piglet cake."

"I don't give a damn. I don't know if I'm going to be here this weekend anyway."

"What?! It's your son's birthday. His first one since you've been back. You *have* to be there!" I couldn't believe he was even considering being gone.

"No, I don't. Remember? Whatever, whenever." With that, he showered and left.

~~~~~~

Over the next few days, Grey didn't spend time with either Tyler or me. In fact, he wasn't home much at all, and if he was, it was only to sleep. I was more concerned about his response to Tyler than I was about our relationship at that point. Our little boy deserved his daddy's time and attention. Grey acted like he could care less.

The weekend of Tyler's birthday, Grey still hadn't given me any idea as to whether he would be there. On Friday morning, Grey told me he was going to Wells, Nevada, to a party for a "friend" who was supposedly being deployed—and was completely defensive when I asked if it was a girl. By Sunday morning, Grey hadn't come home yet. By five o'clock that afternoon, I'd called him several times with no response. He finally showed up forty-five minutes before everyone else, most of whom were his family. The first thing he said when he walked in the door was, "Don't f***in' bitch at me or I'll leave."

"I wasn't going to say anything." How did my mere presence offend him so easily?

"You usually do."

How did he know that? He'd been home a total of two days since I'd picked him up five days ago. I was doing everything I could to give him his space, as I'd promised. So that a fight didn't ensue, I left him alone to get ready for Tyler's party.

Tyler's third birthday party ended up being somewhat of a homecoming for Grey as well. That wasn't my intention, but he hadn't been to see any of his family since returning, so what could I do? Tyler was so excited to have his daddy home he didn't notice anything amiss. We sang *Happy Birthday* to Tyler and opened gifts with him.

While eating cake and ice cream he asked me, "Mommy, why aren't Grandma and Grandpa here?" I hoped he wouldn't notice, but how could he not? They'd been a part of his everyday life since he was born.

"Sweetie, they live in Georgia now. Remember? They would be here if they could."

"Why can't they ride the airplane?"

"Honey, airplane tickets cost a lot of money." I knew I would lose this conversation. Luckily, the phone rang. I guess talking to Grandma and Grandpa made things all better because Tyler was okay after that.

~~~~~~

Over the next several days, the only thing Grey asked of me pertaining to him was whether I could take him to look at a pickup. The pickup was one I had been looking at for him but wanted to wait until he came home to make a final decision. It was a 1988

Chevy 4x4 extended cab. It was a dark tan and in pretty good shape minus the dent in the hood. He wanted to get it because he claimed to hate my car. "It's too girly," he whined.

"If you want to go look at it, you need to call the guy and set a time." I was done doing things for him that he could just as easily do for himself. I'd been bending over backwards to not rock the boat since his return, but it was getting tiresome! Not only was I still on crutches but having him home made my pain more intense.

"Fine. You don't need to bitchy about it." He didn't get it, did he?

A few days later, I took him to look at the truck. It didn't take him long to decide it was what he wanted. He put down a hundred dollars and promised the guy a hundred every month after until it was paid off. How did he think he was going to pay for his truck when we had my car payment, rent, utilities, groceries, and we still had several more payments for his rest and relaxation time spent as a civilian while in Kuwait that hadn't come through yet? He said it shouldn't be more than three hundred altogether. It ended up being WAY more than that, but I wasn't made aware until the bank cleared the payments. It ended up being almost $3,0000. We continued receiving active duty pay so we would be okay for a little while. Who knew how long, though.

Just as soon as he got the registration and insurance put on the truck, he promptly informed me he would be gone the upcoming weekend. He was going to a party that his adoptive mom was throwing him. Why his family wasn't invited, I'd never know. Because he was still technically on his "two-week hiatus" there was nothing I could do. It was almost over and when it was. . .

~~~~~~

Grey's *whatever, whenever* days were over! Like he'd done several times over the last two weeks, Grey came home smelling like cigarettes and alcohol—oh yeah, he'd started drinking again, too! I'd spent the last fourteen nights alone, when by all rights, I shouldn't have. Grey didn't seem to realize, or maybe he just didn't care, but I had adjustments to make too.

When he staggered in the door on April fifteenth, I laid into him without giving him a chance to hide, "I *did not* spend fifteen months alone for you to come home and completely ignore not only me, but our son as well! I've done what you asked and have given you your damn space, and haven't bitched about it, but I'm not doing this anymore! I haven't bothered you about the shit you brought home from Iraq that still graces almost every room in our apartment. I don't bug you about spending time with us, nor do I bug you about attending church with us! You either start acting like you want to be a part of this family or don't, but please stop stringing us along!" I was hoping I could say my piece without crying, but no such luck. Luckily, Tyler was playing at Reghan's so I didn't have to hide my tears. At least, not yet.

Something must have clicked because Grey chose not to sleep on the couch as he had since he came home. To say I was excited was an understatement! Finally, after fifteen months, my wish came true: to be cuddled, caressed, and loved as I'd been dreaming about for so long—to sleep and wake up next to my sweetheart!

What happened, however, wasn't lovemaking! Grey made sure he was properly pleasured, which to an extent wasn't new. Even before going to Iraq, our lovemaking revolved around what he needed. He immediately ordered me onto my knees. "Grey, no." I pleaded. He knew I hated it when he forced me to go down on him. I was scared, but there was a part of my brain that exclaimed, *Bite him! Come on, you can do it!* I had a difficult time keeping up with the fast pace he wanted. He became so enraged that he jerked me up off my knees, forcing me onto my stomach on the bed and, his voice dripping with contempt, growled, "Fine. Have it your f***in' way. If you refuse to suck my dick without gagging, fine, we can do something else." Without another word, Grey grabbed my arms, pinning me beneath him. He then violated me in ways that no one should ever have to experience. There were certain places a man just wasn't supposed to put his dick!

To keep him from hearing my pained cries, I buried my face in the quilt Grandma Kacie made, trying to muffle the sound. Having survived Grey's fantasies before, I knew this had to be another one.

.

Was this rape? Could it even be deemed rape because we were married? How was I ever going to tell anyone about this? Was there anyone I trusted enough to tell? Would he do it again? As for that question, I found myself praying he wouldn't, but my intelligent side feared I would endure such violations and fantasies if Grey wanted it. I knew Tyler and I were in trouble but didn't know what to do.

I laid there thinking to myself, *"Why doesn't anyone care? No one knows, or even wants to know what's going on with my family. Why do I feel so alone and abandoned by everyone?"*

It was up to me to make the best of the hole I'd put Tyler and myself in. The sad part was, even after being violated by the man who was supposed to love me forever, I clung to the hope that he would change. I had to put Grey's actions behind me, for Tyler's sake.

~~~~~~

No matter how hard I tried, I couldn't stop thinking about that awful night. Grey, of course, acted as if nothing was different. Not about that, and not about any other aspect of our life. He still spent a lot of time on the computer playing *Combat Killers* and chatting. Every Thursday he left me at home with Tyler and went dancing at *Renegade* with any and every female he could find. He didn't give me the chance to show him all the dance moves I'd been working on while he was away. He seriously didn't seem to care.

Whenever he wanted sex, I shut down and went somewhere—anywhere—in my mind, other than where I was. I felt more and more like a prostitute and less and less like a wife. No matter how many times I told him no and that I HATED it that way, it didn't matter!

I'd never been a huge drinker, but in my mind, there was only one way to numb the pain and rejection I felt. Taking matters into my own hands, I made sure I had a constant supply of alcohol hidden away—somewhere Grey couldn't find it—so that whenever the feelings cropped up or Grey wanted the prostitute, I knew where to look. He was good at making sure he had his cigarettes. Well, I was becoming exceptional at making sure I was numb. I was extremely careful, however, not to drink when Tyler was awake or to mix too much medication. Most of the time, when my drinking took place, I didn't take my meds because, although I had suicidal thoughts on a regular basis, I was dead set against leaving Tyler alone.

~~~~~~

There was a part of me that couldn't take anymore, but the bigger part felt like I married Grey against almost everyone's advice, so I'd better learn to live with it. Besides that, I saw potential in my husband—he just needed to find it. He could be a great husband and father if he wanted to be. All I could do was be a good mom to Tyler and hope and pray that Grey would come to his senses!

~~~~~~

I wanted so badly to believe the person who came home in my husband's body wasn't my Grey. In doing so, I was determined to make my marriage work. I would do whatever it took to bring out the Grey he'd been working on becoming when he left! Even if it meant hanging out with people I didn't have anything in common with, or didn't necessarily like and doing things that disgusted me to no end.

The first weekend in June, I decided it was time to take Grey on a mini-vacation, even though it was only for the weekend. So, leaving Tyler with Reghan, we drove almost six hours to Boise, Idaho, where Grey's friend, Grace, and her boyfriend, Jack, lived with their kids. It wasn't very long before I realized I had nothing in common with these people. Although I drank most nights, it wasn't so much that I didn't know what was going on around me. These people, however, liked to drink continually. Yes, Grey was drunk most of the time, too. He was mellow if he was drunk, but if he wasn't at the very least buzzed, he was wound tighter than a clock. To say I was grateful when Sunday finally arrived and it was time to leave was an understatement. My hopes of moving towards positive changes had been dashed.

Maybe we'd be better off doing things with Gunner and Shaylie. We'd hung out with them several times in the last few weeks, but since they lived in Salt Lake, it wasn't easy getting together.

~~~~~~

Grey still hadn't done anything about finding employment and I foolishly thought giving him a weekend to breathe might kick him in the ass. He received his last active duty check just before we went to Boise, and he didn't seem at all interested in getting into school or finding a job. Of course, talking to him was like talking to a brick wall, most of the time.

"Grey, are you ever going to look for a job?" I asked one day, purely frustrated.

"I'll do it when I'm damn good and ready," he quipped.

"You either need to look for a job or go to school. I don't care which one you choose, but you need to do something."

"Quit being a cunt and get off my case!"

"You need to take care of your family!" In desperation, I tried to reach him. There was a position I'd been looking into for him at a local lumber company for a CDL driver, but I wasn't sure he wanted to hear it. I could tell Grey wanted to lay into me about how I needed to leave him alone and stay out of his life. It was as if he only kept Tyler and me around just in case.

Trying to stroke his ego, I delved into it, "Look at it this way. Do you know anyone who has a CDL? When you pass, you can get a position just about anywhere."

"I don't need your help to find a job," he answered snidely. Oh, I wanted to say something so clever it would knock him down several pegs, like he did me on a regular basis. I wasn't like him, however, so I didn't do it. He decided he liked the idea of having a CDL endorsement on his license, however, and, of course, took credit for it.

During the next couple of weeks, Grey interviewed, got the job, studied, and, with my help—it seemed it was the only thing I could do that didn't tick him off—passed the CDL licensing test.

~~~~~~

Our marriage went from bad to worse when, one day in late June, he showed up at our apartment with a girl—a college student to be exact. He claimed she was a journalism student named Fran who wanted to write a paper on Grey and his tour in Iraq. She spent entirely too much time with Grey, sometimes at our apartment, and, other times in places I wasn't privy to. The two spent so much time together that, with his job, going out, and his computer usage, I was by all rights a single mom. AGAIN.

I'd spent the first part of Tyler's life without help from Grey, then spent the months of his deployment raising his baby by myself, and now, since his return, being a single mom was worse than it had ever been. I took Tyler with me everywhere—grocery shopping, to pay bills, and to church. Grey hadn't attended church since coming home, although our home teachers checked in with Grey regularly. It didn't matter to him. He'd thrown our family out the window, but he hadn't left for good. So, there was still hope, right?

~~~~~~

Two weeks into Fran's journalism project, I received a phone call from one of the assistant deans at BYU who wanted to know the skinny on Grey and Fran's friendship. Apparently, someone had called with concerns about Fran. According to both Grey and Fran, she was only writing a journalism paper on him, but when we decided to go to Lagoon, Grey invited her. I wasn't happy about it, but Fran told Grey she wouldn't go if I did. I explained this to the dean, while also sharing about how one evening while we were out with friends, Fran called Grey to come pick her up, and when he told her I was coming, she told him to forget it. It appeared even the dean felt there was more to their "friendship."

Grey was spitting mad when he returned home that night. "What the f*** do you think you're doing?" he yelled at me.

"What the hell are you talking about?"

Continuing to yell, he shouted, "You got Fran kicked out of school! She has nowhere to go! She can't go home. It's too far away!" He expected me to feel sorry for her. He blamed me for Fran getting kicked out of school. Not the woman who'd been spending time with a married man, but me!

His anger escalated from there. He did something he had never done before. I watched in horror as, without saying a word and breathing heavily, Grey slapped me, hard. He took a huge chunk of skin from my left cheek with his finger nail, causing it to bleed profusely. I didn't know then, but I would have a scar for the rest of my life to remind me of that day. It took a thick gauze pad to cover the area and to keep it from bleeding through. I wasn't sure how to handle this, but I did know I couldn't let anyone see it. That proved to be harder than I expected. When asked what happened, I told people it was caused by a spider bite. That seemed to stop the questioning.

Grey wasn't at all apologetic for causing physical injury to me, but the Fran thing caused a huge chink in our marriage—a crack bigger than any we'd had up to that point, except maybe Sheryl. Even though I wasn't the one who reported Fran, Grey saw it and his reaction to it that night as my fault.

The incident with Fran was a HUGE downhill slide as far as our marriage went. Other than getting sex and living out his fantasies whenever he felt like it, Grey didn't touch me. The more time that passed, the more it felt like we were more like pimp and prostitute than husband and wife. Even the sex acts I despised so badly were becoming the norm, especially when I would do anything to keep the peace.

~~~~~~

A few weeks later, Grey left without telling me where he was going or how long he'd be gone, as he had become accustomed to doing. I heard nothing from him the whole weekend. He finally came in after midnight on Sunday. When it became apparent he wasn't going to divulge any information, I asked, "Where have you been?"

His response, "It's none of your damn business. If you keep asking me questions about stuff you know nothing about, I'm f***in' outta here."

I didn't comment any further. *What difference would it make, really?* When he was home, which was seldom, he was doing anything and everything that didn't involve being a husband or a father. There were times when I wondered if he wanted a divorce and the only reason he didn't bring it up himself was because he thought he would lose Tyler—a child he hardly ever spent time with or even acknowledged. I didn't think if I were to bring it up—

and I was certain it was what I wanted—he would object. Thing was, I *loved* the man! I knew he could change, but at the same time, he had to *want* to change.

~~~~~~

With our marriage in the gutter—never knowing whether we were okay or not—and needing to boost our finances, I decided to get a job, just in case. In July, I obtained a position taking surveys over the phone. It wasn't an easy job, by any means, because sitting for even the three-hour shift a day I could muster hurt terribly, but every little bit helped. Not only did it help with bills, but it gave me something to do besides think about the demise of my marriage. Unfortunately, It also meant putting Tyler in daycare/preschool.

~~~~~~

As if my problems with Grey weren't enough, barely a week after beginning my new job, the teacher at Tiny's Academy told me when I went to pick Tyler up that he had bruised his ankle while playing.

"It's bruised?" I asked, trying to keep my voice on an even keel as to not startle the children. What I saw was not a bruise! "Did you even look at it?"

"Well, no, but one of our assistants is getting her certified nursing certificate and she looked at it."

"Come over here." The teacher looked at Tyler's foot. "The child can't even put any weight on it! Why wasn't I called when he did this?" I demanded.

"We didn't think it was that bad and we didn't want to bother you," she replied sheepishly.

"Bother me? This is my son!" Picking Tyler up I turned to leave, but not before informing her he wouldn't be returning. The next day I took Tyler to his pediatrician. His ankle was sprained, which made me working nearly impossible until he could put weight on it—two weeks the doctor said. Luckily, I was able to set my own schedule and, with help from Reghan and Shaylie, I was able to work a little during that time. Tyler even handled having his foot wrapped all the time considerably well, which I was grateful for.

CHAPTER TWELVE

As if things between Grey and me weren't difficult enough, in mid-August I had a pregnancy scare. I forgot to change my birth control patch on time, and of course, Grey's needs came first—something I had to endure whether I wanted to or not. I was late. The only way to be sure was to take a pregnancy test, and, when I did, I swore I saw two faint lines. Scared, but at the same time elated, I called Reghan. I needed to share this with someone and I didn't want to say anything to Grey yet.

"Did you take a pregnancy test?" Reghan inquired.

"Yeah. I thought I saw lines." My voice was trembling. "Reg, I can't be pregnant. Not now. If the meds I take aren't bad enough, my relationship with Grey is in the shitter."

"Don't borrow trouble." She sounded just like my mom. "Maybe you're late because of stress. Your life hasn't exactly been the easiest since he came home."

"I know. You're probably right. And I'm only a week late, which isn't something new to me."

Grey came into our bedroom and literally growled at me, "You better not be pregnant, bitch!" He must've heard our conversation.

I was pretty sure Reghan had heard every word. She confirmed my suspicions when she asked, "Is everything okay?"

"Yeah," I wasn't going into it just then. "I gotta go. I'll keep you posted." With that, I hung up.

I turned on Grey, "What will you do if I am?" I couldn't keep my voice from rising no matter how hard I tried, but I held my chin up anyway.

He waved at me, as if to say bye-bye. Then said, "Bitch, you know how I feel about having any more damn kids. What are you trying to do, f***in' trap me?"

How could he be so cold? Especially about a baby? "You think I would do this on purpose? What kind of woman do you take me for? You would leave over a baby?" I couldn't mask my feelings.

"Damn straight and I wouldn't f***in' look back," he replied arrogantly. "You trapped me once—never again." He said nothing more after that, just walked away—something he'd become great at!

~~~~~~

As it turned out, I wasn't pregnant. I wanted desperately to have more children, but even the thought of it, with all the medication I took, scared the devil out of me. Grey didn't want any more kids, and acted as if having babies with me was completely awful. Because of everything, I religiously changed my patch after the scare. I didn't want any more grief from Grey than I was already dealing with!

It seemed to me the pregnancy scare had made Grey angrier, if that was even possible. He told me on a regular basis that if I did or said anything he didn't agree with he going to leave. On the day I found out I wasn't pregnant, Grey came home later than usual. I'd made dinner four hours before and it had been waiting ever since. I was tired of not being included in his life, and even more tired of his threats. When he walked in, I asked him why he was home. "I f***in' live here." He looked at me as if I'd lost my mind.

"Do you?" I countered.

"Uh, duh." He did his level best to make me feel like an insolent idiot.

"Sure as hell can't prove it by us."

"What the f*** are you talking about?" He was losing his cool, but I didn't care.

"You're never here. You have a son that begs, literally begs youi to play with him, and you never have time. When you are here, you're not *here*. You're either on the computer playing that stupid game or chatting with "friends." You swear you aren't cheating, and I'm doing my best to trust you! It sucks! We're married, but we sure as hell don't act like it! Sex is all about you. Living and breathing is all about YOU! You don't give a damn about anyone but yourself!" I could feel my temper rising.

"What the f*** do you want from me? To be here all the time, listening to you bitch and moan about my friends?" Grey demanded, his temper rising.

"We've been over this a million damn times! I seriously need to tell you what I need from you again? Here's a new one for you; I think you should leave," I said it with as little emotion as I could.

"What?!" He looked surprised.

"I can't do this anymore and neither can Tyler." Without saying another word, I went into our bedroom and closed the door. I could hear him tapping away on the computer through the door. Whether he would leave or not remained to be seen. Maybe if he left and had time to think about what he would be giving up, he might see where I was coming from. Of course, because it wasn't Grey's idea to leave, he didn't.

~~~~~~

I was getting fed up being non-existent to Grey. I'd gone to both our bishop and home teachers and they knew I had asked him to move out. I had even packed a bag for him, but he wouldn't go. What the hell did he want? Not me, that was a given. For the life of me, I couldn't figure out why, when I was giving him permission to leave, he wouldn't!

My birthday came and went and was yet again, *just another day*. What hurt the most though, was that Grey, the man who was supposed to love me, didn't even acknowledge it! But that shouldn't have surprised me.

I needed something to help me not worry and de-stress. For some reason, school provided that for me. When I was accepted back into BYU, I decided I wasn't going to quit until I had my bachelors degree. I got accepted into the Early Childhood/Special Needs program and started classes in September. I received my student loans on my birthday so, taking Tyler with me, I headed up to the campus bookstore and bought what I needed for the twelve credits I was taking. I also put Tyler into a new daycare/preschool; one I thought would be better suited to him. Because Tyler wasn't four- years- old yet, I didn't worry too much about the preschool part at that point.

~~~~~~

My marriage added more stress than I could deal with. By September, my pain level had increased, as had my depression and anxiety. I had hoped that after my husband's return, at least the depression and anxiety would subside, but instead, both increased drastically.

Not only were things increasingly worse between Grey and me, but he lost another job! That meant he no longer carried a CDL endorsement on his license. Everyone that knew us, me included, were beginning to wonder if Grey would *ever* keep a job longer than a few months.

~~~~~~

Because I still loved him and desperately wanted to make our marriage work, at whatever the cost, the day of our fifth anniversary—September 20, 2004—I bought the stereo system Grey had been drooling over, complete with brand new speakers and a subwoofer, installed in his truck. After the system was installed, I washed and waxed his truck and picked Tyler up from daycare.

Wanting to show Grey that I still had sex appeal, I had Shaylie come over to help me put together a sexy, but tasteful outfit. I wanted to show him I loved him, no matter what!

As soon as Shaylie and I were done, and she left with Tyler, I called Grey, "Hey."

"What the f*** do you want?" He sounded pissed. Since losing his CDL, Grey was, once again, "working" for Hank's dad.

"I just wanted to let you know I have a surprise for you."

"What the hell for? You know I hate surprises!"

"Humor me, okay." I tried to keep my voice light. "There is a change of clothes in the car. Go over to your mom's, shower, and come home."

"Fine. Whatever." Grey acted like he didn't have a clue what day it was, but I wasn't going to let that bother me. I was bound and determined to open his eyes or die trying! While I waited, I put the final touches on Grey's second favorite dish, stroganoff.

He usually got off work by five-thirty, but when he still wasn't home by eight o'clock, I began to worry. I called his mom, who said he'd left a few minutes before. Apparently, he stayed to hang out after he got there. He told his mom he didn't want to go home. Finally, she made him. As he walked through the door of our home, he didn't even notice the candle lit dinner waiting on the coffee table or the way I was dressed. "So, what's this f***in' big surprise?" He sounded pretentious.

Trying to hide my disappointment, I excitedly belted out, "Happy Anniversary!" I noticed he hadn't bothered to shower and change.

"That's today?" Like he didn't know.

"Um...Yeah—like it has been the last five years."

The next thing Grey said shouldn't have surprised me, and it really didn't, but it did hurt. "What did you get me?"

Giving up on dinner, no longer hungry anyway, I led him outside and stood by his truck without saying a word. "What? You washed and waxed my damn truck? Big shittin' deal!" Still not saying anything, I opened the driver's side door and walked back into the house. Grey didn't even give me a "Kiss my ass" when he realized what I had done; he simply went in the bathroom to shower.

By the time he came out, Tyler was home and I already had him tucked safely in bed. As I'd done many times in Tyler's life, and tons more since Grey came home, I held my little boy close, whispering that I loved him no matter what. I knew I couldn't make up for the absentee male that called himself dad, but I could try. It seemed like I would forever be trying to make up for Grey when it came to Tyler.

~~~~~~

Grey became increasingly bold as far as his "friends" were concerned. For reasons I couldn't fathom, the idiot gave one of his "friends" my phone number and the "friend" texted me. I still had the cell phone I bought while Grey was in Iraq, but since coming home, we hadn't been able to afford to keep the pay-by-minute phone he'd bought in Maryland. Taking matters into my own hands, I called the "friend."

"Who the hell is this and how do you know my husband?"

"Ummm...he's my boyfriend," she sounded mousy.

"What the hell? No way!" I was pissed!

"He told me he was divorced." That statement stung more than I wanted to admit.

"Uh, no, he damn well is not. How long have you known my husband?"

"Over a year." He must've found her on the Internet while he was overseas. Then the "friend" did her best to convince me she and Grey were "just friends."

After hanging up, I confronted Grey. Of course, the only thing he was concerned with was why I didn't give him his privacy. "You need to choose, Grey. It's either Tyler and me or your "friends."

Acting all innocent, as if he didn't know what kind of slippery slope he was on, he said, "Why are you doing this?"

"I'm not. You are. I've been raising Tyler by myself for a long time. If I have to, I'll keep doing it, damn it! I'm tired of your excuses and now you have a girlfriend? What the hell? And, you told her your ass was divorced?" I wondered if *he* knew what he was going to do.

As I looked in the mirror, I couldn't fathom why he would want me anyway. It wasn't as though I was gorgeous, or even pretty for that matter. Even on a good day the pain showed on my face. There were dark circles that had made a permanent home under my eyes. Everything about me was *blah*. I was a fat cow according to Grey, and he'd been ashamed of me our entire marriage because of my Cerebral Palsy. After he said as much not long after we were married, I found I was much more self-conscious about the disability I was born with than I'd ever been. Grey had also warned me several years before that, even after having babies, I'd better not get fat.

The only thing I saw when I looked in the mirror was a failure. Maybe that was the reason he filled his time and energy with other women or girls and pornography. If I was so awful, why was he still with me? It was as if he wanted me to make the choice for him. There was no way I was going to be the bad guy! The sad part was, the bad guy stared back at me. I just didn't know it.

~~~~~~

By October, Grey had found a painting position with a contractor out of South Jordan, after much hassling from me. The only drawback was that, because it was coming on winter, work was more scarce than abundant. He still came and went as he pleased, and spent his time playing on the computer, chatting, and going dancing weekly. He never asked me to go, and pretty much ignored Tyler. Of course, the only time he paid attention to me was when he wanted some action, which meant more forcing, more tears, and more name-calling. Did he realize how badly it hurt me both physically and mentally when he forced me to do the unthinkable? I hoped Grey wasn't *that* unfeeling. But I was beginning to see that I might be wrong.

~~~~~~

One evening in October I decided that just because Grey was indecisive about me, it didn't mean I couldn't give him a taste of what and who he'd be giving up if he chose to leave.

I'd planned a night of fun and seduction. This was something I'd never done before because of Grey's rule regarding my showing sexy to him. First, I wanted to take him out to dinner at La Jolla Groves in Provo, a place neither of us had been. I'd already set up the candles around our bedroom, taken out the fun dice that had never been opened and involved senses and places on the body, and I knew exactly what negligee I was going to wear—the same one I'd bought for his homecoming, but had never used. I hoped by my doing that he would see that I was willing to do whatever it took to keep our family intact, even though he had been excessively mean and ultimately abusive in every way.

Leaving Tyler at Reghan's, I headed home. Even after all that had transpired between us throughout our marriage, the thought of bringing out the Grey that had started to emerge before deployment caused butterflies and giddiness.

He was on the computer when I walked in. "Let's go out," I almost pleaded.

"Nope. Not with you."

"Why not? Reghan has Tyler. It would be just the two of us."

"Hell, no."

I should've known not to push, but we hadn't been on anything even resembling a date since Grey's return.

"Come on, I don't ask you for much. We haven't been on a date in over two years, since just before you left."

Grey boomed, "I SAID NO! NOW LEAVE ME THE F*** ALONE!" His favorite string of profanity followed. Unfortunately, I was becoming accustomed to hearing the F-bomb and any other foul language he chose to let loose.

I didn't say anything to him as he sat at his computer, continuing to ignore me. Instead of risking his wrath again, I picked up my keys and went to pick up Tyler. Reghan tried to get me to talk, but I couldn't.

When I arrived home, Grey was still sitting where I left him. I got Tyler ready for bed and, instead of putting him in his bed, I took him in my bedroom and locked the door. I really didn't want to deal with anymore of Grey's outbursts tonight.

~~~~~~

Grey left early the next morning, claiming he wanted to talk with a recruiter because, although he was technically still military, he had been discharged and demoted upon returning home. He had been demoted from Sergeant to Private. Grey's explanation for being both discharged and demoted was that he'd lost his temper and punched his commanding officer. I still wondered if there was more to the story than Grey was telling me.

When Grey finally came home later that night, I tried talking to him, but all he wanted to do was play *Combat Killers*. It looked like it was going to be yet another lonely night for me. The sad part was, I wasn't in the house by myself; the person I wanted to spend time with was there. But at the same time, he wasn't. He might be physically there, but in the ways that counted, he was gone.

Just as I was about to go to bed, I heard Grey say, "I'm leaving." He didn't even bother to look up from his game or his chatting; whichever he was doing at that moment.

"What?" I wasn't entirely surprised at the piece of news. I had been trying to get him to decide for weeks. Now, he had. "When?" I asked.

"Tomorrow. I'm moving in with Mom. I need to figure some things out, and I can't have you naggin' and bitchin' at me all the time about my smoking, friends, or spending time with you and Tyler."

"What about Tyler? You've been absent almost his whole life." I wanted to get angry, especially for Tyler, but I was tired of the entire deal. This had been going on our entire marriage, and I didn't want things to continue as they had been.

"I'll come over every day to see Tyler after work."

"What for? You live here, and you don't see him. What makes you think it will be any better if you move out? The only change I can see is you bailing. I've asked you twice to leave. Even packed your bags at one point and you wouldn't. Why wait until a few weeks before Thanksgiving?"

"Look, I just need some f***in' time. You *have* to give me this. You owe me that much."

I couldn't believe he said that; that I had to give him anything or that I owed him! *Was he out of his mind?* Like the last five years had meant nothing? Keeping him bolstered while he was overseas? And what about what I'd allowed him to do since returning? None of that was enough? Maybe that was the problem. I'd been so scared of losing him that I let him use me as his whore and doormat whenever his fancy struck.

Having Grey gone wasn't much different than when he was home, except he didn't sleep there. He wasn't home all that much before he moved out anyway.

Grey moved out on Saturday and, to my utter amazement, attended church with me and Tyler the next day! It was fast and testimony meeting, and I bore my testimony; only the second time in my life.

~~~~~~

The one and only other time I bore my testimony was when I was eight. Derek double-dog dared me, knowing I was petrified, to stand up in front of people. He thought he had me, but instead he learned to never dare me!

Standing at the pulpit I looked straight at Grey and expressed how grateful I was for his safe return. I declared my love for him, hoping it might reach my husband and soften his heart. I spoke to Tyler as well—even though he didn't understand much of what I was trying to convey—telling him how special and important he was to me and how much I loved him. Of course, I couldn't do any of it without crying.

Grey didn't say much to me for the rest of our meetings, and afterward he took Tyler to visit his mom.

My mom called while they were gone. "Hunter, are you and Tyler okay?" she asked.

"We're fine. Why?"

"Where's Tyler?"

"Grey took him to visit his mom. They shouldn't be gone too long."

My mom immediately burst into tears. "What's wrong?" I asked.

"I had a feeling I needed to call and check on you and Tyler today."

"Okay."

"I'm afraid Grey wants to take Tyler away from you. I'm scared he will do whatever it takes to prove you an unstable woman and unfit mother."

After reassuring my mom that there was no way I would let that happen, and not wanting to believe he would do such an underhanded thing, I called and asked when he was bringing Tyler back. Talking to my mom brought out that fear in me as well.

"I'll bring him home in a few minutes," Grey responded. "Why? What the hell is going on?" I didn't want him to know about my mom's concerns.

"I know you just moved out, but I feel like I am floundering here." I hoped Grey might give me a hint as to where we were headed. Like how much time he needed.

"Look, I told you, I have some things I need to deal with. If I come back it will be because I want to—nothing you say or do will sway me."

"Are we over then?" I wasn't looking forward to his answer.

"No. I think we can fix things, but you can't bitch at me all the time."

Was he for real? He thought I nagged him all the time? Okay, so maybe I *did* nag a little when it came to the computer, smoking, drinking, and his "friends," but I had every right to feel safe, loved, and wanted, didn't I?

~~~~~~

On Tuesday night, I had a full-blown panic attack. They'd been coming more and more frequently. Thankfully, it hit after Tyler had gone to sleep, but it scared me so much that I called Grey. Not sure how he would react, I explained to him what was going on.

He came over, albeit reluctantly. "What the...?" He exclaimed when he walked in the door.

"I can't get this panic attack to stop." I was trying to slow my breathing and heart rate. Unfortunately, whenever I'd had one before, Grey was never around, or it wasn't bad enough that I couldn't talk myself out of it. I was unaware that this, or the other attacks I'd had, were caused by the stress Grey put me under. The way I constantly worried about our marriage, money, his inability to keep a job, and where I stood with him were all stressors.

"What the f*** do you want me to do? Can't you make yourself stop?" He sounded put out that I would have the audacity to even ask him to come over.

"No. I've been trying that and so far, it hasn't worked."

"Still doesn't explain what the hell you want from me."

"I want you to come home."

"What the f*** for?"

"I need you. Tyler needs you."

"If I move back in, you can't bitch at me."

Surprised by how quickly he agreed to come home, I responded, "Okay." I was willing to do whatever he wanted as long as he came home. I hated being alone and I thought that was where all my fear came from.

~~~~~~

Thanksgiving Day was harder for me that year than ever before, because this was my first Thanksgiving without extended family. Reghan was going to her in-law's, and, since it was Grey's first Thanksgiving home, his family let us do what we wanted. I wanted to make this day memorable for Grey, so I swallowed the tears and did my best.

I got up at six o'clock that morning and put the turkey in the oven. Since Grey and Tyler were still asleep, I laid on the couch and slept until three-year-old Tyler came bounding out of his room at nine o'clock. "Mommy, why are you on the couch?" He looked concerned.

"Oh, sweetie, I put the turkey in the oven and didn't want to wake your daddy up."

"Oh. Can I watch cartoons?"

"Yeah. But keep it low so you don't wake up Daddy." Tyler's favorite cartoon was *Transformer the Movie*. That's what we watched in between making salads and desserts. Because Grey's favorite pie was pumpkin, I swallowed my disgust for it and made it for him. I hoped he would notice, but I doubted it.

Later, I asked Grey to keep an eye on Tyler while I finished making the broccoli salad he liked. Of course, he had better things to do. While Grey took a shower, I, with Tyler sitting near me on the counter, made the salad. I already had the grated cheese, green onions, crispy bacon all thrown into the bowl. Because the knife set we had was extremely dull, I decided to use Grey's new hunting knife to cut up the broccoli. Trying to keep Tyler's fingers away from where I was cutting proved to be a huge challenge. One-minute I was cutting broccoli and the next I was telling Tyler he couldn't be so close. In one split second, though, while keeping Tyler away from the sharp blade, my hand slipped—thanks to my Cerebral Palsy—and I sliced through my index finger. The next several seconds went by in slow motion as I tried to stem the blood flow while not passing out. I did not want to interrupt Grey unless I had to. Unfortunately, I had to.

"GREY!" I yelled, hoping he could hear me above the shower. "GREY, COME HERE QUICK!" I yelled again. While waiting on him I made sure Tyler was okay. He was still sitting on the counter looking scared.

"Mommy! There's lots of blood!" Tyler was hysterical. I was trying to stay standing, doing my best not to pass out. *Where the heck was Grey?* I tried to breathe in and out in order to stay calm while keeping my hand under the cold water and away from where Tyler could see it. The cold water, of course, hurt like a beast, but it slowed the blood flow.

It felt like an eternity before Grey finally came out of the bathroom wrapped in a towel with shampoo still in his hair. "What the f***in' hell is going on?" he demanded. When he saw my pale face and the blood-soaked rag on my left hand, he grabbed a kitchen towel, wrapped it tightly around my finger and walked me over to the couch.

"What the hell were you thinking? If I had known you were gonna cut your damn finger off…" He didn't say anything else for a minute, but gave me a condescending look, as if he never would've done such a thing, making me more painfully aware of my limitations. "Let me get dressed and I'll take you to the damn Emergency Room. You might need stitches." Then under his breath, which I'm sure he wanted me to hear, he said, "Dumbassed woman." Grey had a unique way of making me feel like the stupidest person on the planet even though this could've happened to anyone. Even him!

Luckily for me, the Emergency Room wasn't packed, so we got in fairly quickly. I ended up getting nine stitches in my index finger and was in too much pain to worry about finishing dinner. Not that I didn't already have enough pain to deal with but adding insult to injury…that was my life.

Grey let me know just how he felt about it, too! "You are such a baby! Stitches are NOTHING! Now, because of your clumsiness, I'm missing out on my first Thanksgiving home!" Grey never noticed that pain accompanied my every breathing moment. Nor did he seem to care.

I was in no mood to play this game with him. "Stitches are nothing? Really? How many times have you had stitches?" Not giving him a chance to answer, I continued on, "Have you forgotten that pain is my constant companion, or do you just not give a shit?" I didn't swear often, especially not at Grey. The repercussions weren't worth it. But I'd had it! "I wish, just once, you could change bodies with me. Then, you *might* understand. You *might* have some empathy for me!" Because I hurt so badly, I didn't care whether Grey saw the tears sliding down my cheeks. The rest of the ride home was so full of tension I felt like I was going to choke on it!

It was a good thing that I at least got the turkey, rolls, mashed potatoes, and a relish tray finished before the accident. Luckily, most of those warmed up. Grey's first Thanksgiving home wasn't as bad as it could've been. I was just grateful that it wasn't Tyler that was cut. There was a part of me that was irritated with Grey because, if he had helped me like I'd asked, this very well might not have happened. And all he could do is treat me as if I was a dumb shit..

To say I was relieved by the time Tyler was in bed was an understatement. With all the other pain medications I took, there wasn't anything more the doctor could give me for the pain in my hand. My entire hand felt like it wanted to throw up; that was the best way to explain how it felt—the pain went clear up my arm. The day had been extremely long, but I had a feeling it was going to be an even longer night.

~~~~~~

This year, because my parents lived in Georgia, going up into the mountains to cut down Christmas trees didn't happen. It was Derek's turn for our parents to spend Christmas with them, but no one knew what their plans were yet.

Grey didn't like Christmas much. Getting a tree wasn't a high priority on his list of things to do and, as usual, we waited until the week before Christmas to get one.

"Since this is your first Christmas home and Tyler's first Christmas with you that he will remember, can we go get the tree as a family?" I hated sounding like I was begging, but at that point I didn't really care.

"I don't give a shit. You're gonna make me go whether I want to or not. Let's just get it over with," he grumbled.

Grey was in such an all-fired up hurry to be done with family time that he chose the first, least pathetic tree he could find. "This one." He was extremely demanding. Almost like a child. "Can we f***in' go now?"

Looking at the tree he chose, I was sad that Grey cared so little about making his first Christmas home and the first Christmas Tyler would remember with him fun and memorable. Maybe, though, with a little tinsel, ornaments, and lights, the tree might not look so bad.

Upon returning home, Grey went directly to the computer, leaving me to bring the tree in and get the box of Christmas stuff down from our bedroom closet. Trying to engage him in what Tyler and I were doing, I asked, "Hey honey, why don't you come help us put the lights on?"

Tyler, of course, didn't want to be left out. "Come on, Daddy! It's fun!"

Grey ignored both of us, which didn't surprise me, but I couldn't stand the crestfallen look on my son's face. Trying to make up for Grey's ignorance, I put on the *Chipmunk Christmas CD* and as Tyler and I decorated the tree together, we danced around and sang to the silly music. It appeared that Tyler had forgotten his dad wasn't interested.

By the time we finished putting everything on, even I had to admit the tree didn't look so sad anymore. It actually looked really good.

~~~~~~

My mom called a few days later to let me know she and my dad were coming home for Christmas.

"Really?" I asked. "What about Derek? Aren't you guys supposed to be with them for Christmas this year?"

"We've talked to them. They understand why I need to come home."

"Okay. Do you know when you'll be here?"

"We fly into Salt Lake International Airport on Christmas Eve and fly back out on New Year's Day."

"That's great!" I had mixed feelings about their coming home. I wasn't sure I could pretend Grey and I were okay—not for an entire week. I'd been hoping that, since Grey had moved back in, he would work with me on compromising.

The truth was, nothing had changed. He still played *Combat Killers* and chatted all the time. He had even become brazen enough to chat when and where I might see it. I thought he did it on purpose. As if to say, "You don't own me." I was fairly certain he still had issues with pornography, although I hadn't seen any evidence since the first time I caught him. Along with dancing at *Renegade* every Thursday night, Grey started going up to the college every Wednesday night for country line dancing. As far as work was concerned, he went to work in South Jordan every once in a blue moon, but for the most part he hung out at Hank's dad's house. Working? I doubted it.

Saving money to buy Christmas gifts was difficult because, not only did Grey work very little, but I couldn't work anymore. It was getting too hard and too painful to balance motherhood, school, work, AND work on a marriage—a marriage that, more and more, felt one-sided.

~~~~~

The only things Tyler wanted for Christmas were a bike and transformer toys. He was easy to buy for. Grey, on the other hand, was a nightmare! He wanted a new pistol, new boots, a new paint job on his truck; all things we couldn't afford, but that didn't stop him from dropping hints at me every chance he got. He was even sweet at times, which made me want to give in, but experience had taught me that he was only doing it to get what he wanted.

A few days before Christmas, Grey said, "I need to go to Salt Lake."

"Why?"

"It's none of your damn business," he snarled at me.

"You realize we need to get some Christmas shopping done, right? I have no idea what to get your mom, your sisters, or your brother and their families. Maybe we should go together," I suggested.

Grey shut me down with a resounding "NO."

Just then, the phone rang. When I answered, there wasn't a response, only breathing. The Caller ID told me what I needed to know, however. Trying to keep my cool, I turned to my husband. "I believe *that* was for you. She didn't respond when I answered so... At least now I get why you don't want me to go with you."

My next move surprised even me. I took my wedding ring and the gold diamond studded heart pendant that he'd bought me a few years back off—the two items I held near and dear to my heart and I seldom removed—and quietly put them in Grey's hand.

"Maybe you should give these damn things to someone more deserving than me." I tried to keep my voice from breaking, but with the tears that clogged my throat, there wasn't anything I could do about it. Without saying another word, Grey put the jewelry on the bookshelf and walked out the door. I so badly didn't *want to* care! It was as if the week he moved out was for nothing. And in a couple of days, I was going to need to put on the best fake marriage I possibly could!

While Grey was gone, his boss from South Jordan brought a two-wheeler with training wheels for Tyler. It was something he really wanted, but we couldn't afford. I put it together and hid it in the closet, so Tyler wouldn't find it. As far as the rest of the Christmas shopping, Grey left it to me. I got Tyler a couple new

Transformers—Optimus Prime and Radio Wave. For Grey, I ordered personalized military veteran license plates that read OIF which stood for *Operation Iraqui Freedom*, as well as a new pair of lace up boots. We gave an updated family picture to the rest of our family members.

CHAPTER THIRTEEN

My mom and dad showed up on our doorstep at about ten thirty Christmas morning. Much to their surprise, especially with a three-year-old, we were all still asleep.

When Tyler saw who had come to visit, he squealed at the top of his lungs, jumped at Grandpa Marshall, gave him a huge hug, then gave Grandma a much gentler, but no less intense, hug. It seemed, at least for the moment, Tyler had forgotten about presents.

Of course, once Tyler realized there *were* presents, there was no more patience. Everyone had to wait until Grey had his morning smoke before doing anything else.

"He's finally going to quit," I explained to my parents while he was out of earshot.

"No, he won't," my mom said. I wasn't taking the bait because it usually ended up in a fight. I couldn't do that right now. Not if I was going to pull off my happy marriage.

I loved watching Tyler open each of his gifts because everything was "Wow!" or "Way cool!" He was just so cute!

When Grey opened his license plates and boots, he actually gave me a hug. Whether it was real or not, I didn't have the slightest idea, but at that point, I'd take whatever I could get that was affectionate.

After opening presents, my parents went back to Reghan's to sleep and spend some time with Reghan's family. Due to harsh feelings between Grey and most members of my family, doing things with everyone had pretty much vanished.

Reghan had to work the last couple of days my parents were home, so I got to spend a little time with them. I invited my parents over for dinner and a movie. While we were making dinner my mom asked, "Hunter, have you noticed that Tyler walks on his toes?"

"Yeah. A little."

"How long has he been doing that?"

"I'm not sure. I think it started right after Grey came back."

"Doesn't it worry you?"

"Some. Why?"

"I'm afraid he is being abused. You say he started walking on his toes when Grey came home. Right?"

"That's when I remember it starting, but Grey wouldn't hurt Tyler." Knowing the abuse he heaped on me, I prayed daily he wasn't doing anything to my baby. I hoped he wasn't capable of hurting a child.

With my permission, my mom asked Tyler why he walked on his toes outside of Grey's earshot. "Cuz if I don't it makes my bum hurt." Hearing that, my blood ran cold, but I didn't want to believe Grey could do that. Just like everything else, I did whatever I needed to put it out of my mind.

The last day of my parents' visit, Tyler and I went to lunch with them before taking them to the airport. Grey was too busy to go with me. Even though I promised myself I wasn't going to cry, I did anyway.

My mom gave me a hug and, at the same time said, "Honey, I hope for your sake and Tyler's that Grey will change, but I'm afraid it's not going to happen. I'm afraid you and Tyler are going to be caught in the middle." She said, too, that she was suspicious about Tyler walking on his toes and if he wasn't being abused, he was, at the very least, being neglected and mistreated. "You know you always have a place whenever you need it, with us."

"Mom, there's good in him. I just need to draw it out." As always, I defended Grey.

"That's not your job, sweetie. It's his. He needs to *want* to have you and Tyler now and in the eternities, and he just doesn't seem to want it."

"I'm not giving up on him!"

"Just don't make Tyler the collateral damage," she whispered as she hugged me goodbye.

I had a feeling deep in my heart Grey probably wouldn't change, but I held onto hope for the miracle.

~~~~~~

By the end of January, I had not only returned to school, but decided Early Childhood/Special Needs wasn't what I wanted to do with the rest of my life. I didn't feel any excitement about the prospect. Not like I thought I would. I talked to my mom about it.

"You need to find a major that puts the spark back in your step. Early Childhood Education just doesn't do that for you."

I'd always wanted to be a Social Worker, but never pursued it because my mom was afraid I would become too emotionally attached to my clients. What I really wanted was a career where I could use Social Work and Special Needs degrees together.

~~~~~~

Being back in school and without the income needed to support the family due to Grey's inconsistent employment, we decided to move. Finding something cheaper would help lessen my stress, I hoped. Less than two weeks after turning in several applications, we got a call from a place called *The Cedars*, which happened to be low-income housing. Between classes the next day, I met with the manager, looked at the apartment paid the deposit, and got the keys. I did it all on my own, as Grey had stated he didn't care where we lived.

By the end of that week, we were moved into our new apartment. It was a lot smaller than our current one and was just plain old. It was dark and dank, like a basement apartment. Smelled like my grandma's basement, too. Mold and mothballs. Beggars couldn't be choosers, however, when we were saving almost two hundred dollars a month in rent.

The biggest drawback for me was there weren't any washer and dryer hookups. Instead of putting ours in storage, we decided to let Grey's mom use them. It helped her because her washer was on its last leg and she didn't have a dryer. At the same time, it helped us because we wouldn't have to put them in storage.

Tyler, being almost four, didn't care what the place looked like. His most favorite part was the playground available for all tenants and children. Not to mention all the other kids there were to play with. Since it was the dead of winter, though, there weren't many kids out. That didn't stop him from wanting to suit up and play in the fluffy, cold whiteness, making snowmen and snow angels. I took him outside whenever I had a spare minute. Grey, however, didn't have the time or ambition to do anything with Tyler, much less take him outside to play in the snow. He still preferred being anywhere but home.

~~~~~~

Two weeks after moving into The Cedars, I came home from a long day of school and all I wanted to do was attempt to cuddle with my husband and watch a movie. No homework, no housework, nothing.

Walking in the door, I was greeted with, "I'm either going to stay home and chat or I'm going dancing." Grey knew neither option was a good one, nor ones I would agree to.

"Why don't we do something? Just the two of us?" I asked. I was sure Grey could hear the weariness in my voice, but I didn't think he cared, especially when he replied, "No. I've been working, and I deserve to do something *I* want to do." He sounded like a spoiled child.

Since there was snow everywhere, Grey only worked one day a week in South Jordan; today wasn't that day. He spent most days at Hank's dad's shop.

"You have got to be kidding me. By your own admission, you sit around the shop and do nothing. Exactly what kind of hard work are you talking about?" I knew it was futile and, most of the time, detrimental to stand up to him, but I was tired...tired of having a husband that cared for only himself and tired of having to take care of things he should've been!

"That doesn't even deserve a f***in' response," Grey exploded and, without so much as a good-bye, stormed toward the door, letting it slam behind him.

Sitting alone after putting Tyler to bed, like I had so many times before, I wondered what was wrong with me. Why didn't my sweetheart love me? Had he ever? I found myself wondering if all the times we were doing so well was because I was afraid to face the truth. After writing in my journal—I had been good at that while Grey was in Iraq, but it seemed like the only time I did any writing since was when my emotions were about to explode—I tried to study, but all I could think about was the man I loved dancing with other girls. He had no idea how much time and effort I put into learning his favorite dances—the two step and three step, no matter how bad the pain got—while he was overseas, and he probably never would. Why? If I was honest with myself, I knew the answer. Grey was ashamed of me. Why did I stay? The answer for me was easy... I loved him!

~~~~~~

February came, with Valentine's Day being *just another day*. The funny thing was, Grey was actually narcissistic enough to ask me where his present was! Like I had money to throw around? Still, I'd always gotten him something, and this year was no different.

~~~~~~

A week later, I interrupted Grey's chatting session. "I think we need to talk to the bishop." I cringed at the rage that crossed Grey's face. "It's either that or apply for disability again." I had tried in 2003 while he was overseas, but was turned down. It couldn't hurt anything to try again. I needed something to give a little.

"Why? You don't think I can pay the damn bills? With your student loans and now that I'm working in South Jordan again (when he did), we should be fine."

Did he seriously believe there was anything left of my student loans with all the cigarettes he bought and outings he went on?

"You're not disabled either. You're just a crazy bitch who thinks she deserves more than she's got."

"I didn't say you can't pay the bills. Would you like to trade places? Spend one day in my body? You wouldn't last a minute."

"No, but you implied it. Why are you always such a f***in' bitch?"

"Don't call me that!"

I could tell this wasn't going anywhere. The only question was, should I talk to the bishop without Grey's knowledge? I knew we needed help. He *knew* we needed help. He didn't like people to know he wasn't doing everything in his power to care for his family, though. He'd rather let everyone believe we weren't in trouble.

Grey didn't say anything else; he just continued playing *Combat Killers* and chatting.

Just before bedtime, Tyler tried getting Grey's attention. "Daddy?" Finally, Tyler patted Grey on the leg, when nothing else he did or said worked to get his Daddy to notice him.

Grey exploded, "WHAT THE F*** DO YOU WANT?!"

I was pretty sure Grey could see the tears welling up in our three-year-old's eyes. "I just want to read a book with you," he replied sadly.

"I can't. I'm busy." Grey went back to the computer.

My heart bled as I watched my baby whimper and shakily reply, "O-okay."

Trying to make up for Grey's total and utter lack of caring, I, who had three tests back to back the next day, put my books away and read to the little boy who was my entire world. If it would keep the sadness out of his eyes, I would read *Take Me Out of the Bathtub and Other Silly Songs* a thousand times.

~~~~~~

School was more difficult than it had ever been. All the medications I was on for chronic pain, depression, and anxiety had side effects—the worst one was being tired all the time. Added to that, the depression medication made me feel like I was having an out-of-body experience—as if I was watching myself live my life—and it made going to class almost impossible, and I might as well forget studying. I wasn't going to let that stop me, however.

~~~~~~

Several weeks after talking to Grey about applying for disability, the verdict came back. I'd been turned down, AGAIN! Now what?

It was mid-March, and I had a doctor's appointment in a couple of days. I was told at my last visit that if they didn't receive the delinquent balance—which was way more than I could afford—by the next visit, they would see me one last time in order to taper me off my medications. Of course, we didn't have that kind of money lying around so I freaked when we got the letter. I wanted to scream, yell and swear at anyone and everyone. Why couldn't I catch a break? Was there any hope of ever getting better?

As it turned out, the pain center decided that, because my car accident claim still hadn't settled, they would continue treating me as long as I could make a payment at future appointments. I was still fighting with the insurance company to get a settlement large enough that I might be able to afford medications and doctor appointments at least for the foreseeable future. According to my attorney, the insurance company was allowing us $50,000 to work with. That meant my settlement couldn't go over that. Not knowing how long I would be on pain medications, or whether I would ever be able to function without them, made settling difficult.

~~~~~~

In April, during all the craziness, Tyler turned four. Tyler loved Transformers, so even though it was a little more expensive, I bought him a Transformer cake. We had Reghan and the boys over for a little party, as well as Grey's mom, sister, and his brother and family. As I watched Tyler open his presents, including the ones that my parents sent from Georgia, I couldn't believe how my little boy was growing up so fast!

~~~~~~

The day after Tyler's birthday was just like any other normal day in our lives. I got Tyler up, made Grey's lunch—complete with a little heart-shaped note with a few words of appreciation and love. I put it in his lunchbox, making sure the note wasn't where he could see it before his lunch hour. I didn't know whether he saw them or not, but I wrote them anyway.

I got myself ready while Tyler ate breakfast. I would love to wake Grey up with a kiss, but I learned the hard way that it wasn't allowed. Most of the time, I left him alone. He was a grown man; he had an alarm clock. Grey came into the kitchen a few minutes later. When it was time for Tyler and me to leave, I kissed Grey on the cheek; I wasn't allowed to do any more than that.

"Hunter," Grey barked.

"Yeah?" Maybe he'd changed his own rules and would show me some real affection. I should've known better.

"I work in Orem today." He turned back to his breakfast, saying nothing more.

While sitting in my 9:45 class, Family Dynamics, my cell phone buzzed. Fearing it might be about Tyler, I answered, stepping out of class and taking my backpack with me in case I needed to leave.

It was Grey's boss, telling me he'd taken him to the Emergency Room. Apparently, he had been up on a ladder painting a ceiling in a building they were renovating, and his foot slipped off the second or third rung. He landed on his back, fallen onto some steps that were directly below him.

Without so much as a second thought, I drove as fast as I dared to Salt Lake, worrying the whole time about how badly Grey was hurt. Arriving less than thirty minutes after the call came, I saw Grey lying on a gurney, moaning in pain. "Hey, honey." I leaned down to kiss him on the cheek. "How are you feeling?"

Of course, he wasn't hurt badly enough to be nice. "That is a f***in' dumb question. I fell and landed on concrete steps on my back. How the hell do you think I feel?"

Doing my best to ignore his snide remarks, I asked, "What did the doctor say?"

Grey's boss heard how rude and degrading Grey was to me. Not wanting to cause any more problems for me, he told Grey that unless the doctor said he was physically incapable of working, he

259

would expect him to be at work the next day. He felt if a guy could degrade his wife that much while in so much supposed pain, he deserved to work while being in that pain. He didn't believe Grey was in as much pain as he led everyone to believe anyway—and boy was Grey milking it! He left Grey in my hands, but not before telling me if I needed anything to let him know.

Just then the doctor came in. "We did some x-rays. Nothing is broken or torn. It looks like he's bruised some from landing on the stairs, but other than that, it looks like pulled muscles. All he needs is a day or two of rest and he should be as good as new."

"What can he take for pain?" I was pretty sure he wasn't hurt nearly as bad as he made it sound, but I wanted to cover all my bases.

"Because he's never taken anything stronger than Ibuprofen, we can give him Tylenol with Codeine for today and tomorrow. He should only take one every four to six hours. After that, try the Ibuprofen—just the over-the-counter will do."

"When can he go back to work?"

"If he feels okay enough, tomorrow is fine, but other than that, two days should be okay."

Discharging Grey four hours after being admitted, I called the sitter and let her know I'd be late picking up Tyler. I wanted to get Grey home and settled on the couch first. The child didn't need to see any more degradation than he already had in his young life. Grey moaned and groaned all the way home. It was a LONG thirty-minute drive to our apartment!

~~~~~~

I ended up staying home from school the next day because Grey had turned into a big baby! He wouldn't take a shower, get dressed, or even get a heating pad or ice for himself! Maybe he'd have empathy for what I dealt with on a day-to-day basis. Yeah, right! Empathy was nowhere in his vocabulary *or* his feelings. Grey expected me to take care of Tyler, while being at *his* beck and call, without so much as a complaint. And with a smile!

"Well," I said under my breath, "there's a lot over the last several years I've had to grin and bear. I can sure as hell fake this, too."

Even after returning to work, Grey complained daily that he hurt so badly he couldn't stand it. Funny, though, he didn't hurt severely enough to hinder his sitting at the stupid computer and chatting while playing *Combat Killers*.

Thursday evening, not too many days after Grey went back to work, he came home complaining about how much pain he was in. I was hoping he might stay home and spend some time with me. I put Tyler to bed at eight o'clock then asked if Grey wanted to watch a movie. I should've known better.

"I'm going out." He wasn't nice about it.

I knew where he was going. "If you hurt so badly, do you think dancing is a good idea?"

"I don't care. I want to go, so I'm gonna f***in' go." I'd hoped that over time, the F-bomb would dissipate, but as time went on, Grey continued littering his speech with it.

"Are you ever going to stop?"

"AAAUUUGGHH! Not this AGAIN! We have f***in' been over and over this!"

I should've stopped and let him leave, but I was tired of being his verbal, sexual, physical, and emotional sacrificial lamb. I hated it when he made me feel so worthless and starved for affection that even the negative affection he gave me was better than nothing. Instead of letting him go, I blocked the front door so that he had to go through me to get out. He pushed me so hard that when my back and shoulders hit the door, my entire body exploded in pain. Trying not to let Grey know he hurt me, I moved.

"Look what you made me do! Damn cunt. I'm outta here!" I knew at that moment, if I wanted to keep the peace, I was going to have to let him do whatever he wanted, but more importantly, I just needed to keep my mouth shut.

~~~~~~

My parents flew into Salt Lake on May 10th for Reghan's graduation from the Police Academy in Boise, Idaho. Two months ago, she'd gotten a job working as a jailer, which meant she had to attend the six-week program at the police academy.

My parents didn't want Reghan to know they were coming; they wanted it to be a surprise! Grey had been planning all along to go with me, but when I let him know my parents were coming, he quickly opted out. He'd been a real jerk since then! He didn't care that I'd be driving alone, even with a toddler.

~~~~~~

Over the next few days, between school, being a wife, and being a mom, I continued to try and convince Grey to go with me, to no avail. "Grey, please come with me."

"No. Not if your parents are going to be there."

"What does it matter? You were planning on going until I told you they were coming."

"Well, you never should have told me, huh? You know how much your mom f***in' hates me."

"She doesn't hate you. She has a hard time with the way you treat me and Tyler. That's all."

"See? That's exactly why I'm not going." Grey turned his back to me. I knew this conversation was over.

Thursday came—the day I was supposed to leave—and in one last ditch effort, I persuaded Grey to come. "What if we hang out with Grace and Jack while we're in Boise? We can even stay there if you want." Grey finally relented. Apparently, hanging out with

Grace and Jack held enough appeal for him that he could handle being in my parents' presence for the weekend.

~~~~~~

While I spent the next few days with my family, Grey stayed at Grace and Jack's. This meant I didn't have to be the go-between when it came to him and my parents.

While I was gone on Saturday, Grey had a little heart to heart with Grace. "If Hunter would just lose several f***in' pounds and wear sexier clothes, I wouldn't *need* to look at or chat with other girls." Without my knowledge, Grey asked Grace to help him let me down gently.

When I returned Saturday evening, after getting Tyler settled for the night, Grace asked if we could talk. I wasn't sure what about, but she had always been nice to me, so no alarm bells went off in my head. and

"Sure. What's up?" I asked as we walked to the garage where all their parties happened.

"Grey asked me to talk to you." Grace looked apologetic.

"Okay..." I waited for the ball to drop. Had he found someone else? Did he want a divorce? Had he seen the error of his ways (scoff)? But nothing, I mean nothing, prepared me for some of what she was about to say.

"Grey says that if you would only lose some weight, he wouldn't need to chat or look at other women."

"And you believed the ass?!" I was completely astounded that a woman would think this was okay.

"I can see his point, to some degree. You don't dress sexy, and he needs eye candy."

The more she talked, the hotter my temper became! Grace obviously had no idea who I was. My husband didn't either for that matter—I didn't even know who I was anymore. I possessed many labels. Grey's whore when things were bad, which was most of the time; Grey's wife when he was being nice, which wasn't often; and Tyler's mom, which was my most cherished title. Somewhere along the way I had lost myself, and I wasn't sure how to find "me" again. The way Grace had stood up for me with Grey, I thought we were friends, but after our talk, I didn't think so.

~~~~~~

On June 22, 2005, I had to give a deposition to opposing counsel regarding the settlement for my back injuries. After the insurance company finished their questions, my attorney gave them the itemized list I felt was acceptable in my case—two sets of injections (after the doctors were sure they'd work), two years' worth of medication, doctor visits for two years, a TENS unit, past medical bills (everything I'd paid out of pocket), and gas to get to and from appointments.

"There is no way we will even get close to $70, 000," my attorney said.

"What do they expect me to do? Live with it?" I couldn't believe it! The insurance company *and* my attorney were treating me as if this was my fault.

"You have to be reasonable," one of the insurance agents claimed. "As we informed you previously, we are only allotted $50,000 to work with and we can't change that."

"So, you're saying the pain I live with every day doesn't matter?"

"No one is saying that." This from my attorney who, by then I was pretty sure was helping the insurance company get off without paying much of anything.

"It's not like I'm asking them to pay my medical expenses for the rest of my life!" I exclaimed. My emotions were running at full speed now. "Which I could very well be stuck with."

"We would like to see this case settle outside of court." The insurance agent chimed in, again.

~~~~~~

After giving the deposition and finding out I wasn't going anywhere with my case, except maybe down the crapper, I decided to take my case to trial. I figured even if I came away with nothing, at least I'd fought all the way. When my attorney got wind of this, however, he advised me that he didn't think we could win. Nor did he think pain doctors were reliable witnesses.

"You are *just going to have to live with* the fact that someone else caused the accident." A few days later I received a letter that read:

> *Dear Mrs. Andrews,*
>
> *I regret to inform you that I will no longer be representing you. It is my professional opinion that continuing to pursue your case is to your detriment. If you find an attorney willing to take your case, you will be required to pay me the first $20,000 of your settlement in order to cover the services rendered.*
>
> *Sincerely,*
>
> *Tom Jones, ESQ*

A couple of weeks later, I received another letter from him. In it, he stated that he had gotten an offer of sixteen thousand dollars; that again, he wouldn't take my case to trial. I didn't think this was ethical, so I called a malpractice attorney who explained to me that if it were him, he would take the offer.

I couldn't believe it! Wasn't it my attorney's job to do his best to win? Because it looked like no matter what I did, I was stuck with the pain and years of doctor visits and bills. I didn't have the ambition to go through the whole thing again with another attorney, so I settled. I came away with thirteen thousand after my attorney took his six-thousand dollar cut.

~~~~~~

When my settlement payment finally came in, I put the thirteen thousand in a separate bank account that was password protected. This way, only I could get into it. With our finances being what they were, I didn't know how long it would last. I was afraid we'd end up living on my settlement money due to our bills and my doctor appointments and medications.

Therefore, after talking with my doctors and receiving Grey's whole-hearted approval—he thought my medications made me bitchier than usual—I decided to see if I could survive without medication. With the doctor's help, I began tapering off over the next two weeks. I went the next few weeks after the tapering without any medication in my system. Those weeks were hell! It was impossible for me to do my wifely, much less motherly, duties, which made me feel like I was neglecting Tyler.

The only thing Grey did was piss and moan about how much I cried from the pain. He grumbled about how I should, "Just f***in' suck it up! Back pain isn't that bad!" He jumped on my case on a regular basis, too, because the house wasn't spotless, or dinner wasn't fixed whenever he decided to come home.

~~~~~~

Three weeks after getting off my medications, I had a doctor's appointment to decide whether this was an avenue I felt I could take. Grey, of course, didn't think it important enough to go with me. Luckily, I had a babysitter I could call on short notice who I didn't have to pay an arm and a leg when he watched Tyler.

When the nurse took my blood pressure, it was through the roof, 151/100, so with the doctor's approval, I started on a lower dosage regimen of medications than I was on previously. The reason, the doctor said, was because my body has gotten used to having nothing for so long, they had to slowly build it back up. It was all I could do not to cry in front of him. I wanted to live my life drug free, but that didn't look like it would happen.

After filling my prescriptions, I headed home. Blake had some bad news I didn't want to hear when I got there. Tyler had been bugging Blake to play on the computer, even though he knew he wasn't allowed to touch it. Somehow, he convinced Blake that I okayed it. "What happened?" I asked, afraid of the answer.

Blake, looked at the floor and was about to tell me when Tyler, in his little four-year-old voice, whimpered, "Mommy, I broke Daddy's game." He promptly began to cry.

Part of me wanted to be angry with my son, but there was another part that knew all too well the starvation for his daddy's affection and attention. "Tyler, Mommy told you never to touch the computer. Do you remember why?"

Between hiccups, Tyler answered, "Because Daddy has a very important game he doesn't want to lose?"

"That's right. Now, why did you tell Blake it was okay for you to play the computer?"

"I wanted to see why Daddy likes it so much. Maybe I could play, too, if I learned how."

"You just wanted something you and Daddy could do together?" I felt tears welling in my eyes.

"Uh-huh." Knowing he needed some sort of discipline for disobeying me, but at the same time understanding the kid's logic, I sent Tyler to bed thirty minutes early.

Tyler was in bed asleep by the time Grey came home. I readied myself to tell him about the game, and totally wanted to crawl under a rock, but I knew he would find out either whether I told him or not. Taking a deep breath and, after setting his dinner in front of him, I explained what happened.

"HE F***IN' ERASED THE WHOLE DAMN CHARACTER?! Little asshole!" Grey growled and yelled at the same time—how that was possible, I didn't know. He balled his hands into fists like he did when he wanted me to know he was furious. This time, though, I was afraid he would use them. He stood up, knocking the chair over in the process, and I watched as he seethed and stomped around the living room, swear words spewing from his lips.

"Grey, he wanted to learn to play it, so you and he would have something to do together." I tried to stay calm, but Grey was ANGRY! "He was only trying to get your attention," I mumbled.

"WELL! The little shit's got it now!" Grey's face was beet red and his nostrils flared. "I spent the last two f***in' years making that character and getting to the level I was on!! Now it's gonna take another two! Damn kid!" Under his breath, he said, "I should've just stayed away." But not quiet enough that I didn't hear it.

"Grey, calm down. It's only a game." I couldn't believe he could get this bent out of shape over a computer game.

"Did you punish him?"

"I sent him to bed early, and he will apologize to you in the morning."

"Man, if I were here when he did it, I would've beaten his ass!"

"That is exactly why he was in bed when I told you. He is a four-year-old little boy starving for his daddy's attention. You haven't spent more than five damn minutes doing anything he likes, and you've been home over a year." I figured giving Grey time to cool off was the best thing.

I was shocked at the way Grey handled the situation. The next morning, instead of talking to Tyler, he shunned him to the point that, even when Tyler apologized, Grey turned his back on him.

This made me severely angry with my husband —because he put so much stock in a game, he snubbed his son. It wasn't like Grey spent much time with Tyler anyway, but this was ridiculous! It made me wonder if my mom had been right. Was Tyler being abused? In any way? The thought made me gravely nauseous.

CHAPTER FOURTEEN

As if the issues Grey had with our four-year-old weren't bad enough, a few days later, I came home from running errands and, as usual, listened to the answering machine. What came through the speaker rocked me to my core, to say the least.

It was a woman's voice. "Grey, I went in for a check-up today and was found positive for gonorrhea. You might want to get tested. Soon."

My body shook and turned hot and cold at the same time, whether in fear, anger, anxiety, or all three, I wasn't sure.

When Grey came home, I didn't give myself time to think, but let him have it. "Who the hell is she?!?"

"Who's who?" Grey actually had the nerve to act dumb.

"HER!" I played the message.

"I don't know who the f*** that is." Grey was defensive; something he usually did when he had to remember what lies he'd told and when.

"Why would she tell you to get tested?"

"I don't f***in' know!"

"How did she get our *unlisted* telephone number then?"

"I have no damn idea who that is and, besides, why would I sleep with someone with STD's? What kind of asshole do you take me for?"

"I don't have any idea why you'd want to sleep with anyone else. But with all your so-called "friends," you should understand why I am leery. If I had any guy "friends" you would be livid, even if there wasn't anything beyond friendship."

"You? What man in his right mind would want you? Not only are you damaged goods, but you are the bitchiest woman I've ever met!" The last words that spewed from his lips were more horrific than any foul named he'd ever come up with. "I only married you out of pity. Saved some poor sucker from a life of hell." He smirked as he sauntered away.

I felt like I'd been punched in the gut! Did he seriously mean that? Why was he still around then, if he only married me out of pity? I knew I should leave. The sad part was, as I watched him walk away, I still held onto the hope he would change. That part of my faith in him hadn't died. I could handle all the low blows as long as he stayed.

~~~~~~

I watched Grey over the next several days, hoping Tyler deleting his character on *Combat Killers* might stop him from being on the computer as much. Wrong again! He spent that much more time chatting and whatever else he did. He opened a *Lookatme.com* account and threatened if I deleted or tried getting into it or his email he would leave, no questions asked.

I wasn't exactly scared he'd leave; he'd already done that and come back. I was more scared of being alone, but he didn't know that. I wondered if the real reason he stayed was because he thought he'd receive some of the insurance payout from the car accident— what was left of it anyway—but if we divorced, he'd get nothing. I was also going back to school full-time in September and applied for student loans, so he was probably thinking, *money bags*! Who knew the reasons he was still with me?

~~~~~~

My life went from hanging on, to *barely* hanging on by my toenails. First, Grey and Tyler were in a car accident. On the way to take Tyler to school, Grey wasn't watching where he was going and slammed on his brakes. He had missed a stop sign and rear-ended a jeep. Grey tried bribing the driver of the jeep into leaving the police out of it because he didn't want me or the police to know he was driving on a suspended license, again. If that wasn't careless enough of Grey, instead of Tyler being in the back seat, Grey let Tyler sit up front with no booster *and* unbuckled! When he slammed on the brakes, Tyler's head smashed into the windshield. He didn't just hit it; his head broke the glass! Due to Grey's disinterest in Tyler's wellbeing and safety, not to mention he'd been driving on a suspended license, the officer took his license right then and there.

~~~~~~

To say I was furious Grey allowed our four-year-old to be unbuckled and out of his booster seat was an understatement. I made sure Tyler was okay. The kid didn't have anything more than a goose egg, for which I was grateful. As far as Grey was concerned, he was going to have to get Hank's dad to come get him on the days he "worked" because I was certainly not going to help him tinker the day away at Denny's having coffee! The idea sounded good, but I ended up dropping him off every morning at coffee before taking Tyler to daycare because Grey informed me it was my job as his wife to make sure he got where he needed to go; not Hank's dad.

Secondly, Tyler had begun having problems with some of the older kids at the playground outside our apartment. The kids were mean; Tyler didn't even want to be outside, and this was his favorite pastime. He spent a lot of that summer indoors. One day, the father of the kids who were giving Tyler trouble came pounding on our door. Of course, like most days and nights, Grey was nowhere to be found so I got to take care of it—nothing new there. I had never seen the man before, but I recognized the kids right away. "Can I help you?" I asked.

"You can keep that shittin' kid of yours away from mine!" The guy was big, fat, and bald and looked as if he might pop a blood vessel at any moment.

"What's going on? Tyler came in terrified and in tears a few minutes ago and told me you threatened to have the police take him away! He's four years old! Why would you do that?"

"Yes, I did tell him that. He told my daughter that his daddy has damn guns!"

I didn't see the big deal. Most everyone I knew owned guns. "And?"

"It scared the hell outta her. You don't allow him to use the guns, do you?"

I was utterly dumbfounded he would even ask that! "No, he has never even seen the guns. They are under lock and key." In fact, the guns weren't even at our apartment, but I didn't tell him that.

"WELL! Just keep your brat away from my kids *and* my house or I'm going to get a restraining order!" With that, he turned abruptly and stomped away. After such a stimulating conversation, I talked to Tyler about why he shouldn't talk about Daddy's guns. I explained that they weren't toys and not to talk about them unless he was asking me questions. I didn't even think it a good idea for him to talk to Grey about them for fear of what he might tell him was okay.

Not even fifteen minutes after the guy left, a police officer came knocking at the door. "I'm here about a complaint made by one of your neighbors."

"Geez. Is he serious? Yes, officer. I know what this is about."

"Look, I think it's a stupid reason to call the police, but I have a job to do."

"I understand." I explained to him what the neighbor said and that I had talked to Tyler as well. I promised to make sure Tyler was nowhere near the neighbor or his kids. It didn't matter, however, because, although I did everything within my power to keep Tyler away from the neighbor, his kids still taunted and heckled Tyler whenever they were outside at the same time. In fact, the issue continued to escalate so much so that, not a month later, I wanted to move even though our lease wasn't up yet. My son should not fear playing outside.

~~~~~~

We found a place about ten minutes away in Orem. It was a house which had been converted into a main level apartment and a basement apartment. The house was in a cul-de-sac with a lot of other kids around for Tyler to play with, and it had a huge yard. Grey wouldn't go with me to look at the apartment, so, taking Tyler, I did a walkthrough of the main level apartment, signed the lease, and started moving the next day.

Grey's new friend, Kaden, had a truck and, with Grey's truck, Kaden's, and one other from our ward, we were able to get things boxed and moved in a couple of days. I did most of the packing, because according to Grey, I was better at it. It didn't matter to him how much it hurt my back to do it. In all reality, he couldn't care less whether I hurt or not, as long as he got to do the bare minimum. Cleaning the old apartment took me the longest. It took me two full days to get the place clean. I knew no matter how clean I made the place, we weren't getting our deposit back because we broke the lease. I didn't care. I had to get Tyler out of there.

~~~~~~

Grey went out every week night and most weekends, too. Sometimes he drove, knowing he didn't have a license. On other occasions, Kaden picked him up. He spent an awful lot of time with Kaden. Kaden made it clear he did not like me; and he treated me with such animosity. I couldn't figure out why he hated me so much. I fed him when he happened to be at our place, and I didn't say much of anything when he came to get Grey, either. I didn't know what his issue was. Grey took his cues from Kaden, because whenever Kaden was around, Grey was meaner than usual. They both thought it fun, instead of using my name when they needed something, to call me "Cunt." This happened whether Kaden was at our house or not.

~~~~~~

When Grey *was* home, we spent most of our time with Gunner, Shaylie, and their kids. Because money was tight, we either barbecued or made egg rolls while the kids played outside. Or we hung out at Shaylie and Gunner's playing cards or board games while the kids played together. More of the same old, same old. We seldom went out as couples. I did, however, notice that Grey seemed to talk to Shaylie a lot, but because she was married, I didn't think much of it. Maybe I should have.

~~~~~~

Because I was conquering another semester, I decided it was time to put Tyler in preschool in September. He'd be going into kindergarten next year, and, even though he was still going to be spending some time at daycare, I felt he needed to see what a school environment looked like. When I asked Grey what he thought—I included him in parenting decisions although he acted like he wanted no part of it—he grunted, "I don't care. Do whatever you want." That was pretty much *all* he said to me unless he was calling me some disgusting, demeaning name.

I had to get a schedule worked out around my classes and Tyler's preschool so I could pick him up. We started school on the same day, so this all had to be figured out beforehand.

~~~~~~

Preschool was good for Tyler. He made several friends quickly and liked the learning and playing he did there. Unfortunately, this didn't last long.

I learned through the grapevine there was one lead teacher a lot of parents had issues with. She picked on at least one student during each year of preschool, and made that child's life at school horrendous. The year before there had been a little girl who started preschool loving it, but by the half-way mark the same little girl had tantrums and crying spells about going, much like Tyler began exhibiting. Even after she told one of the other adults that the teacher had been calling her names and making her the last in line when it was lunchtime, nothing was done, making her feel like she didn't belong there, and she didn't matter.

By the end of the month, I started to see Tyler withdrawing from school, and even from his friends. He wanted to go to school with me, which I couldn't do. One day, however, when I went to pick Tyler up, what I was greeted with wasn't respectful. The lead teacher pulled me aside and said, "Tyler was being a butt today." I couldn't believe my ears! What kind of teacher made comments like that? When the teacher told me Tyler and another child were fighting over a toy, I was floored because that was normal for that age.

"They are four-year-olds. Things happen!"

"I know, but neither of the boys would listen to me."

"Did you call the other child a "butt" to his mother, too?"

"Well. No." There wasn't anything said after that, but I was so far from done with it!

I wrote a letter to those who were above the lead teacher and filed a formal complaint. There were several parents in both the morning and afternoon classes who backed me up and even signed a petition to get a replacement. The only other decision I had to make was whether to leave Tyler in preschool or not. I wanted him to learn everything he could, but at the same time, I couldn't let this continue. I let him stay but watched his reactions closely. Not two weeks after writing the letter, however, the lead teacher was replaced with a grandma-like teacher. The new teacher treated each of the children with the same respect she expected them to give her—lead by example. The turnaround in Tyler was amazing! He was back to loving school again and couldn't wait to attend every day.

~~~~~~

October arrived and, of course, nothing slowed down. I was having a heck of a time keeping up with my class schedule, volunteering to help at the preschool, and essentially being a single mom.

Tyler had, for a long time now, wanted to be Darth Vader for Halloween. "I like it cuz Daddy likes it." He explained to me.

I vowed to make sure my son had an awesome costume. Since I had a class on Halloween and only about thirty minutes to get Tyler ready and get to school, I took Tyler with me to my Geography class. Afterward, in the bathroom, I spray painted his hair black and painted his face black because he wasn't allowed to wear his mask or take his lightsaber to school. He looked cute with his hair and face black. When I dropped him off at school the local news station was there because they were doing a story about Tyler's class.

I called Grey, but as usual, he didn't answer and let it go straight to voicemail. "Grey, this is...Oh! You know who the hell this is! My guess is that's why you're not picking up. I think you need to be here. TXMP 8 is here doing a story on the preschool and Tyler will be on the news. He really, really wants you here. Guess if we see ya, we see ya. I love you." I didn't know whether Grey would check his voicemail in time, but I had to try. Of course, he didn't make an appearance.

That night, after getting Tyler's makeup off and getting him into bed, I waited for the ten o'clock news to come on. I wanted to tape it for Grey because he hadn't been there. For some reason, I missed it.

When Grey finally came home after midnight, he was angry because I hadn't taped the segment for him. "How hard is it to hit the record button when the news starts? What are you, dumbass?"

By nature, I wasn't a submissive person. I thought that by surviving his deployment and my ability to take care of Tyler, Grey might see I'd changed. I'd grown up. Maybe that was our problem—I had grown up. When he called me names and belittled me, I somehow lost the stubbornness. I found it was easier to be submissive most of the time—like tonight. Oh, how I *hated* letting him see me like that! I didn't give him the satisfaction of knowing he'd, once again, renewed the belief I was lower than the scum on the bottom of his boots.

Not wanting to hear anymore negativity from Grey, I quietly went into our bedroom. I left the door unlocked, not knowing whether he would come in or sleep on the couch. I was in NO mood to deal with him, but the part of me that wanted his love and affection won out again. I lay in my bed crying. I sobbed so hard I was sure Grey could hear me. Oh, how badly I wanted him to come in, apologize, and hold me all night. I fell asleep with that wistful dream still in my head.

~~~~~~

By the first part of November, our marriage wasn't getting any better. I had never been so grateful for school in my life! It gave me the reprieve I needed from the realities of my life. We had been advised by the bishop to go on a monthly date, but so far, I hadn't been able to get Grey to take me out.

I was beginning to wonder if it would ever happen when, one night, much to my surprise, Grey said, "Hey, let's go out."

I wasn't sure if this was a joke or not. Raising my eyebrows, I asked him, "Are you serious?" I was totally baffled.

"Do you want to go or not? You know I've been wanting to see the *Work and the Glory* movie that just came out. Let's go!" He was losing his patience. Hurrying as fast as I could, I called the babysitter, changed into a cute blouse, and touched up my make-up.

There had to be an ulterior motive, I was thinking, and I asked, "How are we going to pay for it?

"That fat-ass settlement check you got."

I wanted to be angry he would use me that way, but I had been put down so many times, and I was so starved for his love and affection, I couldn't see he was using me. All I saw was Grey and me on a date—a real date.

~~~~~~

Sitting at *Foundry Grill* in Provo several minutes later, waiting for our food, I did whatever I could to engage Grey in conversation. I wanted my husband to remember the strides he'd been making before deployment.

"Honey, I am so glad we are on a date."

"Yeah, whatever."

"What made you decide you wanted to go out?" I was a bit curious seeing as how whenever I brought it up, he shut me down quick.

279

"How the f*** should I know?" he responded.

"Well, you have to admit it was kind of sudden."

"So?"

"I'm just curious. That's all." I could tell it was going to be like pulling teeth to get him to talk much.

The movie was much the same. I tried several times to cuddle and hold hands, but it was a washout too. I seriously hated the fact that even after everything he had said and done, Grey still had the power to make me feel jittery; especially when he wore his green Henley and his black cowboy hat. Oh, and don't forget the Stetson. My mom told me once, "That's how you know you love someone. When, no matter what, they can elicit those kinds of feelings." He didn't even have to say anything; he was the man I loved, and I really wanted to be with him forever. I was at a point that it didn't matter anymore if he stopped smoking, but I didn't think I could ever be okay with the girlfriends—even if they were "just friends."

~~~~~~

I'd been thinking for quite some time that Grey and I needed to try marriage counseling again. I had no idea whether it would help, or make things worse, but we needed to do something. I had an agenda which was as follows: first, get Grey to agree to go, and second, convince him to come with me to talk to the bishop. My hope was to find a counselor that could get through to Grey, even though our financial and personal circumstances made it clear there was no way we could pay for such an expense ourselves.

One day in early December, I had an overwhelming feeling. I needed to talk to Grey *that* day. Knowing not to ignore such promptings, I decided to talk to him when he got home. Of course, my nerves were on edge when he walked in the door.

"Grey, can I talk to you?" I asked, feeling submissive and passive, both of which I hated.

"What?" He sounded impatient. Like I'd interrupted something.

"Are we okay?"

"What the hell are you talking about?"

"I think it might be a good idea if we try marriage counseling again. It can't hurt."

"Didn't work the first two times. What makes you think it will now?"

"It did help some. Don't you remember all the changes you were making before you were deployed?"

"Are you really that f***in' stupid? Haven't you figured out the only reason I did that shit was to get you off my back?"

Such an admission shouldn't have knocked me for a loop, but it did. I wasn't sure how to respond to him. Swallowing the lump in my throat, I went on. "What do you think?"

"About counseling?"

"Yes." I got the feeling I was keeping him from something...or someone.

"If I agree to it, will you leave me the f*** alone?"

"Okay." I didn't know what made him agree, but I would take it. I'd promise anything if it meant he at least acted like he wanted our marriage to get better. "Will you go with me to meet with the bishop?"

"I knew there was some damn catch," Grey moaned. "Can I go now?"

"Where are you going?"

I didn't remember it was Thursday until Grey said, "It's Thursday, duh."

"Do you have to go?"

"Don't give me any of your f***in' shit about it. You knew when we got together that I liked to go to the club. I've been doing it for the last six years, so you should be used to it by now."

"Why don't you take me?" I'd asked this question several times and I knew the only answer he gave. I guess I thought there should be more to it..

"You know why."

"The only thing you've ever said about it is that you can't dance left handed and you don't want to learn."

"No, I've always said I hate dancing with you because everyone can see what a fat-assed cripple you are." He said nothing more, but slammed the door on his way out.

I tried not to think about his last comment, but it kept echoing in my head. Out came the journals. I had homework to do, but at that moment, there was no way I could concentrate. As the tears fell, soaking the pages, I angrily wiped them away as I ferociously wrote in my journal. My feelings, the way I saw myself, and the way my husband saw me appeared on the pages. Luckily, Tyler didn't have to see his mommy in tears.

~~~~~~

The first night of marriage counseling was awful! Grey puked out whatever he thought the counselor wanted to hear. He explained to the counselor during our first session that we didn't have any problems other than the mundane marriage issues. Everything else was peachy.

"And I'm not gone as much as Hunter wants you to think. I'm home enough and can't figure out why she thinks I don't spend enough time with her and Tyler."

"Hunter, do you feel he's gone a lot?" The counselor asked me.

"Yes. He is either out dancing with his friend, Kaden, or he's hanging at his best friend's dad's house; don't forget dancing."

"Do you do those things, Grey?"

"Sometimes."

It was all I could do not to jump in and let it all out. I wasn't sure what the counselor thought, but it was blatantly obvious Grey didn't want to be there. His slouching in the chair and scowl on his face as he answered questions was a dead giveaway.

The counselor thought it best if we both attended individual counseling along with the marriage counseling. Each week we would have marriage counseling, and one of us would have individual counseling that same day as well. Oh boy! I wasn't looking forward to this, but our marriage was important.

~~~~~~

With Christmas quickly approaching, my plan was to get all the Christmas shopping done. It was called power shopping. I had just enough left from my settlement to make a decent Christmas for my family. Between monthly bills, doctor bills, and the cost of my medication, my settlement money got eaten up faster than it should have, but I had no other choice. I took Tyler with me to get Grey's Christmas present, explaining to him that it was a surprise for Daddy and he couldn't say anything. Tyler was still young enough I could buy his gifts and leave him completely oblivious that they were his. I'd known since our second Christmas together what I could expect from Grey, because each year he bought the same thing, either Bath & Body Works Bubble Bath, usually a scent he liked that I didn't particularly care for, or a book. It had gotten so redundant I didn't bother dropping hints to him anymore. He never put much thought into gifts for me anyway. Why should Christmas be any different from any other important day in my life?

~~~~~~

As far as counseling went…well, it went. There weren't any epiphanies or major changes. In fact, it was the exact opposite.

During one marriage session in February, the counselor gave Grey an assignment. "Grey, I want you to romance Hunter."

"Romance her? What the hell are you talking about?" He furrowed his brow.

"Yes, romance her. I want you to think about what romance means to her and do it."

~~~~~~

In my individual session that same evening, the counselor asked me to do a homework assignment he hadn't given Grey, nor would he. My assignment was to write down what I needed from Grey, as well as what I needed from other people in my life — namely my extended family; my parents in particular. That wouldn't be hard. I'd known for a long time what I needed from them.

Grey chose to go dancing after our counseling. He shouldn't have been driving, but he didn't care. Once again, since I was home alone, I sat down to write in my journal after putting Tyler to bed. I'd written the list the counselor wanted in my journal. My list went something like this:

*I need my parents to support me, no matter what. The fact that I chose Grey should be reason enough.

*I need to know my whole family matters, not just me and Tyler.

*I need my parents to stop leaving us out when making plans with the rest of the family.

*I need to know that I matter enough for them to at least TRY to get along with Grey.

To Grey:

*I need to know I am the most important person in your life.

*I need to know that when I need you, you will come running, no matter how small you might think the issue is.

*I need you to realize how important Tyler and I are and, even though it isn't easy, let us know every day.

*I need to be shown and told that you love me.

*I need to spend time alone with you with no interruptions.

And finally, to them all: *I shouldn't have to choose between my parents and my husband!*

~~~~~~

During our next session, the counselor asked me to read the part of my list pertaining to Grey. Taking a deep breath and wiping the sweat from my palms, I began—feebly at first, but with the counselor's encouragement, my stubbornness won out.

"How do you feel about what your wife said, Grey?"

"She is so damn needy! I don't have the f***in' time to give her what she wants!"

My eyes were glistening, and the counselor said, "Look at her, Grey. What do you see?"

Rolling his eyes, Grey remained silent. All I could do was curl into the other side of the couch and will the tears away.

Changing the subject, the counselor asked, "Grey, have you romanced Hunter yet?"

"Nope." Putting emphasis on the P.

"Have you done anything we've discussed, either here or in our individual sessions?" Grey wouldn't answer. The session ended with Grey, again, promising to do his homework. I had severe doubts.

~~~~~~

A few days later, Grey came home from work and promptly went into the bathroom. No "Hi, how was your day." No "Kiss my ass." While he was occupied, his cell phone rang. As it did every time it rang, my stomach fell to my toes. My blood ran cold when I saw the name on the caller ID—*My Lover*. Who was the woman who got the title that was mine? Should I confront Grey or leave it alone? Not knowing what to do, I acted as normal as possible when he finally emerged. It didn't work because he obviously heard the ring tone, and the first thing he said was, "Who was that?"

"My lover."

"No. Who was on my cell?" He actually thought I was that half-witted. I was furious.

"That's the name on the caller ID."

"Oh."

"Who the hell is she? Why does she have a damn pet name that should be reserved for me?"

"None of your f***in' business." Not wanting to cause problems, I didn't bring it up again until...

~~~~~~

Our next counseling session was a doozy. The counselor saw right off the bat that I wasn't okay, nor did he miss the icy glare from Grey. I was at the point where I didn't care whether I made him mad or not. It was all I seemed to accomplish.